THE BEST AMERICAN RECIPES 2001–2002

The Year's Top Picks

from Books, Magazines,

Newspapers, and the Internet

THE BEST AMERICAN RECIPES

2001–2002

Fran McCullough
SERIES EDITOR

With a Foreword by

Marcus Samuelsson,

executive chef of Aquavit

Houghton Mifflin Company
Boston   New York
2001

ACKNOWLEDGMENTS

I'm very grateful to the superb people at Houghton Mifflin who bring these books into the world. This book wouldn't exist at all without the help of dozens and dozens of people all across the country whose tips and cooking talk and generosity are invaluable.

This year I've been especially lucky to have Molly Stevens working with me as an alter ego—searching out recipes, testing, bringing her fine kitchen intelligence and high good humor to the project.

ISSN: 1525-1101
ISBN: 0-618-12810-7

Designed by Anne Chalmers
Cover photograph by Beatriz Da Costa
Food styling by Anne Disrude
Prop styling by Betty Alfenito
Asparagus Baked with Roncal Cheese (page 207),
Roasted Red Onions with Thyme and Butter (page 210)
and The Best Grated Potato Pancakes (page 220).

Printed in the United States of America

DOW 10 9 8 7 6 5 4 3 2 1

contents

foreword

My JOURNEY TO BECOMING A CHEF was a circuitous one. My older sister, Linda, and I were orphaned in Ethiopia at the height of the famine in the early 1970s, when I was three years old. Food was scarce in the Red Cross hospital where we spent time before being adopted by a Swedish family from Gothenburg in southwest Sweden. I have no memories of that period, but my mother tells us that the first night we arrived at our new home, Linda and I banged on the door of the refrigerator all night long.

In a short time, the ample food in the Western world made us forget the hunger of our early years in Ethiopia, but even so, food continued to shape my life. My grandmother was a terrific cook—she'd worked at an inn on the Swedish coast where she cooked three meals a day, six days a week, for several years—and by the time I was six I was spending countless hours with her in the kitchen. She had an immense respect for food, and she passed along to me her passion for fine ingredients and flawless techniques. We made breads and cookies and all the traditional Swedish dishes, like gravlax, meatballs and salt-cured duck. I loved everything she prepared, and my parents introduced me to a host of new tastes and flavors when we traveled throughout Europe on vacation.

When I moved to New York in 1993, I was amazed at the city's cultural and culinary diversity. I'd been raised to think that Europe was the only place for serious food. But here in America, I found every type of dish imaginable, including vegetables, fruits and spices that I'd never heard of. On my days off, I'd eat at small ethnic restaurants throughout the five boroughs and travel the subway to visit one neighborhood after another, exploring the Indian food shops in Jackson Heights, the Fulton Fish Market and the labyrinth of streets in Chinatown. New York, I learned, was rapidly becoming a culinary mecca unlike any other, with ingredients and influences from around the globe.

The longer I've been in America, the more I've come to realize that this enthusiasm for new flavors and quality ingredients is not limited to New York but is present everywhere. You can buy lemongrass at midwestern grocery stores and eight different types of potatoes at markets in Texas. As more and more Asian, African, Middle Eastern, South American and European influences find their way into the melting pot, the menus in restaurants and home kitchens reflect these changes. American comfort foods will always be with us — as well they should — but more and more people are open to experiencing and enjoying the foods of India, Brazil or even my native Ethiopia.

Two years ago, when I returned to Ethiopia for the first time since 1973, I was struck by the deep-rooted hold that cooking and eating have over the country's social life. Each meal is a carefully prepared feast of slow-cooked stews and *injera,* a spongy, sour bread that perfectly complements the spicy heat of most main dishes. Entire families spend three to four hours each day preparing and eating dinner. It is as though Thanksgiving were every day of the year.

This attitude appeals to me because I've always felt that something vital is missing when the connection between meals and socializing is lost or neglected. And that's one of the reasons I am so pleased about *The Best American Recipes 2001–2002.* Bringing eating and cooking back to the center of social life in America is the point of this book. With recipes for every level of ability, from casual chips and dips, simple main courses and homey desserts, to the more challenging preparations of four-star cuisine from the country's most luminous culinary stars, this volume makes cooking fun and accessible. Moreover, the collection bursts with recipes from around the world, making it a genuine reflection of America today.

The recipes come from many sources, from top chefs like Jean-Georges Vongerichten in New York and Ben and Karen Barker in North Carolina, to food writers like Michael Bauer of the *San Francisco Chronicle,* to home cooks like Rita Cayea, whose recipe for Potato Chip Cookies came to light in a *Newsday* baking contest. *The Best American Recipes* proves what I've always believed about this most democratic of industries: It doesn't matter where you come from or what your age, race or sex is. As long as you are passionate about food, you can go far.

MARCUS SAMUELSSON
Executive chef, Aquavit
New York City

introduction

As THIS EDITION of *The Best American Recipes* goes off to the printer, we've been musing about what's changed since the series was inaugurated two years ago. Certainly we have a stronger idea of what delights our readers and what they find useful, and that in itself has influenced the way we track down recipes. After two seasons on the road all across the country, talking with cooks and chefs and the food media, we know that it's the simple but sophisticated recipe that we're after. It has to be a recipe that tastes great, one that we'd eagerly make again, and one that we want to tell our cook friends about too. If it can be made ahead, if it's versatile, if it looks gorgeous, so much the better. (After all, we all have an inner Martha by now, who gets crabby if the food doesn't look ravishing.) These are the recipes we want for our own kitchen repertoire. But we can't resist including an occasional recipe that requires a little more work when it's truly a knockout.

In the last couple of years, we've discovered some great little tips that we pocketed and kept to ourselves as the search went on. This year, however, we decided to feature those that we found especially useful. As with the recipes, they come from pro and amateur alike. The wine suggestion of Karen MacNeil-Fife, a California wine expert, alone (see page 149) could save you a lot of money.

Intuitive food savvy turns up everywhere. The recipes in this collection are as likely to come from a stranger encountered in a parking lot or a UPS clerk (as two did this year) as they are to emanate from the kitchens of internationally known chefs. We agree with superchef Jacques Pépin, who says, "No one knows it all."

So is this a definitive collection? Not at all; to provide that, we'd need dozens of scouts and a full-time test kitchen with a full staff to do the testing and tasting and evaluating. (And even then, it's doubtful that we'd be able to look at even a decent percentage of the literally millions of recipes that are published and floating in cyberspace every year.) Instead, we offer a cornucopia of recipes that's probably entirely unlike the list any other food professional would find. Our selection is quirky, very much to our taste, and cheerfully mindful of the limitations of time. With no pretensions to being "comprehensive," we can promise you that these recipes not only work, they're exceptionally tasty.

But simply finding good recipes is not our

only goal. *The Best American Recipes* is also a unique way of looking at what's happening in American food. And frankly, this is our favorite part of the job: looking at the thousands and thousands of recipes from every possible source to get a sense of what's really going on and bringing our readers what we consider the best of it. It takes us a while each year to get the scent of a particular direction the food world is moving in, but once we have it we start to notice it everywhere—that's the origin of our list of top ten trends (see "The Year in Food," page x).

Our favorite recipes bring something new and exciting to the table. Sometimes it's a new ingredient chefs have been playing with that has suddenly started turning up in home kitchens; at other times it's a technique that simplifies everything enormously or produces the best possible version of a dish. Sometimes it actually involves doing something "wrong" or backward, when all the rules get broken and something amazing is the result. British TV cook Delia Smith's coconut-lime cake (page 282), which turns cake-mixing principles upside down, is a good example. In fact we had to make this cake twice, once the "right" way to be sure it wouldn't be better (it wasn't). The year also saw a number of culinary experts trying to come to terms with something as basic as how to hard-boil an egg. We share the one we prefer on page 7.

But this year's big news was the revolution in fish-cooking techniques. Our favorite was Chef Michael Roberts's "crimping" technique (see page 22), one of those great discoveries that was the result of a kitchen accident.

Oddly enough, chefs, blamed so long for giving us useless recipes designed for restaurant kitchens, have become much more interested in home food. Chefs like Alfred Portale, Mario Batali, David Waltuck and Caprial Pence really do cook at home with and for their families, and it shows in their books. And for their part, home cooks seem to be cooking a bit more like chefs, wanting to play with new ingredients and becoming more conscious of presentation.

What brings the creators of these recipes together—chefs and amateurs alike—is the enduring embrace of comfort food. There are certain things we Americans love more than anyone else, such as ice cream, doughnuts, onion rings, macaroni and cheese, meat loaf, meatballs, potato chips and fried chicken. We bring to these foods our great gifts of invention, our deep fascination with novelty and our seemingly endless creativity, not to mention the amazing potential of our evolving melting-pot culture. That's the real story of American food. That's how we end up with Japanese bread crumbs (panko) on onion rings and harissa in fried chicken. And besides, who else in the world would stick potato chips in cookies?

the year in food

WE STILL DON'T KNOW quite how this phenomenon happens, this wave of excitement about particular dishes or ingredients or techniques or attitudes. But it definitely happens, usually beginning with the chefs and quickly reaching the alert home cook.

This year there were two remarkable invasions: The British came, more or less by stealth. We counted among them the distinguished food writer Nigella Lawson, the always reliable Delia Smith and some lively newcomers (to us), such as restaurant chef Gordon Ramsay, TV star Jamie Oliver (aka the Naked Chef), the Indonesian cook Sri Owen, the bouncing-off-the-wall TV chef Ainsley Harriott, the exuberant London restaurateur Italian chef Antonio Carluccio . . . the list goes on and on.

Part of the reason for the immigration is the plethora of British TV food shows available to us. As we all know by now, watching food shows is mainstream entertainment, even for people who never cook. These British cooks have become familiar visitors in the living room, and we now want them to join us in the kitchen as well. What may seem surprising is the high quality of British food, so long the subject of scorn, and the fresh take these writers have to offer.

The other invasion came from Southeast Asia. Despite the increasing popularity of Asian cuisines in restaurants, home cooks have been reluctant to take on the battery of ingredients they require and the reschooling in techniques. Once again, chefs have shown the way by using just an element or two in a dish to transform it—and we're eager to follow their lead.

Other trends from previous years are continuing to evolve, such as brining meats, poultry and seafood to tenderize them and make them more succulent. This year, we've picked up some tips from ethnic cooks who know that just a smear of coarse salt directly on the food to be cooked will accomplish the same thing with much less effort required.

THE TOP TEN

1. COMEBACK OF THE YEAR
Soufflés

Banished partly because French food went into eclipse during the low-fat era and partly because they're old-fashioned (not to mention tricky), these ethereal creations were rediscovered this year. Anne Willan's brilliant way of twice-baking them not only is foolproof, it lets you make the soufflé ahead of time and serve it with panache (see page 103).

2. HERB OF THE YEAR
Mint

We finally had to declare a moratorium on including mint recipes, since they were turning up everywhere. Whether fresh or dried, this humblest of herbs, the one most likely to be in your backyard, is king this year. Exotic mints such as chocolate and orange (among hundreds of others) were showcased in chefs' and gardeners' recipes, but we're sticking with good old spearmint.

RUNNER-UP: Tarragon, the anisey French favorite, back again after a long absence.

3. SPICE OF THE YEAR
Cardamom

You might think cardamom had a publicist this year, it has so completely blanketed the food world. We're used to seeing it in Scandinavian recipes but not much elsewhere. This year, however, it took off in all directions, partly because of the interest in all those sweet spices associated with Indian cuisine.

RUNNER-UP: Coriander, the dried seed of the cilantro plant, which couldn't be more different from fresh cilantro. Coriander used to be the most popular baking spice in America in early days, but until now we'd forgotten all about it. Check out the coriander mashed potatoes on page 218, which George Washington might have appreciated.

4. VEGETABLE OF THE YEAR (UNCONTESTED)
Beets

Although they are beloved almost everywhere else in the world, beets have been scorned in America. But this year our eyes were opened to the delights of this sweet, earthy root, which turns up in salads, soups and even pasta. It seems we couldn't get enough of beets.

5. TECHNIQUE OF THE YEAR
Fish cookery

We were amazed by the number of new (to us) ways of cooking fish we encountered this year. Our favorite was a no-fuss cooking method we learned from Chef Michael Roberts, called "crimping." You make a flavored broth, simmer it in a heavy pan for about 5 minutes, add the fish or shellfish, cover and cook for 1 minute, then remove, still covered, to rest for about 5 minutes, or until the temperatures of the fish and the liquid are equal. Presto: The fish is perfectly cooked without its proteins being disturbed and toughened, there's no fishy smell, and there's a flavor exchange between the broth and the fish, so you have the basis of a tasty sauce in the broth. Brilliant!

Another technique that captivated us is poaching in olive oil, a Mediterranean way of cooking fish that leaves it silky, infused with flavor and gently cooked (see page 142).

6. FRUIT OF THE YEAR
Plums

The field is crowded here, with everything from dates to blueberries to persimmons—and our winner (see the plum galette on page 300). Somehow the millions of advertising dollars spent to transform poor old prunes into fashionable "dried plums" ended up focusing attention on plums, not prunes.

7. DRINK OF THE YEAR
Rum, especially dark rum

This makes perfect sense, now that eggnog is back and punch is back and cocktails are back. A good dark rum is a serious drink on its own and does wonderful things to food. It's even a traditional secret ingredient in tapenade, says Mediterranean cooking authority Paula Wolfert.

RUNNER-UP: Cider. Cider hot, cider cold, boutique ciders, cider jelly as an ingredient, cider in soup . . . this American classic is finally being given its due. It's right up there with coffee as our favorite companion for our favorite food, doughnuts.

8. NEW ETHNIC CUISINE
Southeast Asian

Thai food paved the way, but now we're ready for some more serious exploration of these fascinating cuisines, which includes everything from Indian to Indonesian. A landmark cookbook–adventure book, *Hot Sour Salty Sweet* by Jeffrey Alford and Naomi Duguid, crystallized this curiosity, but a number of other cookbooks and articles contributed to the wave of interest. Most important, the conference on Southeast Asian food held this year at the Culinary Institute of America at Greystone, in St. Helena, California, brought together cooks from all over the area and introduced their foods and their culture to American professional cooks and the media, so we know we'll be seeing even more next year.

9. TOOL OF THE YEAR
Spice spoons

It's hard to imagine why it took so long for someone to come up with this idea, but it did. Now we have these great little measuring spoons, narrow tiny shovels that dive into spice jars with no trouble and easily fill those badly designed salt and pepper mills with small openings. The heavy-gauge stainless spoons sport European equivalents so you can use European cookbooks too. Now, if you need a $^{3}/_{4}$ teaspoon measurement, you've got it.

10. ADDICTION OF THE YEAR
Caramel

How sweet it is. This year, everything is caramelized, from scallops to milk. Americans just don't seem to be able to get enough of this entrancing flavor of sugar taken to the next power. We're no exception; we always have a jar of the Mexican version, cajeta, in the refrigerator, ready to be spooned over ice cream for an emergency dessert. But for true aficionados, the over-the-top sophisticated taste is the not-too-sweet, not-too-rich Burnt Caramel Ice Cream on page 314.

starters

Southern-Style Spicy Pecans   2

Baked Greek Olives   4

Asian Tea Eggs   6

Porcini Dust Twists   8

Charred Tomatillo Guacamole with Seeded Tortilla Triangles   10

Bacon-Wrapped Scallops with Tamari Glaze   13

Moroccan Tapenade   16

Spinach Dip with Jicama and Sweet White Onions   18

Gorgonzola Mascarpone Torta   20

Crimped Shrimp   22

Albóndigas (South-of-the-Border Meatballs)   24

Martabak (Savory Indonesian Meat Pies)   26

southern-style spicy pecans

We've always loved southern spiced pecans, with their crunchy egg-white coating. But the Barkers, chef-owners of the famous Magnolia Grill in Durham, North Carolina, have taken these tasty little nuts a step further by adding punchy cayenne pepper. These are sweet, hot, crisp and crunchy all at once—and very hard to stop eating.

SOURCE

Not Afraid of Flavor: Recipes from Magnolia Grill by Ben and Karen Barker

COOKS

Ben and Karen Barker

They come out of the oven all blobby and mis-shapen, not as individually coated spiced nuts. They also make a big mess as they're cooking, so if you have one, use a Silpat or other baking sheet liner.

The nuts are obviously perfect with cocktails, but they also perk up a green salad as a surprise garnish.

makes about 4 1/2 cups

2 large egg whites	1 tablespoon cayenne pepper
1 1/2 teaspoons salt	2 teaspoons Worcestershire sauce
1/2 cup sugar	
2 tablespoons sweet paprika	4 1/2 cups pecan halves

Preheat the oven to 350 degrees.

In a large stainless steel bowl, whisk the egg whites until foamy. Whisk in the salt and gradually add the sugar, beating the egg whites to stiff peaks. Add the paprika, cayenne and Worcestershire sauce and whisk to combine.

Using a spatula, fold in the pecan halves, making sure to coat them evenly with the egg-white mixture. Turn the nuts out onto a non-stick baking pan or Silpat-lined baking sheet (see note), arranging them in a single layer.

Bake the nuts for 5 minutes. Remove from the oven and, using a metal spatula, turn them over, breaking up any large clumps. Return the nuts to the oven and bake for 5 minutes more. Repeat, turning and stirring the nuts every few minutes until they are dry and evenly browned, 10 to 15 minutes total.

Remove from the oven, separate into single pecan halves, and allow to cool. Store in an airtight container for up to 5 days.

cook's note

Silpats or other baking sheet liners are made of space-age material that's nonstick and releases easily. Just wipe them off, give them a good rinse and use them over and over.

starters

3

baked greek olives

SOURCE

Ainsley Harriott's
Barbecue Bible
by Ainsley Harriott

COOK

Mama Tahsia

The irrepressible Harriott seems to have done the impossible: given credibility to England as a source of great barbecue and delivered it all, in bible form, to the New World. It's his charm, energy and passion for food as well as his fascinating combinations that make all this work. He was served these terrific olives at the home of a Greek friend years ago, but he never forgot the taste.

These marinated olives are very mellow, especially when served warm. They go right on the grill, in little packets, as a sort of barbecue first course. Be sure there's plenty of bread to dip into the delectable juices. Pita bread warmed briefly on the grill would be perfect.

Don't ignore these olives just because you don't have a grill; put the packets in the oven and they'll be just as good (see note).

serves 4

4 ounces pitted kalamata olives
4 ounces pitted green olives
1½ tablespoons crushed coriander seeds
2 strips of lemon zest, halved
2 strips of orange zest, halved
2 small bay leaves, halved
2 garlic cloves, sliced

2 sprigs of fresh thyme, leaves only
¾ cup olive oil
2 tablespoons fresh lemon juice
2 tablespoons fresh orange juice
Salt and freshly ground black pepper

Mix all the ingredients together in a bowl and set aside to marinate for at least 2 hours. Shape two 12-inch squares of heavy-duty foil into little bowls and divide the olives between them, making sure each bowl has a strip of orange and lemon and a piece of bay leaf.

Pinch the sides of the foil together to make well-sealed packages and place them to the side of the barbecue for 5 minutes, or until heated through. Remove, allow to cool slightly, then open and serve warm with plenty of crusty bread and chilled spicy white wine.

cook's note

Instead of cooking these olives on the barbecue, you can bake the packets in the oven at 350 degrees for 5 to 10 minutes, or until heated through.

asian tea eggs

SOURCE
The Good Egg
by Marie Simmons

COOK
Marie Simmons

These gorgeous, tasty eggs look like fine porcelain with a crackled, marbleized glaze. They're twice-cooked, hard-cooked the first time and then simmered in a smoky fragrant broth with star anise, sherry and orange zest.

The tea eggs make a good hors d'oeuvre—try tucking them into a nest of watercress—or a snack, and they're also very good in salads. For a starter salad, cut an egg into quarters and reassemble it on top of the greens.

Our favorite way with these eggs is to serve them deviled. Mince some scallions and cilantro with the mashed egg yolks and add a few toasted sesame seeds and a touch of grated ginger. Add a little mayonnaise to bind it.

serves 4 to 6

8 eggs, preferably medium-size
½ cup dark soy sauce
½ cup dry sherry
4 star anise
1 strip (½ x 2 inches) orange zest

3 cups water
3 Lapsang Souchong tea bags, strings removed
Toasted sesame oil for rubbing the eggs (optional)

Place the eggs in a single layer in a saucepan. Cover with water and bring to a boil over medium heat. As soon as the water boils, remove the pan from the heat, cover and let stand for 10 minutes. Drain off the water, cover the eggs with cold water and let stand until cool enough to handle.

---

to drink
Asian beer

Meanwhile, combine the soy sauce, sherry, star anise, orange zest and water in the saucepan and bring to a simmer. Add the tea bags.

When the eggs are cool, gently tap them with the back of a tablespoon so the shells are evenly cracked. Do not peel. Using the spoon, carefully lower the eggs one at a time into the simmering liquid. If it does not cover the eggs entirely, add more water. Cover the pan and simmer for 1 hour.

Transfer the eggs to a bowl or small casserole with a lid. Cover with the hot liquid and cool to room temperature. Cover and refrigerate, preferably overnight.

Drain, peel and pat each egg dry. Rub with sesame oil, if desired. Serve halved or quartered.

---

tip

We were bemused this year to discover a lot of people reinventing the wheel in the hard-boiled egg division. We thought this question had been settled eons ago, but Alice Waters (in the *Washington Post*), Corby Kummer (in *The Atlantic Monthly*) and Shirley Corriher (in *Gourmet*) thought otherwise. In our own testing, we came to agree with the Alice Waters method (very similar to the Corby Kummer method), which gives firm whites and deep golden orange yolks that are slightly moist at the center. No gray rings, no nasty greenish yellow yolks. Here's what you do:

Have the eggs at room temperature. In a saucepan just large enough to hold them, bring enough water to cover them to a full boil over high heat. Using a slotted spoon, lower the eggs gently into the boiling water, reduce the heat slightly, and cook for exactly 8 minutes for salads and eating out of hand, 10 minutes for deviled eggs. Have a bowl of ice water ready.

Remove the eggs from the hot water and immediately plunge them into the ice water to cool. After a minute or so, when they're cool enough to handle, crack them all over and then return them to the ice water for another 5 minutes to make peeling easier. Peel off the shells under cold water.

---

porcini dust twists

The crisp cocktail puff-pastry twists everyone loves are given a magical new taste: wild mushroom. If you can manage to keep frozen puff pastry on hand (the best is made with butter—check the label) and

SOURCE

The Mushroom Lover's Mushroom Cookbook and Primer by Amy Farges

COOK

Amy Farges

dried porcini mushrooms in your cupboard, you can make these at a moment's notice, and have an emergency hors d'oeuvre or an elegant accompaniment to soup or salad in just 10 minutes.

makes 15 cocktail-size twists

8 ounces (½ package) frozen puff pastry, thawed in the refrigerator
Flour for rolling dough

2 teaspoons porcini powder (see note)
1 large egg, beaten with a fork

Preheat the oven to 400 degrees.

Carefully unfold the pastry. Roll it out on a lightly floured surface to a 14-x-10-inch rectangle. Sprinkle the porcini powder over the pastry. Cut the pastry into 7-x-³/4-inch strips. Twist each strip loosely as you lay it on an ungreased baking sheet. Leave about 1 inch between twists. Brush the twists with the egg on the unpowdered side and refrigerate for 10 minutes.

Bake until golden brown and crisp, 10 to 12 minutes. Transfer to a cooling rack. (The twists may be made ahead and stored for 2 or 3 days in an airtight container. If they get at all soft, crisp them in a 350-degree oven for about 4 minutes.)

---

cook's notes

- To make porcini powder, check a 3-ounce packet of dried porcini to be sure they're completely dry and stiff. If not, dry them on a baking sheet in a low oven until they're completely dry. Grind the porcini in a blender and keep in an airtight container.
- If you like, you can sprinkle ¼ cup of grated Parmesan cheese over the dough along with the porcini powder.

---

charred tomatillo guacamole with seeded tortilla triangles

SOURCE

Gourmet

COOK

Mary Sue Milliken

If there's a more beloved dip in America than guacamole, we don't know about it. So a new twist on our old favorite is an enticing prospect, and this delicious version, by one of the Two Hot Tamales team of TV chefs, completely delivers. Acidy little tomatillos get charred and then mashed into the basic seasonings before the avocado is added for a whole new taste.

Chef Milliken has taken the tortilla chips for a spin as well: These crunchy scoops come crusted with all kinds of seeds. The tortilla scoops don't have a particularly Mexican taste, so you can use them with any dip that would be good with the seeds. They're also delicious all by themselves.

For a party, you can make the tortilla scoops a day ahead and the guacamole up to 8 hours ahead. Just be sure to bring it to room temperature before serving.

Seeded Tortilla Triangles

makes about 32 triangles

¹/₄ cup flaxseed
¹/₄ cup sesame seeds
¹/₄ cup poppy seeds
4 (10-to-12-inch) flour tortillas

1 large egg, beaten with
  2 tablespoons cold water
  and 1 teaspoon salt

to drink
Margaritas or Mexican beer

Preheat the oven to 350 degrees.

Stir together the three kinds of seeds. Put 1 tortilla on each of two baking sheets and brush with some egg mixture. Sprinkle with seeds to coat, then cut each tortilla into long thin triangles with a sharp knife.

Bake in the upper and lower thirds of the oven, switching the position of the sheets halfway through the baking, until crisp and lightly golden, 15 to 20 minutes total.

Transfer the triangles to wire racks to cool. Repeat with the remaining tortillas.

---

cook's notes

- Flaxseed is delicate and best bought at a natural foods store that re-stocks frequently. If you can't find it, just leave it out and replace with 2 more tablespoons each of the other seeds.
- If the triangles lose their crispness, recrisp them in a 350-degree oven for about 5 minutes.
- Try other seeds, such as cumin.

Charred Tomatillo Guacamole

makes about 3½ cups

6 ounces tomatillos (6 or 7), husked and rinsed

½ small red onion, finely chopped

3–4 fresh serrano chiles, seeded and finely chopped

½ cup finely chopped cilantro

1 teaspoon salt

½ teaspoon freshly ground black pepper

2 large California avocados (about 1 pound)

Preheat the broiler.

Broil the tomatillos in a flameproof shallow baking pan about 4 inches from the heat until the tops are charred, 7 to 10 minutes. Turn the tomatillos over with tongs and broil until charred, about 5 minutes more.

Combine the onion, chiles, cilantro, salt and pepper in a large bowl. Add the tomatillos, 2 at a time, mashing with a fork or pestle to form a coarse paste.

Pit and peel the avocados. Add to the bowl and continue mashing until incorporated but still chunky. Serve with the Seeded Tortilla Triangles.

bacon-wrapped scallops with tamari glaze

The famous San Francisco caterers who are twin sisters took on the overlooked topic (in food, at least) of skewering this year and came up not only with brownies stabbed with candy canes but also with this intriguing twist on an

SOURCE

Skewer It! by Mary Corpening Barber and Sara Corpening Whiteford

COOKS

Mary Corpening Barber and Sara Corpening Whiteford

old cocktail-party classic. Scallops and smoky bacon are wonderful together, enhanced with tamari, maple syrup, lime and rosemary. These succulent little morsels will disappear immediately.

serves 12

TAMARI GLAZE

2 tablespoons reduced-sodium tamari sauce

2 tablespoons maple syrup

1 teaspoon fresh lime juice

8 strips applewood-smoked bacon, stacked and cut in 3-to-4-inch lengths (see note)

24 medium sea scallops (about 1 pound) or 12 large sea scallops, cut in half vertically (see page 49)

1 heaping tablespoon fresh rosemary leaves

24 toothpicks, soaked in water for 15 minutes
Freshly ground black pepper, to taste

24 sturdy 3-inch rosemary sprigs (strip the leaves from the bottom inch of each sprig)

---

to drink

Long tall cocktails (try Ginger-Berry Lemonade, page 321, spiked with vodka)

---

starters

13

Soak 24 toothpicks in water for 15 minutes.

MEANWHILE, MAKE THE TAMARI GLAZE

Combine the tamari, maple syrup and lime juice in a small saucepan. Boil over medium heat, whisking frequently, until reduced by half, 5 to 7 minutes. Keep a very close watch to avoid burning. Remove from the heat.

Preheat the broiler. Line a baking sheet with aluminum foil.

Lay several pieces of bacon on a work surface, vertically. Place a scallop flat side down on each bacon strip and place 3 or 4 rosemary leaves on each scallop. Wrap with the bacon (not too tightly, because the bacon will shrink as it cooks) and place seam side down on the baking sheet. Repeat the process until all the scallops have been wrapped. Secure the wrapped scallops with a soaked tooth-

---

cook's notes

- ✿ The bacon (don't use thick-cut bacon) should be cut according to the size of the scallops so that it barely overlaps each piece. Test a bacon strip to determine the right length before you cut all the pieces.
- ✿ Applewood-smoked bacon (Nueske's, in Wittenberg, Wisconsin, is a good brand that's widely distributed) is especially delicious with the scallops, but any good smoked bacon will be fine.
- ✿ Do-ahead: You can get the scallops wrapped with bacon and ready to broil the day before and refrigerate them overnight. Bring to room temperature before proceeding.
- ✿ Use only tiny leaves of rosemary when wrapping the scallops; the large leaves can be overpowering.

---

pick so the bacon won't come undone during the cooking. Liberally season each bacon-wrapped scallop with pepper.

Broil the scallops about 5 inches from the heat source until the bacon is partially crisp and brown around the edges, 10 to 15 minutes. Keep a sharp eye on the scallops, since the bacon can easily burn. Remove from the oven and let cool slightly. Warm the tamari glaze. Brush the scallops with the glaze and skewer each one on top with a rosemary sprig. Serve hot.

moroccan tapenade

SOURCE

Simple to Spectacular
by Jean-Georges
Vongerichten
and Mark Bittman

COOK

Jean-Georges
Vongerichten

This heady tapenade is full of toasted spices that are freshly ground and folded into a voluptuous olive base with a little salt and pepper to spike up the flavor. That's it, but the taste is haunting. And this tapenade is also one of the easiest dips imaginable— if you have a mortar and pestle, a coffee grinder or a spice mill, you're only going to spend about 5 minutes making it.

Once you have the tapenade, you can serve it not only with crudités and drinks, but also with roasted chicken, or as Vongerichten suggests, drop a little into the cooking mix for braised chicken. It's also delicious with grilled fish.

makes about ¾ cup; serves 6

Seeds from 4 cardamom pods
(discard the husks)
½ inch cinnamon stick
1 teaspoon coriander seeds
½ teaspoon cumin seeds
8 ounces pitted brined black
olives (about 1 cup), rinsed

2 tablespoons extra-virgin
olive oil
1 tablespoon water
Salt and freshly ground black
pepper

to drink

A chilled steely dry rosé from
the south of France

Combine the spices in a small dry skillet and turn the heat to medium. Toast, shaking the skillet periodically, until the spices are fragrant, just a minute or two. Use a mortar and pestle or coffee grinder (reserved for that purpose) or spice mill to grind the spices to a powder.

Combine the olives, oil, water and spice mix in a food processor, preferably a small one. Blend until pureed but not too fine. Add more water if necessary.

Taste for salt and add the pepper. Use right away or refrigerate for up to 2 days. Bring to room temperature before serving.

---

cook's notes

- ℞ Serve the tapenade with fennel, carrot and celery, or try jicama.
- ℞ If you can't find the specified olives, kalamatas will be fine.
- ℞ Fresh-ground spices are so superior that it's worth getting an extra coffee grinder to use just for grinding them.

---

spinach dip with jicama and sweet white onions

SOURCE

Time Out New York

COOK

**Colin Alevras,
The Tasting Room**

Remember spinach dip? Everyone loves dips; they're a communal kind of thing, with everyone dipping in and talking about how good the dip is. This one updates an old warhorse on the hors d'oeuvres trail. There's still plenty of cream cheese and sour cream to feel guilty about, but there's a new sweet, crunchy note here from the jicama and the sweet onions (look for the Del Monte brand if Vidalias or Walla Wallas are out of season).

One more reason to like this dip: It actually tastes better if you make it a day ahead.

makes about 4 cups; serves 10

4 cups fresh spinach, cleaned, with stems removed

1 cup cream cheese, softened

1 cup sour cream

1 cup finely chopped sweet onion

1 cup finely chopped jicama

Salt and freshly ground black pepper, to taste

Thinly sliced dark rye bread and/or crackers

Drop the spinach into a large pot of boiling salted water for only about 15 seconds to blanch it. Remove and plunge into a large bowl of ice water to cool. Drain the spinach and squeeze as much water out of it as you can with your hands. Finely chop it.

to drink
A buttery Chardonnay

In a medium bowl, combine the cream cheese and sour cream. Fold in the chopped onion and jicama, and stir in the chopped spinach. Season with salt and pepper.

Serve at room temperature with rye bread or crackers.

gorgonzola mascarpone torta

At the famous Oakville Grocery in the Napa Valley, cheese is a big specialty—and the hands-down biggest seller is this magnificent torta. These two Italian cheeses go beautifully together and the toasted nuts not only look attractive, they contribute both taste and crunch to the torta. At Oakville, they use an aged mountain Gorgonzola that's especially tasty. If you can't find something similar, use a mild Gorgonzola dolce, which is widely available.

SOURCE

The Cheese Course
by Janet Fletcher

COOKS

**Richard Tarlov
and Joyce McCollum**

Although making the torta is a snap, it needs at least 4 hours in the refrigerator to set and another 4 hours to come to room temperature. The best solution is to make it a day ahead, then just toast the nuts and place them all over the torta before serving.

This dramatic hunk of cheese begs for a glass of sherry or a dessert wine—and it works as well to finish a meal as to begin one.

serves 12

1 pound aged Gorgonzola or mild
Gorgonzola dolce, well chilled
10–12 ounces mascarpone, well chilled
¼ cup slivered almonds

If the cheese hasn't been cut (see note), hold a piece of dental floss taut between your hands and cut the cheese horizontally into three 1-inch layers.

to drink

Andalusian fino sherry or, for
dessert, Pedro Jiménez

Put the bottom wedge of Gorgonzola on a cutting board or a small tray. Top with a ½-inch-thick layer of mascarpone, spreading it evenly. Add the second layer of Gorgonzola and once again spread it with mascarpone. Top the mascarpone with the remaining wedge of Gorgonzola. Frost the top and rind of the Gorgonzola with ¼ inch of mascarpone.

Cover the torta with an inverted crock or plastic container to protect it from the drying air of the refrigerator. Refrigerate for at least 4 hours or as long as overnight.

Preheat the oven to 325 degrees. Toast the almonds on a baking sheet, stirring occasionally, until lightly browned, about 10 minutes. Let cool completely. Remove the torta from the refrigerator at least 4 hours before serving and press the almonds onto the mascarpone-covered top and rind. Set the torta on its side so that the layers are face up, cover and bring to room temperature before serving with crackers or bread.

---

cook's notes

℞ The easiest way to deal with the Gorgonzola is to have the cheese merchant cut it into 1-inch layers for you when you buy it.

℞ Sometimes the Oakville Grocery uses toasted pecans instead of almonds —your choice.

℞ For sheer drama, serve the torta standing straight up, like a wedge of cake. It will be slightly harder to serve, however.

---

crimped shrimp

SOURCE

Michael Roberts,
Los Angeles Times

COOK

Michael Roberts

In perhaps the most fascinating article we read this year, French-trained California chef Michael Roberts teaches an incredibly easy, superb way of cooking fish, which the English call "crimping." Roberts discovered it one day when he accidentally turned off the burner under a poaching salmon. Later he found a reference to the technique in a book by Madeleine Kamman, who'd learned about crimping from a British friend.

The idea is to make a flavored broth, bring it to a boil, turn down the heat, add the fish, cover, and cook for 1 minute without boiling. Then the fish comes off the heat in its pot, still covered, and sits for a few minutes, until the temperature of the fish and the liquid are equal. The texture is perfect, the oils in the fish aren't heated enough to release any smell and the fish picks up the flavor of the broth and vice versa. The steeping time is about 6 minutes for each half-inch thickness of fish, but of course it all depends on the fish and the pot.

Here's how it works for shrimp—no more mushy shrimp!

serves 6

- 3 cups water
- 1 cup white wine
- 1/4 cup rice or malt vinegar
- 1 carrot, coarsely diced
- 1 celery rib, coarsely diced
- 1/2 onion, coarsely diced
- 2 teaspoons salt
- 1 teaspoon dried thyme
- 2 bay leaves
- 6 black peppercorns
- 24 jumbo shrimp (about 2 pounds), peeled, with tails on

to drink
Sancerre

Bring everything but the shrimp to a boil in a medium heavy pot, covered. Reduce the heat and simmer for 5 minutes. Add the shrimp, cover again, and simmer for 1 minute.

Remove from the heat and steep, covered, for 4 minutes. Remove the shrimp from the liquid and chill well, at least 1½ hours, before serving with your favorite cocktail sauce.

cook's notes

❧ If you're defrosting shrimp, do it in the refrigerator, placing the frozen shrimp in a bowl of salted water to improve their flavor.

❧ You can freeze the poaching liquid to use again or to make a sauce. Just strain it before freezing.

albóndigas
(south-of-the-border meatballs)

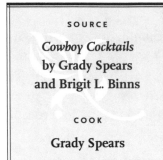

SOURCE

Cowboy Cocktails
by Grady Spears
and Brigit L. Binns

COOK

Grady Spears

Grady Spears is an actual cowboy turned chef for the famous Reata chain in Texas. His food is also kind of wild, full of hearty flavor and surprises, but he never strays far from his Texas roots. These albóndigas are meatballs gone south of the border. It's hard to say why they're so very good (is it the sugar?), but you just can't stop eating them. They're also very easy to make, so they're perfect party food.

makes about 60 meatballs

2 pounds ground chuck, 80% lean

3 large eggs, beaten

3 jalapeño peppers, stemmed and diced small

1 large yellow onion, diced

1 large red bell pepper, stemmed, seeded, and diced small

4 large garlic cloves, minced

½ cup ketchup

3 tablespoons Worcestershire sauce

2 teaspoons sugar

1½ teaspoons kosher salt, or to taste

to drink
Cold lager beer,
and plenty of it

Preheat the oven to 425 degrees.

In a large mixing bowl, combine all the ingredients and mix thoroughly by hand. Divide the mixture into balls the size of large walnuts, rolling them between the palms of your hands until firm and round.

Place the albóndigas on a lightly oiled baking sheet and bake for about 15 minutes, or until firm, bubbling and golden on the bottoms. Serve on a napkin-lined plate.

cook's notes

🔖 When the albóndigas bake, they leave a little custard-like foot around the base of each meatball, which looks a bit weird. But when you take them off the baking sheet, they look fine.

🔖 Be careful not to overmix the meatballs, or they'll be tough.

martabak

(savory indonesian meat pies)

We'd just had a terrific lunch in the Greystone kitchens, and the afternoon's conference offerings included an Asian-style street-food extravaganza. The stalls looked and smelled enticing, but who had room for another bite? A friend came up to whisper that we had to try the little spicy meat pies that Sri Owen, the famous Indonesian cook from London, was making. Can't, we said, too full. No, she said, just a bite, you have to . . . .

That's how we met the martabak, a treat

SOURCE

Recipe handout,
Southeast Asian
Conference, Culinary
Institute of America
at Greystone

COOK

Sri Owen

so delicious we ended up eating three of them in short order. Each crunchy, crisp little square seemed to be begging us to nibble at the corners, then bite into the warm, fragrant spicy filling. Because the martabak are made with wonton wrappers, they're really a cinch to prepare. Serve hot with beer or a spicy white wine. We think they make a great Sunday supper too—just add a green salad.

makes 20 to 25 martabak; serves 8 to 10

2 tablespoons olive oil
2 large onions, finely sliced
2–4 garlic cloves, finely chopped
2 teaspoons finely chopped
   fresh ginger
1 teaspoon ground coriander
1/2 teaspoon ground cumin
1/2 teaspoon turmeric or curry
   powder
1 pound 2 ounces ground beef
   or lamb

1 teaspoon salt
1 cup chopped scallions
   or chives
6 tablespoons chopped fresh
   Italian parsley
2 tablespoons finely chopped
   fresh lemongrass (see tip,
   page 185)
2–3 large eggs
6 ounces wonton skins
1 cup peanut oil, for frying

Heat the olive oil and onions in a wok or a wide shallow saucepan, stirring most of the time, until the onions are softened. Then add the garlic and ginger. Continue to cook, stirring, for 2 minutes, then add the ground seasonings.

Stir again to mix, and add the ground meat and salt. Continue to stir and mix for 10 to 15 minutes, or until the meat is cooked through. Put the mixture in a large bowl and leave it to cool. (You can make the recipe a day in advance up to this point, keeping the filling well covered in the refrigerator.)

Just before you're ready to fry the martabak, mix the scallions or chives, parsley, lemongrass and eggs into the meat mixture. Adjust the seasonings.

Lay a few wonton skins on a flat plate or tray. Put a tablespoon of filling onto each one, then put a second wonton square on top. Press the edges together so that they are more or less sealed (see note).

Pour $^1\!/_2$ to $^3\!/_4$ cup of the peanut oil into a skillet and place over high

---

cook's notes

- You may like about twice as much seasoning if you love spicy food—these seasonings are subtle.
- If the wonton skins won't seal, dip your fingertip into a little water and trace a line around the filling, but not all the way to the edges. Press down again and they should stick.

heat until you see a haze coming off the oil, or until it reaches 350 degrees on a deep-fry thermometer.

Transfer the first few wonton squares to the pan and press the martabak down to submerge them in the oil for a few seconds. Cook for 2 minutes or so, then turn them over and continue cooking for 2 more minutes. The casing should be quite crisp around the edges, but not in the middle, and the finished martabak should be flat and evenly filled with meat almost to the edge. Repeat the process until all the ingredients are used up. The oil in the pan will need renewing once or twice. Serve the martabak hot or at room temperature.

to drink

A light American
or Alsatian Riesling

soups

Broccoli Soup with Stilton   30

Zucchini Soup with Mint   32

Scallion and Mushroom Soup   34

Beet Soup in Roasted Acorn Squash   36

Brasserie Gazpacho   38

Chilled Curried Cucumber Soup   39

Avocado Vichyssoise   40

Asian Chicken Soup   41

Fresh Corn Soup   42

Garlicky White Bean Soup with Chicken and Chard   44

Crab Soup with Sweet Spices and Ginger Juice   46

Scallop and Corn Chowder   48

broccoli soup with stilton

SOURCE

Jonathan Reynolds,
New York Times Magazine

COOK

David Chambers

Every time we walk into the venerable Rules restaurant in London's Covent Garden, we feel a little frisson of anticipatory pleasure. The food is always the traditional English food of your dreams, which you so rarely get to eat anywhere else. So we were completely delighted to see that playwright Jonathan Reynolds had managed to tease out several of their terrific recipes.

This broccoli and Stilton soup is just about perfect—a vegetable-stuffed, lightly creamed soup is taken to nirvana by adding grated Stilton and a garnish of toasted almonds. Yes, it's rich, so a small cup would be plenty before a meal (though at Rules you get a generous amount, and proceed on to even heartier fare). But the soup's so good that we like to make it the centerpiece of the meal and just add a salad with some sharp greens and crusty bread.

serves 8

- 2 tablespoons olive oil
- 2¹/₂ cups thinly sliced leeks, including the firm green
- 1 cup chopped onion
- ¹/₂ cup finely chopped celery
- 2³/₄ pounds broccoli, stems peeled and diced, florets chopped
- 7 cups chicken stock
- 1 cup heavy cream
- ³/₄ pound Stilton cheese, coarsely grated
- Salt and freshly ground black pepper
- 1 cup thinly sliced almonds

to drink

A small glass of fine, medium-bodied ruby port

Heat the oil in a heavy-bottomed pot over medium-low heat. Add the leeks, onion and celery, sweating them for 20 minutes without letting them brown; keep an eye on them and stir frequently. Add the broccoli and sweat for 10 minutes more. Remove any browned bits before proceeding.

Add the stock and bring to a rolling boil over medium-high heat, then lower the heat and simmer until the vegetables are tender, about 15 minutes.

In a food processor, puree the vegetables in their broth (check for any lumps and puree again), rinse out the pot and return the pureed vegetables to the pot. (The soup can be prepared several hours ahead to this point.)

About 10 minutes before serving, stir in the cream and the Stilton. Heat gently until the cheese is melted and the soup is hot. Taste for salt and pepper. Meantime, toast the almonds over low heat in a small skillet until golden brown — watch them carefully and shake the skillet frequently.

Serve the soup as soon as it's ready, and pass the almonds separately in a bowl for each diner to garnish the soup.

---

cook's notes

- It's easiest to grate the Stilton if it's quite cold.
- You may find you need more stock to cook the vegetables; they shouldn't be sticking out of the liquid.

zucchini soup with mint

This is a pure soup, made just with water and the humblest vegetables and brightened with three fresh herbs. The texture is pleasingly rough, almost slushy, and the lovely pale green soup is flecked with bits of darker green herbs.

SOURCE

Simply Tuscan
by Pino Luongo

COOK

Pino Luongo

You really taste the zucchini, so look for small, fresh, thin-skinned ones, which will have the best flavor. The big baseball bat zucchini of late summer won't give you the same delicious results.

serves 6

1/4 cup extra-virgin olive oil
2 cups finely chopped Spanish onion (about 1 large onion)
1 pound Idaho potatoes, peeled and cut into 1/4-inch dice
Salt, to taste

3 pounds zucchini, trimmed and cut into 1/2-inch dice
10 large fresh mint leaves
10 fresh basil leaves
1/2 bunch fresh Italian parsley, leaves only

In a soup pot over medium heat, warm 2 tablespoons of the olive oil. Add the onion and cook until translucent, about 5 minutes. Stir in the potatoes. After 2 minutes, season with salt and add enough water to cover the potatoes and onions.

Simmer for 10 minutes, then add the zucchini. Add an additional ½ cup water, cover and continue simmering until the zucchini is cooked through, about 5 minutes. Remove from the heat and add the herbs. Puree in batches, or in its entirety, using a food processor or an immersion blender and adding the remaining 2 tablespoons olive oil to keep the puree from becoming too thick while blending. Taste for seasoning and serve immediately.

---

cook's notes

❧ We like this soup best served with a little olive oil drizzled over it, with some sizzling croutons fried in olive oil on top.

❧ The soup is also delicious cold, in which case you might want to swirl in a little heavy cream.

soups

scallion and mushroom soup

SOURCE

Joy of Cooking:
All About Soups & Stews

COOK

Dione Lucas

We can't remember ever seeing a scallion soup before, so this recipe stopped us in our tracks. There are other unusual elements as well; you beat the butter until it's light and fluffy, a direction we've never seen before in a soup recipe. Then the mushroom element isn't cooked at all, just dropped into the soup for a moment once it comes off the heat.

We had to try it, and indeed, it's extraordinary, with a delicate but deep flavor that's quite addictive. We called Maria Guarnaschelli, the editor of the new *Joy of Cooking*, to find out where the soup came from. We'd guessed it was French, and sure enough, it's from a long-forgotten book by Dione Lucas, the brilliant French cook who held forth in New York City in the fifties and sixties.

Part of the magic of the soup is that it's so simple to make and delivers such amazing flavor for the tiny amount of work involved.

serves 4

4 tablespoons (¹/₂ stick) unsalted
   butter, at room temperature
5 bunches of scallions, including
   the firm green, very finely
   chopped
1 teaspoon salt
¹/₂ teaspoon ground white pepper
2 tablespoons all-purpose flour

4 cups chicken stock
12 ounces mushrooms with
   stems
¹/₄–¹/₂ cup half-and-half
   Sprinkle of cayenne pepper,
   for garnish
   Dollop of sour cream, for
   garnish

In a soup pot, beat the butter with a wooden spoon until it's light and fluffy (see note). Add the scallions and stir together well. Add the salt and white pepper and cook, covered, over low heat for about 10 minutes.

Remove the pot from the heat and stir in the flour. Return to the stove and cook for 1 minute. Whisk in the chicken stock.

Bring the soup to a boil, whisking, over medium heat. Reduce the heat and simmer for 10 minutes. Meanwhile, wipe the mushrooms clean and remove and discard the tough ends of the stems only. Slice the mushrooms very thin.

Remove the soup from the heat and stir in two-thirds of the mushrooms. Immediately push through a sieve or food mill (see note). Stir in the half-and-half. Gently heat the soup until hot, then stir in the remaining mushrooms.

Ladle the soup into warmed bowls and top each serving with the cayenne pepper and sour cream.

cook's note

Easy as this soup is, you can make it even easier by not beating the butter and by pureeing the soup in a blender instead of using a food mill or sieve.

beet soup in roasted acorn squash

This soup is stunning—just the thing for a truly sensational start to a Thanksgiving dinner. The acorn squash bowls, sculptural in their own right with their deeply lobed sides and scalloped tops, are roasted to a deep orange and filled with a Technicolor-red beet soup. This

SOURCE

Katy Massam, *Gourmet*

COOK

Katy Massam

combo isn't just a visual thrill; it also tastes delicious. You get a little bite of sweet squash with every taste of beet soup.

The roasted squash bowls can be prepared a day ahead and reheated in a 350-degree oven.

serves 8

ROASTED SQUASH

8 acorn squash (1–1¼ pounds each)

3 tablespoons vegetable oil

1 tablespoon kosher salt

BEET SOUP

1 large red onion, chopped

1½ tablespoons vegetable oil

5 medium beets (2 pounds without greens), peeled and cut into 1-inch pieces

1 red apple, such as Gala or Braeburn, peeled and cut into 1-inch pieces

2 garlic cloves, minced

4 cups chicken or vegetable stock

4–5 cups water

2 tablespoons cider vinegar

1 packed tablespoon light brown sugar

Salt and freshly ground black pepper, to taste

TO ROAST THE SQUASH

Preheat the oven to 375 degrees.

Cut off the tops of the squash (about 1 inch from the stem end) and set aside. Scoop out seeds and discard. Cut a very thin slice off the bottoms of the squash to create a stable base. Brush the squash bowls and tops all over with oil and sprinkle the insides with salt. Arrange the squash bowls with tops alongside, stem ends up, in 2 large shallow baking pans.

Roast the squash in the upper and lower thirds of the oven, switching the position of the pans halfway through baking, until the flesh of the squash is just tender, about $1^{1}/_{4}$ hours total.

MEANWHILE, MAKE THE SOUP

Cook the onion in the oil in a 5-quart heavy saucepan over medium heat, stirring occasionally, until softened. Add the beets and apple and cook, stirring occasionally, for 5 minutes. Add the garlic and cook, stirring, for 30 seconds. Add the stock and 4 cups of the water and simmer, covered, until the beets are tender, about 40 minutes. Stir in the vinegar and brown sugar.

Puree the soup in three batches in a blender until very smooth, at least 1 minute per batch, transferring to a large bowl. Return the soup to the pan, season with salt and pepper, then reheat. If the soup is too thick, add enough water to thin to the desired consistency.

Serve the soup hot in the warmed squash bowls.

---

cook's notes

𝔼 You can make the soup up to 3 days ahead and chill it, well covered.

𝔼 If you don't blend the soup for a full minute, you'll end up with grainy soup. Don't use a food processor here. Use caution when blending hot liquids.

---

brasserie gazpacho

Florence Fabricant calls this gazpacho "stunning," and indeed it is. A cross between a Bloody Mary (in looks) and a martini (it's served in a martini glass),

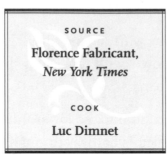

SOURCE

Florence Fabricant,
New York Times

COOK

Luc Dimnet

it's intensely spicy, extremely refreshing on a hot day and topped with a luxurious puff of mint-flavored whipped cream.

serves 6 to 8

- 3 ripe beefsteak tomatoes, diced
- 2 red bell peppers, cored, seeded and diced
- 1 cucumber, peeled, seeded and diced
- 1 small red onion, diced
- 3 garlic cloves, chopped
- 2 jalapeños, minced
- 1/4 cup sherry vinegar
- 3/4 cup extra-virgin olive oil
- Salt and cayenne pepper, to taste
- Chilled tomato juice, if necessary
- Whipped cream, for garnish
- Finely chopped fresh mint, for garnish

In a medium bowl, mix together the tomatoes, peppers, cucumber and onion. Add the garlic, jalapeños, vinegar and olive oil. Cover and marinate in the refrigerator for 6 to 8 hours.

Place the mixture in a blender, puree it, then strain it into a clean bowl. Add salt and pepper and, if the mixture is too thick, some chilled tomato juice. Serve the soup in martini glasses, garnished with whipped cream and chopped mint—or fold the mint into the whipped cream.

chilled curried cucumber soup

Alan Harding is the chef at Pastis, the extremely fashionable bistro in Manhattan. His very refreshing made-in-a-moment soup is wall-to-wall cucumbers in a base of yogurt with Indian

SOURCE
The Greenmarket Cookbook
by Joel Patraker
and Joan Schwartz

COOK
Alan Harding

spices. The spices and the lemon juice and wine vinegar perk it up considerably. With low-fat yogurt, it's really a diet soup; with full-fat yogurt, it has a creamy consistency and a rich flavor.

serves 4

8 medium cucumbers, all but one peeled and coarsely chopped
1/4 cup fresh lemon juice
2 teaspoons kosher salt
1/4 teaspoon freshly ground black pepper

2 tablespoons white wine vinegar
1 1/2 teaspoons hot curry powder
Pinch of cardamom
Pinch of cayenne pepper
1 cup plain yogurt

Put everything but the reserved cucumber and the yogurt in a large bowl and combine thoroughly. Working in batches, puree the mixture in a blender. Pass through a fine strainer into a large bowl and whisk in the yogurt. Adjust the seasoning to taste.

Quarter the remaining cucumber lengthwise. Remove the seeds and slice thinly. Serve the soup in individual bowls and garnish with the chopped cucumber.

avocado vichyssoise

A disarmingly simple soup inspired by a Paris food purveyor, this is a silky, velvety-smooth cream that needs to chill overnight in the refrigerator to bring out its true character. The make-it-ahead feature is a huge plus.

SOURCE

Paris in a Basket
by Nicolle Aimée Meyer
and
Amanda da Pilar Smith

COOKS

Nicolle Aimée Meyer and
Amanda da Pilar Smith

When Florence Fabricant reviewed the cookbook featuring this recipe in the *New York Times*, she suggested adding lemon juice to bring up the flavor. We completely agree, so we've added it here.

serves 6

1¼ pounds medium boiling potatoes, peeled and quartered
Salt
2 Hass avocados, chopped
4 cups chilled defatted chicken stock

¼ teaspoon ground cumin
Juice of 1 lemon
Freshly ground black pepper, to taste
Cilantro leaves, for garnish

Cook the potatoes in plenty of salted water until tender. Drain.

Place half the potatoes and 1 avocado in the blender with 1 cup of the chicken stock, the cumin and lemon juice. Process to a smooth puree, gradually adding another 1 cup of stock. Transfer to a bowl. Puree the remaining potatoes and avocados with the remaining 2 cups stock, and combine with the first batch. Season to taste with salt and pepper. Refrigerate overnight.

Serve chilled, garnished with a few cilantro leaves.

asian chicken soup

Every day there's a new what's-for-dinner recipe featured in the "Express Lane Cooking" columns that run in newspapers all across the country. This extremely simple meal-in-a-bowl soup struck us as just right for a cold evening, and it also seemed to have great restor-

SOURCE

Express Lane Cooking,
syndicated column

COOK

Bonnie Tandy Leblang

ative powers. Best of all, dinner's ready in 10 minutes.

Instead of using rice or noodles, the soup uses orzo, the rice-shaped pasta, which offers a pleasant bite and cooks perfectly in the short simmering time.

serves 4

- 2 quarts chicken stock
- ²/₃ cup orzo
- 1 pound boneless chicken, cut into small cubes
- 4 scallions, including some of the firm green, minced

- 2 tablespoons soy sauce
- 2 teaspoons toasted sesame oil
- 1 tablespoon minced fresh ginger
- 2 tablespoons rice wine vinegar
- 4 ounces snow peas, trimmed

In a large saucepan, combine everything but the snow peas and bring to a boil. Reduce the heat and simmer for 5 minutes. Add the snow peas and cook for 5 more minutes, or until the orzo is tender and the chicken is cooked. Serve hot.

cook's note

You can use fresh or bottled ginger juice instead of fresh ginger. For fresh ginger juice, see page 47.

fresh corn soup

This is, in our opinion, one of the great soups of the world, revived this year in the omnibus edition of Diana Kennedy's oeuvre on Mexican food. It's a delicate, comforting soup with the little piquant touch of poblano chilies and the crunch of crisp fried tortillas. It's also a very easy soup to make if you have a food mill, and it uses one of the great convenience foods, frozen corn kernels. Anyone who still thinks Mexican food is coarse and fiery will be stunned by the elegance of this simple soup.

Because the soup freezes well, you can make lots and keep it on hand for a consoling meal anytime.

SOURCE

The Essential Cuisines of Mexico by Diana Kennedy

COOK

Diana Kennedy

serves 6

4 cups corn kernels (about 1½ pounds), fresh or frozen

1 cup water

4 tablespoons (½ stick) butter

3½ cups milk or light chicken stock

½ teaspoon salt, or to taste

2 poblano chiles, charred, peeled and seeded, then diced and briefly fried in a little oil

6 tablespoons crumbled queso fresco (see note)

6 small tortillas, cut into small squares, fried until crisp in oil

If you're using frozen corn, measure it frozen and then let it defrost. Blend the corn with the water at high speed until you have a smooth puree. Put the puree through the medium disk of a food mill or a coarse strainer.

Melt the butter in a large saucepan but do not let it get too hot. Add the corn puree and let it cook over medium heat for about 5 minutes, stirring all the time.

Add the milk or stock and salt to the mixture and bring it to a boil. Lower the heat and let the soup simmer for about 15 minutes, stirring it from time to time to avoid sticking. It will thicken slightly.

Put about ½ tablespoon diced chile and 1 tablespoon crumbled cheese into each bowl. Pour the soup over them and top with the crisp tortilla squares to serve.

---

cook's note

The quality of queso fresco, a Mexican cheese, is iffy in the United States, except for the excellent product made by the Mozzarella Company in Dallas (1-800-798-2954). To substitute, use a fresh crumbly cheese that has a little acid, such as ricotta salata or feta.

garlicky white bean soup
with chicken and chard

SOURCE
Food & Wine

COOK
Judith Barrett

This rustic meal-in-a-bowl soup is a no-brainer, using canned white beans, quick-cooking skinless chicken breasts, and canned chicken broth to produce a wonderfully satisfying supper. The chard contributes a slightly sweet, slightly earthy taste with a touch of pleasant bitterness. Just add some crusty bread and a lively green salad and you've got a great weeknight meal.

You can even make the soup the night before and dinner will be ready when you get home.

serves 4

- 2 tablespoons extra-virgin olive oil
- 1 large onion, finely chopped
- 1½ tablespoons minced garlic Crushed red pepper
- 4 cups homemade chicken stock or canned low-sodium broth
- 1 pound Swiss chard, stems and tough ribs removed, leaves coarsely chopped

- 1 19-ounce can white beans, such as cannellini or Great Northern, drained and rinsed
- ½ pound boneless, skinless chicken breast, sliced crosswise ⅓ inch thick Salt and freshly ground black pepper

to drink

A dry Orvieto Classico from Umbria or a Gavi from the Piedmont

Heat the oil in a large saucepan until shimmering. Add the onion, 1 tablespoon of the minced garlic and a pinch of crushed red pepper. Cook over medium-high heat, stirring frequently, until the onion is softened, about 6 minutes. Add the stock, Swiss chard and beans and bring to a boil. Reduce the heat to medium-low and simmer until the chard is tender and the soup is slightly thickened, about 15 minutes.

Add the chicken and the remaining ½ tablespoon garlic and simmer gently over medium-low heat until the chicken is just cooked through, about 5 minutes. Season with salt and pepper. Ladle the soup into bowls and serve.

crab soup with sweet spices and ginger juice

SOURCE

*Raji Cuisine:
Indian Flavors, French
Passion* by Raji Jallepalli

COOK

Raji Jallepalli

his sensational soup is hands-down one of the best we've ever tasted. It's also one of the richest we've ever tasted, jammed with crab and luxurious with cream and saffron. You might want to serve very small cups of it—but then your guests may be frustrated, because they'll feel deprived if they can't have more. So save this for a very special occasion, such as New Year's Eve, or serve it as the centerpiece of an otherwise sparse meal when you need a big treat. It's actually a quick recipe to put together once you have the ginger juice on hand.

The soup is based on one from Jallepalli's Indian childhood, given a push into the style of French bisque. Everything about this soup is delicate and elegant, from its use of ginger juice instead of the harsher chopped ginger, to its tiny bit of garlic, blanched first to remove its bite. The saffron, the cream, the crab, the sweet spices with the touch of chili—everything comes together perfectly here.

serves 6

- ³/₄ pound jumbo lump crabmeat, picked over to remove cartilage and shell bits
- 1 fresh cayenne chile
- 3 tablespoons canola oil
- 1 large garlic clove, blanched and minced
- 1 tablespoon finely chopped onion
- 2 teaspoons garam masala
- 2 tablespoons fresh ginger juice (see note)
- 1 teaspoon saffron powder
- 4 cups heavy cream
  Coarse salt, to taste

> **to drink**
> Champagne

Set aside ¼ cup of the crabmeat for a garnish.

Wash the chile and remove the stem. Cut it in half crosswise and mince the top half (save the lower half for another purpose).

Heat the oil in a large heavy-bottomed saucepan over medium heat. Add the garlic, onion and minced chile. Sauté for about 3 minutes, or just until the vegetables begin to brown slightly. Stir in the garam masala. When well combined, add the ginger juice and stir well again.

Add the crabmeat and bring to a simmer again. Simmer for 5 minutes, stirring gently from time to time. Stir in the saffron and stir for an additional minute. Add the cream and bring to a simmer again.

Lower the heat and allow the soup to just barely simmer for about 15 minutes, or until it is slightly reduced. Taste and adjust seasoning with salt, if necessary.

Pour an equal portion into 6 shallow bowls. Divide the reserved crabmeat among the bowls and serve immediately.

---

cook's notes

- To make ginger juice: In a blender, combine 1 cup chopped ginger with 3 tablespoons warm water and blend to a paste. Strain the ginger in a sieve over a glass measure. Ginger juice is more delicate than chopped ginger and will freeze perfectly, so it's worth making a double batch.
- You can also buy bottled ginger juice at specialty stores or through Williams-Sonoma.

scallop and corn chowder

This rich, sweet chowder is also quite stunning to look at, so it's perfect winter dinner party fare. Richard Blais, the chef at Fishbone in Atlanta, has created a truly inspired dish. Even people who don't particularly like scallops love them in this chowder, perhaps because they're so tender you can eat them with a soup spoon.

Show off the chowder in wide, shallow soup bowls; even pasta bowls would work. Set two nicely seared scallops in the center of each bowl and then ladle the chowder around them.

SOURCE

Marcia Langhenry,
*Atlanta Journal-
Constitution*

COOK

Richard Blais

serves 8

2 cups canned creamed corn
1 quart heavy cream or
    half-and-half
½ pound applewood-smoked
    bacon or another smoked
    bacon
½ cup diced onion
½ cup diced celery
½ cup diced leeks
2 cups diced all-purpose or waxy
    potatoes

2 cups low-sodium chicken stock
    Sea salt and freshly ground
    black pepper, to taste
16 large sea scallops, cleaned
1 tablespoon vegetable oil
8 tablespoons (1 stick) butter
¼ cup chopped cilantro
2 tablespoons chopped fresh
    chives
    Juice of 1 lime

to drink
Chenin Blanc

Simmer the corn with the cream for 5 minutes.

Meanwhile, in a large saucepan, cook 2 strips of the bacon until crisp. Drain and reserve. Pour off the bacon grease. Combine the onion, celery, leeks, potatoes and the remaining slices of bacon in the saucepan. Add the chicken stock and the cream-corn mixture. Simmer for 30 minutes and season with salt and pepper.

Season the sea scallops with salt and pepper. Heat a nonstick skillet and sear the scallops until caramelized all over and medium-rare, just a couple of minutes on each side. Remove from the pan, add the oil and let it heat, then return the scallops to the hot pan, cooking for an additional minute. Add 4 tablespoons of the butter and simmer for 1 minute, taking care not to overcook.

Season the chowder with cilantro, reserving a little for a garnish, and chives. Dice the remaining 4 tablespoons of butter and swirl it in, along with the lime juice to taste. Arrange the scallops in the center of the soup plates, ladle the chowder around them and crumble the reserved bacon on top. Sprinkle with the remaining cilantro and serve.

---

tip

The editors of *Saveur* magazine say the way to get the best scallops is to know what to ask for. Since most scallop boats stay out for a long time, the catch is preserved on board with phosphates, which degrades their flavor and makes them ooze a milky liquid when they're heated. These sad scallops are called "wet" and are to be avoided by asking for "dry" scallops, which haven't been treated. They may also be known as dayboat scallops. Another scallop to avoid is the calico, often sold as bay scallops, which they are not. True bay scallops are sweeter, tenderer and more expensive by about half—true bays are usually about $20 a pound.

salads

Green Salad with Grapefruit and Warm Shrimp   51

Jicama-Mango Tortilla Salad with Citrus Vinaigrette   54

Herbed Farfalle and Grilled Chicken Salad   56

Warm Mushroom Salad   59

Fennel, Red Pepper and Mushroom Salad   61

Haitian Coleslaw   62

Fennel Slaw   64

Singapore Salad   66

Beet and Spinach Salad with Lemon, Cilantro and Mint   68

Roasted Bell Pepper Salad with Pine Nuts   70

Tomato, Avocado and Roasted Corn Salad   72

Turkish Bulgur Salad with Tomatoes and Nuts   74

Quick Pickled French Green Beans   75

green salad with grapefruit and warm shrimp

SOURCE

The Secrets of Success Cookbook by Michael Bauer

COOK

Fabrizio Laudati

It's hard to say why this straightforward combination of hot shrimp, cool greens and zingy grapefruit is so exciting, but in fact it's just about irresistible. Grapefruit and almost any kind of fish is an intriguing combination, and here it's perfectly balanced. Chef Laudati concentrates on the classics at his small neighborhood restaurant, Baraonda, on Russian Hill in San Fran-

cisco, but he likes to add a little twist like the grapefruit element here.

For home cooks, this salad is not only delicious but useful; you can make all the elements ahead and just put them together at the last minute. The winter salad makes a great first course for an elegant dinner but it's also delicious on its own for a light meal.

serves 6

MARINADE AND SHRIMP
- ¼ cup extra-virgin olive oil
- ¼ cup fresh grapefruit juice
- 2 garlic cloves, minced
  Salt and freshly ground white pepper
- 12 shrimp (¾ pound), peeled and deveined

VINAIGRETTE
- ¼ cup extra-virgin olive oil
- 2 teaspoons balsamic vinegar
- 2 teaspoons fresh grapefruit juice

- 3 garlic cloves, minced
  Salt and freshly ground white pepper

SALAD
- 3 ounces mixed baby greens
- 2 heads Belgian endive, separated into spears
- 2 pink grapefruit, peeled and cut into segments

- 1 tablespoon butter
- 1 teaspoon minced fresh Italian parsley

TO MARINATE THE SHRIMP

Combine the oil, grapefruit juice and garlic in a medium bowl. Season to taste with salt and white pepper. Add the shrimp and toss to coat. Transfer the mixture to a resealable plastic bag. Seal and refrigerate for at least 6 hours and up to 24 hours.

TO MAKE THE VINAIGRETTE

In a mixing bowl, combine the oil, vinegar, grapefruit juice and garlic, whisking until well blended. Season to taste with salt and white pepper.

TO MAKE THE SALAD

Place the greens, endive and grapefruit segments in separate bowls (reserve any of the juices from the grapefruit segments). Toss each gently with some of the vinaigrette.

---

cook's notes

- To cut grapefruit segments, slice off the top and bottom of the grapefruit, including all the bitter white pith. Over a bowl to catch the juices, slice off the peel from top to bottom, exposing the pink flesh. Be sure no white remains. To release the segments, cut as close as you can to either side of the membrane that separates each section, then pop out the fruit. Squeeze the skeleton of the grapefruit in your hand to release the remaining juice.

- To serve the salad as a meal, slice the endive and add it to the greens along with some diced avocado and chunks of grapefruit. Top with the shrimp and toss with the vinaigrette just before serving to 2 or 3 people.

TO COOK THE SHRIMP

Heat a skillet large enough to hold all the shrimp over high heat. Add the shrimp and marinade and stir until the shrimp are pink and curled and the sauce reduces slightly, about 3 minutes. Add the butter and toss until the butter melts. Remove from heat. Add the reserved juices from the grapefruit segments to the skillet and stir to blend.

TO ASSEMBLE THE SALAD

Place 3 or 4 spears of endive in a starburst pattern around the edge of each of 6 plates. Add a grapefruit segment on top of each spear. Pile a mound of greens in the center. Top with 2 hot shrimp and another grapefruit piece. Drizzle with a little of the sauce. Sprinkle with the minced parsley and serve.

---

to drink

A buttery Chardonnay from California (if you like it oaky) or Italy (if not)

---

salads

jicama-mango tortilla salad
with citrus vinaigrette

SOURCE

Southwestern Vegetarian
by Stephan Pyles
and John Harrison

COOK

Stephan Pyles

Our notes on this recipe start out "WOW!" You might think this will be a spicy salad, but no, there's not even a hint of spice here. Instead, it's all about texture and balance—the crispness of the fried tortillas, the watery crunch of the jicama and the pepper, the soft, voluptuous mango. All of these elements are brought together with a sharp lime and olive oil dressing.

On top of everything else, this is a gorgeous salad full of blazing colors, a particularly welcome one in midwinter when all the elements are available and an interesting salad seems like a big treat. It's great by itself or with fish or with Mexican dishes.

Stephan Pyles is a chef in Dallas, the southwestern heartland, and he has no trouble finding three colors of tortillas. For those who have difficulty finding even one good brand, just go with the plain ones— you'll still knock everyone's socks off.

Although you can make all the elements a few hours ahead, even frying the tortillas, don't put the salad together until the last minute before serving.

serves 4 to 6

3 cups vegetable oil

2 yellow corn tortillas, cut into matchstick slices

1 red corn tortilla, cut into matchstick slices

1 blue corn tortilla, cut into matchstick slices

1/4 cup fresh lime juice

1/2 cup olive oil

Salt, to taste

1 jicama, peeled and cut into matchstick slices

1/2 ripe mango, peeled, pitted, and cut into matchstick slices

1/2 red bell pepper, cut into matchstick slices

1/4 cup cilantro leaves

In a sauté pan, heat the vegetable oil until lightly smoking. Add the tortilla strips and fry over high heat until crisp, about 2 minutes. Remove from the oil with a slotted spoon and drain on paper towels.

Pour the lime juice into a mixing bowl and gradually drizzle in the olive oil, whisking until an emulsion forms. Season the vinaigrette with salt. In a large mixing bowl, combine the jicama, mango, bell pepper and cilantro leaves. Pour the vinaigrette over the salad and toss to combine. Add the fried tortillas and toss gently, being careful not to break up the tortillas too much. Serve immediately.

herbed farfalle and grilled chicken salad

SOURCE

Fine Cooking
by Joanne Weir

COOK

Joanne Weir

It's hard to imagine a more refreshing summer salad than this one, with its masses of cooling fresh herb leaves that are torn, not chopped—a fine point that only increases the pleasure of this dish, since the leaves don't wilt or bruise. The salad is also incredibly light. It's just the frilly little pasta, the herbs, some arugula and the grilled chicken,

all refreshed further with wedges of lemon served at the table. A bit of cumin punches it up.

Although the grilled chicken is perfect with these ingredients and gives the salad a rustic feeling, you could also use pulled chicken from a takeout roast chicken or some poached chicken (see tip) if grilling chicken seems like too much work.

serves 6

Coarse salt

12 ounces farfalle pasta

1/2 cup plus 2 tablespoons extra-virgin olive oil

2 large boneless skinless chicken breasts (about 1 pound)
Freshly ground black pepper

7 tablespoons fresh lemon juice

2 garlic cloves, minced

1 teaspoon ground cumin

1/4 cup packed fresh Italian parsley leaves

1 cup packed cilantro sprigs

1/2 cup lightly packed fresh basil leaves, torn

1/4 cup packed fresh mint leaves, torn

1 cup packed fresh arugula leaves, heavy stems removed

6 lemon wedges

Bring 6 quarts of water and 2 tablespoons salt to a boil in a large pot. Add the farfalle and cook until al dente, 10 to 12 minutes. Drain the pasta and toss it immediately with 1 tablespoon of the olive oil. Let the pasta cool completely in the refrigerator.

Heat a cast-iron ridged grill pan or an outdoor barbecue. Brush the chicken breasts with 1 tablespoon of the olive oil. Grill until golden on one side, 4 to 5 minutes. Turn the breasts, season with salt and pepper and continue to grill until golden and cooked through, another 6 to 8 minutes. Let the chicken cool and then cut it on the diagonal into thin strips. Set aside.

---

tip

This great Chinese way of poaching chicken (from New York cooking teacher Rosa Ross) is similar to the crimping technique for cooking fish (see Crimped Shrimp, page 22). You make an aromatic broth for the chicken — the Asian version uses a couple of slices of fresh ginger, a couple of scallions and 1 tablespoon of Szechwan peppercorns, but you can use any combination of herbs and vegetables. Put the flavorings in a large pot and add enough water to cover a 3-pound chicken. Bring the broth to a boil and simmer, covered, for 10 to 15 minutes, or until it smells good.

Insert two large metal spoons into the cavity of the chicken to transfer the heat to its interior. Submerge the chicken in the hot liquid and return the liquid to a boil.

Immediately turn off the heat and cover the pot. Let it sit for at least 1 hour. Remove the chicken from the liquid and let it cool completely. Remove the skin and cut or tear the flesh into bite-size pieces. The chicken will be juicy and moist and have a silken texture. Bonus: You have chicken stock left over.

---

salads

In a large bowl, whisk the remaining $\frac{1}{2}$ cup olive oil with the lemon juice, garlic and cumin. Season to taste with salt and pepper. Add the pasta, chicken and remaining ingredients, except the lemon wedges, and toss well. Taste for seasoning.

Put the salad into a serving bowl and serve immediately, garnished with the lemon wedges.

serve with

Brasserie Gazpacho
(page 38)
Crusty sourdough rolls

℘

Santa Rosa Plum Galette
(page 300)

to drink

A white wine with some
body and a little bite,
such as a Fumé Blanc
from California

warm mushroom salad

We don't usually think of salads being warm, but this one is absolutely delicious, full of savory flavors that are perfect for midwinter and especially good with leftover roast beef. Although the salad is made with plain old

SOURCE

Marcia Kiesel,
Food & Wine

COOK

Marcia Kiesel

white mushrooms, it gathers plenty of complex taste from sherry vinegar, soy sauce and Marsala.

You can make the vinaigrette up to 3 hours ahead and the mushrooms can be made a half hour ahead and reheated.

serves 6

- 3 pounds medium white mushrooms, trimmed and quartered
- 3 tablespoons fresh lemon juice
- 2 tablespoons butter
- 2 tablespoons plus 1 teaspoon olive oil
- Salt and freshly ground black pepper
- 1 tablespoon soy sauce
- 3 tablespoons extra-virgin olive oil

- 3 tablespoons sherry vinegar
- 2 tablespoons Marsala
- 2 teaspoons tomato paste
- 2 garlic cloves, minced
- 3 large shallots, thinly sliced
- 6 cups coarsely shredded romaine lettuce
- 2 cups coarsely shredded Boston lettuce
- 1/2 cup shredded Gouda cheese, aged Gouda or goat Gouda (1 ounce)

Preheat the oven to 300 degrees.

In a large bowl, toss the mushrooms with the lemon juice. In a large skillet, melt the butter with 2 tablespoons of the olive oil over medium-high heat. When the butter starts to brown, add the mushrooms and season with salt and pepper. Cover and cook until the mushrooms release their liquid, about 3 minutes. Uncover and continue to cook, stirring occasionally, until the liquid has evaporated and the mushrooms are deeply browned, about 8 minutes. Add the soy sauce and cook, stirring, for 2 minutes longer. Transfer the mushrooms to a rimmed baking sheet and keep warm in the oven.

In a small bowl, whisk the extra-virgin olive oil with the sherry vinegar, Marsala, tomato paste and minced garlic. Season with salt and pepper.

Add the remaining teaspoon of olive oil to the skillet. Add the shallots, cover and cook over medium heat until softened, about 3 minutes. Uncover and cook, stirring, until lightly browned. Stir in the sherry vinaigrette and remove from the heat.

Toss the lettuces in a salad bowl and add the mushrooms and shallots; toss well. Arrange the salad on 6 plates, sprinkle with the cheese and serve at once.

---

cook's note

Don't leave any of the delicious mushroom juices behind on the baking pan. Tip them right into the salad.

fennel, red pepper and mushroom salad

This extremely good salad is made of everyday ingredients but manages to take off and fly because they're so perfectly balanced. It's a chopped salad with mostly Mediterranean flavors. Shulman served it at a cookbook fair in Austin, Texas, and had so many requests for the recipe, both from casual passersby and her

SOURCE
Martha-rose-shulman.com

COOK
Martha Rose Shulman

fellow cookbook authors, that she posted it on her Web site.

It's a great salad to serve at a party or on a buffet because the ingredients hold up very well. It's also a hit for the holidays, because its colors are so festive and it's so refreshing in a season of overindulgence.

serves 6

SALAD

2 pounds fennel bulbs, trimmed, quartered and cut crosswise into very thin slices

2 large red bell peppers, seeded and cut into thin 2-inch slices

8 mushrooms, cleaned and thinly sliced (about ¼ pound)

2 tablespoons minced fresh Italian parsley

1 tablespoon minced fresh

chives

2 ounces shaved Parmesan cheese

DRESSING

¼ cup fresh lemon juice

2 tablespoons sherry vinegar

1 garlic clove, very finely minced or pressed

Salt and freshly ground black pepper

½ cup olive oil

Combine the salad ingredients in a large bowl. Whisk together the dressing ingredients in a small bowl. Toss the dressing with the salad and serve.

haitian coleslaw

Eileen Hruby of New Jersey can't forget how great the coleslaw tastes at Pusser's (of Pusser's rum fame) in Cruz Bay on the island of Saint John. So she enlisted the help of *Bon Appétit* to secure the recipe. As she points out, it's cool and hot all at the same time. How does the

SOURCE

Bon Appétit

COOK

Pusser's, Virgin Islands

restaurant do it? The secret is the serrano chiles for the fire, fresh lime juice to cool it down and a little sugar to pull it all together.

It's an unusual coleslaw that's perfect with grilled meats, chicken and fish.

serves 6

- ¼ cup mayonnaise
- ¼ cup olive oil
- ¼ cup fresh lime juice
- 2 tablespoons apple cider vinegar
- 2 tablespoons Dijon mustard
- 2 tablespoons chopped fresh dill
- 1 tablespoon sugar
- 2 small serrano chiles, seeded and minced (about 2½ teaspoons)

- 1 garlic clove, minced
- 1 teaspoon celery seeds
- 8 cups packed shredded cabbage (about 1¼ pounds)
- 2 cups packed shredded carrots (about 2 large carrots)
- Salt and freshly ground black pepper, to taste

Whisk the mayonnaise, olive oil, lime juice, vinegar, mustard, dill, sugar, chiles, garlic and celery seeds in a medium bowl to blend.

Put the cabbage and carrots in a large bowl and toss with enough dressing to coat. Season with salt and pepper. Serve cold or at room temperature.

cook's note

You can make the salad up to 1 hour ahead and let it sit at room temperature, or refrigerate for up to 4 hours.

fennel slaw

SOURCE

Gourmet

COOK

**River's End Restaurant,
Jenner, California**

Like so many of the best recipes, this one was discovered by food magazine readers, in this case the Duncans, tourists from Texas who dined on this slaw at a restaurant along the road and found it so addictive they had to ask for the recipe. Good thing: This is an unusually fresh, zesty, crunchy slaw that's indeed hard to stop eating. Even people (like the Duncans) who don't like fennel love it. It goes with almost everything, from chicken to fish to pork.

The only trick here is that the recipe calls for a mandoline or an inexpensive Japanese slicer. If your knife skills are good, you can just cut thin slices by hand.

serves 4

- 1/3 cup mayonnaise
- 2 tablespoons cider vinegar, or to taste
- 2 teaspoons sugar
- 1 1/2 tablespoons chopped fresh dill
- 1/2 teaspoon finely grated lemon zest
- 1/8 teaspoon salt
- 1/2 teaspoon freshly ground black pepper, or to taste
- 1 1/2 pounds fennel (about 1 1/2 large bulbs)

---

cook's notes

❧ It's easiest just to whisk the dressing together in the same bowl you'll serve the salad in, reserve a little in a separate bowl, then add the fennel and toss. You need only enough dressing to coat the fennel.

❧ The salad tastes best within 2 hours of being made. It loses its crunch and starts to weep if it sits longer than that.

In a small bowl, whisk together all the ingredients except the fennel.

Trim the fennel stalks flush with the bulb, discarding the stalks, and remove any discolored outer layers. Halve the fennel through the root end and discard the core. Thinly slice the fennel with a mandoline or other manual slicer.

Place the fennel in a medium bowl and toss with just enough dressing to coat. Taste and adjust the seasonings, adding salt and pepper if needed, and serve.

singapore salad

SOURCE

New York Times

COOKS

**Chris Schlesinger
and John Willoughby**

This exuberant salad was inspired by a visit to Singapore, where peanuts appeared in all kinds of dishes, even salad. This one is a little sweet, a little tart and very savory—and intrepidly hot, with both fresh chile and more Tabasco sauce than you've ever seen listed as an ingredient. Another surprise is the cilantro, used here as a salad green. The combination is simply winning, and it's also visually appealing, with its bright red, orange and deep green against a backdrop of pale green napa cabbage. Topping it all off are the spicy, crunchy peanuts.

However many people you're serving this salad to, we guarantee there won't be any left, even if it's just two eager diners.

serves 4 to 6

- ⅓ cup toasted sesame oil
- ⅓ cup rice wine vinegar (not seasoned)
- ½ cup soy sauce
- ¼ cup sugar
- 2 tablespoons minced fresh ginger
- 1 teaspoon minced fresh chile pepper, or to taste
  Salt and freshly cracked white pepper
- ½ cup shelled raw peanuts
- 2–3 tablespoons Tabasco sauce
- 1 tablespoon vegetable oil

- ½ head napa cabbage, outer leaves removed, inner leaves washed, dried and cut into thin strips
- 1 cup loosely packed cilantro leaves
- 3 scallions, white part and bottom 2 inches of green, thinly sliced
- 1 medium-size carrot, peeled and cut into very thin strips
- 1 red bell pepper, seeded, halved and cut into very thin strips

Preheat the oven to 350 degrees.

In a small bowl, combine the sesame oil, vinegar, soy sauce, sugar, ginger, chile pepper and salt and pepper to taste. Whisk together and set aside.

In another small bowl, combine the peanuts, Tabasco and vegetable oil, and mix well. Spread the peanuts on a small ungreased baking sheet and roast in the oven until nicely browned, 12 to 15 minutes. Cool the nuts and then chop coarsely.

In a large bowl, combine the cabbage, cilantro, scallions, carrot and red pepper. Stir the dressing well, pour on just enough to moisten the ingredients (you'll have leftover dressing) and toss to coat. Garnish with the peanuts and serve.

Garlicky Fried Peanuts

Sri Owen, the Indonesian cook and author, makes the best garlicky fried peanuts we've ever encountered. They're incredibly crisp and completely greaseless, great on salads such as this one, on noodles, in rice dishes or just eaten out of hand. Here's how she does it.

Put 1 to 2 pounds of large raw (unroasted) peanuts, minus their papery skins, in a large heatproof bowl and cover with boiling water. Stir in 4 crushed garlic cloves and 2 tablespoons sea salt and let the nuts soak for 45 minutes. Strain the nuts and spread them on a tray, patting them dry with paper towels.

Heat about 2½ cups oil — peanut oil is perfect — in a wok or fryer. When the temperature hits 360 degrees, add the nuts (in several batches) and fry for 4 to 5 minutes, stirring frequently. Scoop the fried nuts onto a tray lined with paper towels and leave them to cool and crisp. Store for up to several weeks in airtight containers.

beet and spinach salad
with lemon, cilantro and mint

This simple but terrific salad showcases beets perfectly, accenting their earthy sweetness with the cutting freshness of lemon, mint and cilantro. The mystery ingredient here is coriander,

SOURCE
Los Angeles Times

COOK
Deborah Madison

cilantro's alter-ego spice.

You can serve this salad as a first course, as a side salad or as a light meal in itself, with a little cheese —such as havarti with dill —and dark bread alongside.

serves 4 to 6

2 pounds beets (about 6 medium)	2 tablespoons chopped fresh parsley
Grated zest of 1 lemon	2 tablespoons chopped cilantro
2 tablespoons fresh lemon juice	2 teaspoons fresh mint leaves, slivered
2 tablespoons finely diced red onion	6 tablespoons extra-virgin olive oil
1/2 teaspoon salt	5 cups tender spinach leaves
Freshly ground black pepper, to taste	1/4 cup black oil-cured olives (optional)
1/2 teaspoon ground coriander	

Leaving 1 inch of stem and all of the roots, steam the beets until they're tender-firm when pierced with a knife, 20 to 25 minutes. Let cool, then slip off their skins. Cut the beets in quarters or sixths and place in a medium bowl.

Whisk the lemon zest, juice, onion, salt, pepper, coriander, herbs and oil in a small bowl. Taste on a bit of beet and correct the seasonings if necessary. Toss the beets with enough dressing to cover lightly. Toss the spinach with the remaining dressing and arrange on salad plates. Add the beets and the olives, if using, and serve.

---

cook's notes

❧ Beets leave you with telltale Lady Macbeth fingers. If you'd rather avoid them, use plastic gloves when you're peeling beets.

❧ You can microwave the beets, wrapped in plastic wrap, but check them often; they can easily overcook and get wrinkly.

---

roasted bell pepper salad with pine nuts

SOURCE

Rozanne Gold,
Bon Appétit

COOK

Rozanne Gold

If you're giving a big dinner party or going to a potluck, this great little salad could save the day. It's a rustic-looking pile of brightly colored roasted peppers dotted with toasted pine nuts. The only other ingredients (besides salt and pepper) are olive oil and balsamic vinegar, but they conspire to bring out a complexity of flavor and a sweetness that's delightful.

More delightful yet is the amount of time you'll spend actually making this salad. We clocked it at about 8 minutes of actual work, since we decided not to peel the peppers (which would have added a few more minutes). And you could do it all the day before and just mix the salad and scatter the toasted nuts on top a couple of minutes before serving.

Once you know about this recipe, you can make it in any quantity. It's so simple you won't even need a recipe except for the oven temperature and cooking time.

serves 24

6 large red bell peppers, halved and seeded

6 large yellow bell peppers, halved and seeded

6 large orange bell peppers, halved and seeded

8 tablespoons extra-virgin olive oil

Salt and freshly ground black pepper, to taste

3 tablespoons (or more) balsamic vinegar

1/2 cup pine nuts, toasted (see tip, page 227)

Preheat the oven to 400 degrees. Place all the peppers in a large bowl. Pour 6 tablespoons of the oil over them and toss to coat. Place the peppers, cut side down, on 2 large rimmed baking sheets and sprinkle with salt. Roast until the peppers are soft and slightly blackened, about 1 hour, reversing the sheets after 30 minutes. Cool slightly and peel if desired.

Cut the peppers into 1/4-inch-wide strips and transfer to a large bowl. Add the accumulated juices from the baking sheets. Add the 3 tablespoons vinegar and the remaining 2 tablespoons oil; toss gently. Refrigerate the peppers for at least 1 hour or up to a day.

When ready to serve, drain the peppers and discard the juices. Transfer the peppers to a serving platter. Season with salt, pepper and more vinegar if desired. Toss gently and sprinkle with the pine nuts.

---

cook's notes

- Cleanup will be much easier if you line the baking sheets with foil before roasting the peppers.
- We like the roasted pepper skin but suggest you remove any large blackened pieces that have separated from the flesh.
- To our taste, the salad is best just slightly chilled, so let it warm up a bit before serving.
- Discount grocery stores and warehouse clubs have started importing big sacks of multicolored peppers from Israel and Holland; they're a bargain, as are peppers at the farmer's market in the summer.

---

tomato, avocado and roasted corn salad

SOURCE

Jessie Carry,
Food & Wine

COOK

Elizabeth Falkner

San Francisco pastry chef Elizabeth Falkner, who owns Citizen Cake, is also an avid soccer player with a group of women known as the Follies. Falkner likes to host post-game lunches for the players and their kids, and she tosses together this salad at the last minute. All the work (which is minimal) can be done the day before.

It has a definite Mexican accent, but it's also very versatile, great with grilled chicken, meat or fish. Vegetarians can find enough sustenance here for an entire meal.

Part of what makes this salad so good is roasting the corn, an easy step that delivers a huge amount of extra flavor.

The salad serves a crowd, but it also cuts in half easily.

serves 12

5 ears of corn, shucked

1/2 cup plus 2 tablespoons extra-virgin olive oil

Salt and freshly ground black pepper

1/2 cup raw pumpkin seeds

3 tablespoons fresh lime juice

2 tablespoons sherry vinegar

1 teaspoon sugar

1/4 teaspoon hot sauce

1/8 teaspoon ground cinnamon

1 1/2 pounds arugula (4 bunches), large stems discarded, leaves torn into bite-size pieces

3 ripe avocados, cut into 1/2-inch dice

2 large red tomatoes, cut into 1/2-inch dice

2 large yellow tomatoes, cut into 1/2-inch dice

2 medium cucumbers, peeled, seeded and cut into 1/4-inch dice

3 ounces queso fresco (see note, page 43) or ricotta salata, crumbled (3/4 cup)

Preheat the oven to 500 degrees.

On a rimmed baking sheet, drizzle the corn with 2 tablespoons of the olive oil. Season the ears with salt and pepper and roast for about 25 minutes, turning a few times, until the kernels are browned. Let cool. Cut the kernels from the cobs and transfer to a bowl.

Turn the oven down to 400 degrees. Spread the pumpkin seeds in a pie plate and bake, stirring occasionally, for about 4 minutes, or until lightly browned. Transfer to a plate to cool.

Put $\frac{1}{2}$ cup of the corn kernels in a blender. Add the lime juice, sherry vinegar, sugar, hot sauce and cinnamon and puree. With the machine on, add the remaining $\frac{1}{2}$ cup olive oil in a thin stream and blend until emulsified. Scrape the vinaigrette into a bowl and season with salt and pepper.

In a large bowl, toss the remaining corn kernels with the arugula, avocados, red and yellow tomatoes and cucumbers. Add the vinaigrette and toss well. Mound the salad on a large platter, scatter the pumpkin seeds and crumbled cheese on top and serve.

---

cook's notes

- You can make the corn and the vinaigrette a day ahead; just don't mix them together. The roasted pumpkin seeds will keep for several days in an airtight container at room temperature.
- This salad looks prettiest, we think, if you don't add the corn to the vinaigrette. Just toss the extra $\frac{1}{2}$ cup of kernels into the salad.
- You can use cherry tomatoes instead of regular tomatoes.
- This salad has no oniony element and doesn't need one. But if you'd like, you can toss in some chopped scallions or chives.

turkish bulgur salad
with tomatoes and nuts

We'd passed this salad by initially because it seemed a bit plain and slightly odd, but in fact it's neither. It's intensely flavored and so simple that it's a pleasure to make. You don't soak this bulgur in boiling water in the usual way; instead, the liquid all comes from tomatoes. In winter you can use canned diced tomatoes and it will still be wonderful.

Among this salad's many virtues is the fact that it holds up well for a day in the fridge, so you can make it ahead.

SOURCE

*The New Book of
Middle Eastern Food*
by Claudia Roden

COOK

Claudia Roden

serves 4 to 6

³/₄ cup fine-ground bulgur
(cracked wheat)
1 pound tomatoes, peeled and
pureed in the food processor
1 teaspoon tomato paste
3–4 tablespoons olive oil
Salt, to taste

Pinch of chile flakes or ground
chile pepper, or to taste
1 smallish mild onion or
5 scallions, finely chopped
¹/₂ cups walnuts or pistachios or a
mixture of the two

Mix the bulgur with the blended tomatoes and tomato paste and let stand for an hour, or until the grain has become tender. Add a little water if it hasn't.

Add the oil, salt and chile flakes or ground chile. Before serving, stir in the onion or scallions and walnuts or pistachios.

---

cook's note

The salad is even tastier if you lightly toast the nuts first.

---

quick pickled french green beans

Chef Harry is a health-minded TV chef (star of *Chef Harry and Friends* on PBS) with an avid Hollywood following. His fresh pickled beans are a little reminiscent of dilly beans but much crisper and livelier.

The beans pickle—and look—best when

SOURCE

Healthy Mind, Healthy Body, Oxford Health Plans

COOK

Chef Harry Schwartz

they're almost jammed into the jar—French jam jars are about the right size. Be sure you use the skinny French green beans. Regular supermarket green beans will be too thick and tough for this treatment.

The refreshing beans are especially good for a picnic or barbecue.

serves 4 to 6

8 ounces French green beans (haricots verts), rinsed and trimmed

2 tablespoons red wine vinegar

1 teaspoon or 1 cube sugar

1/4 cup chopped purple onion

2 tablespoons minced fresh dill

Salt and freshly ground black pepper, to taste

About 1 cup water

Place the beans lengthwise in a jar (about 2 cups) with a tight-fitting lid. The beans should fit somewhat tightly in the jar. Pour in the vinegar, and add everything else but the water.

Add enough water to fill the jar and seal. Shake the jar to blend the ingredients and refrigerate overnight or for up to 3 days before serving.

breakfast and brunch

christmas morning melon wedges

For Oregon chef Caprial Pence, breakfast on Christmas morning is almost more important than the big-feast dinner. But she's also not a morning person, so anything that can be prepared the night before gets a thumbs-up.

SOURCE

Caprial Cooks for Friends
by Caprial Pence

COOK

Caprial Pence

These marinated melon wedges are deliriously good —fragrant, lightly sweet, a bit exhilarating with ginger and mint delicately added. They're just as good for dessert, especially refreshing after a holiday dinner.

serves 6

- 1 large, ripe seasonal melon, seeded, rind removed, cut into 12 wedges
- 1/2 cup sugar
- 1 cup Riesling or other sweet white wine
- 1/4 cup orange liqueur, such as Grand Marnier or Cointreau
- 1 large slice of fresh ginger
- 1 cinnamon stick
- 1 teaspoon frozen orange juice concentrate, thawed
- Dash of pure vanilla extract
- 1 teaspoon chopped fresh mint
- Sprigs of fresh mint, for garnish

Place the melon in a high-sided baking dish. In a saucepan over high heat, combine everything but the mint sprigs. Bring the mixture to a boil and cook until the sugar has dissolved, about 5 minutes. Let the syrup cool completely, then pour it over the melon. Cover and refrigerate for at least 1 hour or up to 24 hours.

To serve, place the melon on a platter, pour the marinade over the top, and garnish with the mint sprigs. Serve cold.

new orleans broiled grapefruit

In New Orleans, where brunch is a much-beloved institution, ordinary breakfast foods tend to get the grand treatment. Plain old grapefruit leaves the kitchen at Commander's Palace not only tipsy with

SOURCE

Commander's Kitchen
by Ti Adelaide Martin
and Jamie Shannon

COOK

Jamie Shannon

dark rum but warm, wearing a crunchy little brown sugar and cinnamon topping. If it's a ruby red grapefruit, so much the better. What a great way to start the day!

serves 4

2 grapefruit
1/4 cup dark rum

1/2 cup packed light brown sugar
1 teaspoon ground cinnamon

Cut the grapefruit in half around their equators. Using a grapefruit knife or other serrated knife, cut the flesh into sections by running the knife along each side of the membranes that separate them. Cut around the edge of the fruit to separate it from the rind, but do not remove the flesh.

Place the prepared grapefruit halves in a casserole dish or baking pan. Drizzle a tablespoon of rum over each half. If it doesn't soak in, poke a few holes in the flesh.

Combine the sugar and cinnamon and divide equally among the grapefruit, sprinkling it over the top. Broil for 4 to 5 minutes, or until the sugar and juice boil and the sugar starts to darken. Serve each grapefruit half in a small bowl and pour any excess liquid on top. If desired, splash with a little extra rum before serving.

glazed bacon

If you need to serve break-fast to a crowd, or you're just looking for something new and interesting to do with bacon, this recipe is for you. It calls for thick-

SOURCE

Jacqueline Higuera
McMahan, Sfgate.com

COOK

Jacqueline Higuera
McMahan,
after James Beard

sliced, meaty bacon—we'd make it double-smoked—and brown sugar. In the oven, the bacon loses almost all its fat and turns crunchy and sweet.

serves 6

½ pound thick-sliced, meaty bacon

1 tablespoon brown sugar per strip of bacon, or to taste (see note)

Preheat the oven to 350 degrees.

Lay out the bacon on a jelly-roll pan and bake for 10 minutes. Pour off the fat. Sprinkle a tablespoon of brown sugar over each bacon strip. Return to the oven for 8 minutes. Turn the bacon over and bake for 2 to 3 minutes longer. Watch carefully; the bacon can easily overbrown and burn.

Remove the bacon from the oven and place on a plate to cool slightly before serving.

---

cook's notes

✎ You can use light or dark brown sugar, as you please (we prefer light). You may find 2 teaspoons is plenty of sugar for each slice.

✎ Although it's only a little unwieldy to pour off the bacon grease, it's even easier if you cook the bacon on a rack in the pan and just lift out the rack to drain the grease.

---

pecan praline french toast

One of the specialties of the Stage Stop Ranch, which is in the Texas Hill Country in a little town called Wimberley, is this rich French toast for a crowd. It's custardy inside

SOURCE

Virtualcities.com,
1st Traveler's Choice
Internet Cookbook

COOK

Stage Stop Ranch

with a crisp brown sugar topping that doesn't, according to the ranch, require syrup (though some at your table may beg to differ). It's a very simple dish that's always very popular.

serves 6 to 8

³/₄ cup (1¹/₂ sticks) butter
1 cup packed light brown sugar
1 cup coarsely chopped pecans
8 large eggs
1¹/₂ cups milk

1 teaspoon pure vanilla extract
Several dashes of ground cinnamon
1 loaf of French bread, cut into 1-inch slices

Preheat the oven to 350 degrees.

In a 12-x-15-inch baking pan, melt the butter in the oven as it heats, being careful not to burn it. Stir in the brown sugar. Sprinkle with the pecans.

serve with

New Orleans Broiled Grapefruit (page 78)
Little sausages

to drink

Café au Lait

In a medium bowl, beat the eggs and stir in the milk, vanilla and cinnamon. Dip the slices of bread into the egg mixture. Arrange the slices over the brown-sugar mixture in the pan. Pour any remaining egg mixture over the bread.

Bake for 35 to 40 minutes, or until the toast is golden brown. Invert each slice onto plates and serve.

---

tip

If you're making breakfast for a smaller group, you can make the French toast in a 9-x-13-inch baking dish or a deep 12-inch ovenproof skillet and use the following proportions:

- 8 tablespoons (1 stick) butter
- 2/3 cup light brown sugar
- 2/3 cup coarsely chopped pecans
- 5 large eggs
- 1 cup milk
- 3/4 teaspoon pure vanilla extract
- 2 dashes of ground cinnamon

Use as many slices of bread as will fit in the pan. This is two-thirds of the original recipe and will serve 4 to 6.

zucchini, rice and mint frittata

SOURCE

Fall Downunder
(travel newsletter)

COOK

Roz Warner

Karolyn Wrightson conducts wine tours in Australia and New Zealand, and one of her favorite areas is the lush Marlborough region of New Zealand, the source of this terrific frittata. At Gillan Estate winery, this Greek-accented frittata is served for lunch, but it's also excellent for brunch or breakfast. Simple as it is, the frittata almost qualifies as soul food; once you taste it, you want to have it again and again.

For maximum flavor, serve the frittata just barely warm. The tomato salsa looks lovely served with it, but to our taste it mutes the delicate quality of the frittata. Add it or leave it out as you wish.

serves 4

- 2 tablespoons (¹/₄ stick) butter
- 2 medium zucchini, chopped (about 1³/₄ cups)
- 4 scallions, sliced, including the firm greens
- 1 cup cooked long-grain white rice
- 2 tablespoons chopped fresh mint

- 2 tablespoons chopped fresh dill
- 6 large eggs
- 2 tablespoons water
- ³/₄ teaspoon salt
- ¹/₄ teaspoon freshly ground black pepper
- ³/₄ cup crumbled feta cheese
  Tomato salsa, for garnish (optional)

---

cook's note

Frittatas are born to use leftovers. You could use little bits of cooked pasta instead of rice (Karolyn Wrightson uses orzo, the rice-shaped pasta) or leftover rice for that matter (though we prefer the soft texture of just-cooked rice here). Diced cooked squash or pumpkin are also delicious in this dish. But try it first in its purest form.

Preheat the oven to 400 degrees.

Melt the butter in a medium nonstick ovenproof skillet over medium heat. Add the zucchini and scallions and sauté until soft, about 5 minutes. Mix in the rice and herbs.

Whisk the eggs, water, salt and pepper in a medium bowl to blend. Pour the egg mixture over the vegetable-rice mixture in the skillet. Sprinkle with the cheese. Cook, without stirring, until the bottom begins to set, about 3 minutes.

Transfer the skillet to the oven and bake until the eggs are set, about 12 minutes. Run a rubber spatula around the sides of the frittata to loosen it and slide the frittata onto a serving plate. Cut into wedges and serve slightly warm or at room temperature, with salsa, if desired.

---

serve with

Spinach salad tossed with pine nuts and a not-too-sharp vinaigrette
French bread

℘

Plum Crumb Cake (page 278)

to drink

This region's Sauvignon Blanc is just the right companion to the herbal frittata.

---

morning-after scrambled eggs with bacon

SOURCE

Details

COOK

Eric Ripert

When asked what a cool bachelor should prepare for a new love's breakfast, Chef Ripert of Manhattan's Le Bernardin came up with a simple but not ordinary solution—really good soufflé-like scrambled eggs. Ripert is more or less shocked by the state of this classic dish in America: He thinks most scrambled eggs are so tough they need to be cut with a knife and are concocted with old, tired eggs from chickens who haven't been dining well.

Enter the French chef, with whisk. There are just a few key elements to Ripert's French-style eggs, which have the liquid added after they're cooked, not before, to stop the cooking at the perfect moment and give them an extra creaminess. You'll need very fresh organic eggs, and in place of the half-and-half you can substitute whatever you put in your coffee—cream, milk or even soy milk. To pull out all the stops, serve the eggs topped with caviar.

serves 2

4 slices double-smoked bacon, cut into 1-inch pieces
6 very fresh large organic eggs

Fine sea salt and freshly ground white pepper, to taste
1 tablespoon half-and-half
1 teaspoon chopped fresh chives

---

serve with

Toast with Cranberry Butter
(page 100)

to drink

Champagne
or Bloody Marys

Fry the bacon. While it's cooking, crack the eggs into a bowl and season each one with salt and pepper (this will save seasoning later). Whisk the eggs briefly so the yolks and whites are just mixed (too much whisking will introduce too much air into the mixture).

When the bacon is cooked, drain off the fat and pour the eggs directly into the pan with the bacon. Cook them for about 3 minutes over medium heat, stirring with a wooden spatula and scraping the sides of the pan constantly.

Take the eggs off the heat when they reach a consistency somewhere between a soufflé and polenta—they'll continue to cook off the heat. Stir in the half-and-half and keep stirring for about a minute to stop the cooking process and add creaminess. (If you cook the eggs too much, you can rescue them by adding a little more cream.)

Sprinkle with the chives and serve immediately.

whiskied jungle oats
with vanilla brown sugar

This intriguing recipe turned up in a couple of sources this year, and it reminded us of how wonderful a similar spiked oatmeal is at breakfast in Ireland. At the Halfpenny Inn in West Hartford, Vermont, it's called Jan's Oatmeal and it's made with Irish whiskey. In Ireland, it's made with Irish whiskey, of course (except in the north, where it might be Scotch or Drambuie), and the sugar is demerara sugar, a crunchy

SOURCE

The African Kitchen
by Josie Stow
and Jan Baldwin

COOK

Josie Stow

brown sugar that has recently become widely available here. And in South Africa, cooks infuse the brown sugar with vanilla bean and sometimes use a syrupy cream liqueur made from the fruit of the marula tree, which is reportedly a popular snack among elephants.

This is a bracing, great morning-after breakfast, not your usual oatmeal by a long stretch.

serves 2

2¹/₂–3¹/₂ cups milk
1 cup rolled oats
¹/₂ teaspoon salt
4 tablespoons whipped cream

4 tablespoons vanilla brown sugar (see note)
2–4 shots whiskey (see note)

serve with
Raspberries or strawberries

to drink
Espresso

In a large saucepan, bring 2½ cups of the milk to a boil. Whisk in the oats and salt and cook for 3 to 5 minutes, or until thick. If you prefer your oatmeal thinner, gradually add more milk until it's right.

Spoon the oatmeal into individual serving bowls. Place a large dollop of whipped cream in the center of each serving and sprinkle with the vanilla brown sugar. Drizzle the whiskey over the top and serve.

---

cook's notes

ꤷ To make vanilla brown sugar, split a vanilla bean in half and place it in a jam jar filled with light brown sugar or brown sugar crystals, such as demerara. Leave, tightly sealed, for several days for the flavor to develop. Remove the bean and use it for another purpose, such as flavoring custard.

ꤷ Cooking the oatmeal in milk, as this recipe does, is very luxurious, but we prefer to use water.

ꤷ Teetotalers will love this oatmeal without the whiskey. We like to serve it the Irish way, putting the whiskey over the oatmeal first, then the sugar, then the cream.

ricotta hot cakes with honeycomb butter

SOURCE

Gourmet

COOK

Kemp Minifie

On a trip to Australia, *Gourmet*'s editors tasted honeycomb, that airy, crunchy candy staple of the British Isles. Down under, the candy was turned into a compound butter and served over ethereally light pancakes, which make a great special-occasion breakfast.

The pancakes are made of both ricotta and cottage cheese; the lightness comes from the beaten egg whites. They not only cook perfectly, they hold up well in the oven while you get everything else ready. As the butter melts over and between them, the crunchy little bits of honeycomb emerge as a delicious surprise.

Although the pancakes are excellent without it, the honeycomb is easy to make. You'll have leftovers, which are great mixed into ice cream or just drifted over it. If you make the honeycomb butter the night before, the pancakes will be ready in the morning in no time.

serves 4 to 5

HONEYCOMB BUTTER

- 1/2 cup sugar
- 1 tablespoon light corn syrup
- 2 tablespoons water
- 1 tablespoon plus 1 teaspoon honey
- 1/8 teaspoon baking soda
- 8 tablespoons (1 stick) unsalted butter, at room temperature
  Scant 1/4 teaspoon salt

RICOTTA HOT CAKES

- 1 cup whole-milk ricotta
- 3/4 cup milk
- 1/3 cup cottage cheese
- 4 large eggs, separated
- 1 cup all-purpose flour
- 1 3/4 teaspoons baking powder
- 1/4 teaspoon salt
- 2 tablespoons unsalted butter, melted

TO MAKE THE BUTTER

Combine the sugar, corn syrup, water and 1 teaspoon of the honey in a 2-to-3-quart heavy saucepan. Bring to a boil, covered, over medium heat, stirring occasionally, until the sugar is dissolved. Increase the heat to medium-high and boil, uncovered, without stirring, swirling the pan occasionally, until the sugar turns a deep golden color. Remove the pan from the heat and immediately stir in the baking soda—the mixture will foam up and look creamy.

Pour onto a large sheet of foil. Cool the candy completely and remove the foil. Coarsely chop enough candy to measure $\frac{1}{2}$ cup (see note). Blend the butter, salt and remaining tablespoon honey in a food processor until smooth. Add the chopped candy and blend until combined well. Transfer to a sheet of wax paper and roll to form a 6-inch log. Chill, wrapped in wax paper, until firm, about 2 hours.

TO MAKE THE HOT CAKES

Preheat the oven to 200 degrees.

Whisk together the ricotta, milk, cottage cheese and egg yolks in a large bowl. Sift the flour, baking powder and salt over the ricotta mixture and whisk until just combined. Beat the egg whites with

---

cook's note

The easiest way to break up the honeycomb is to place it inside a kitchen towel, still wrapped in the foil, and then scrunch it apart with your hands or hit it with a meat mallet.

---

an electric mixer in a separate bowl until they just hold stiff peaks, then fold into the batter gently but thoroughly.

Brush a 12-inch nonstick skillet with some of the melted butter and heat over medium heat until hot but not smoking. Scoop ¼-cup measures of batter into the skillet, 4 to a batch, spreading to form 4-inch hot cakes, and cook until the undersides are golden brown, 1 to 3 minutes. Flip with a spatula and cook until golden brown and the hot cakes are cooked through, 1 to 2 minutes more. Transfer the hot cakes as they're cooked to an ovenproof platter and keep warm in the oven, covered with a kitchen towel. Serve with the honeycomb butter over and between the hot cakes.

serve with

Mixed berries with crème fraîche
Italian Shortbread with Almonds and Jam (page 272)

to drink

Spumante–Vodka Cocktail with Lemon Sorbet (page 328)

stollen

Recipes turn up in the oddest places. This one was discovered in a parking lot, when Karyl Bannister, the editor of a recipe newsletter in Maine, ran into a complete stranger outside a gourmet shop and they started talking. Nina Buric was there to buy some key ingredients for her traditional German stollen, a recipe she knows by heart and happily rattled off.

As Bannister says, it's rich, luscious and easy. In fact, the hardest part is assembling the ingredients. Suet is usually available at the butcher's, especially if you ask in advance, or you can use the trimmings from a roast beef. Almond oil can be found at the natural foods store; lemon oil is usually at gourmet shops (Boyajian is a good brand).

Don't let yourself be daunted by the ingredient hunt, because this is really a killer holiday treat, and the recipe makes enough for a crowd. Well wrapped, it keeps for several days at room temperature, so you can make it ahead.

We've put this recipe in the breakfast section because we think it's the ultimate Christmas-morning breakfast. But of course stollen is great for afternoon tea, for a snack or to accompany a variety of sweetmeats for dessert. It won't last long on a holiday buffet.

SOURCE

Cook & Tell
by Karyl Bannister

COOK

Nina Buric

serves 12

serve with

Christmas Morning Melon
Wedges (page 77)
Canadian bacon

to drink

Mimosas, fresh-squeezed
orange juice or Champagne

breakfast and brunch

4 1/3 cups all-purpose flour
2 teaspoons baking powder
1 teaspoon salt
1 cup plus 3 tablespoons sugar
1 teaspoon pure vanilla extract
4 drops lemon oil (see note)
4 drops almond oil (see note)
4 drops rum flavoring (see note)
Pinch of cardamom
Pinch of freshly grated nutmeg
2 large eggs
8 tablespoons (1 stick) unsalted butter, chilled and cut into 16 pieces

Scant 1/4 cup finely chopped suet
8 ounces ricotta cheese
4 ounces dried currants
4 ounces raisins
4 ounces hazelnuts or almonds, finely chopped
1/4 cup chopped candied citron

Melted butter (about 3 tablespoons)
Powdered sugar (about 2 tablespoons)

Preheat the oven to 400 degrees. Line a baking sheet with parchment paper.

Sift the flour, baking powder and salt into a large bowl. Make a well in the center and drop in everything but the melted butter and powdered sugar. Knead until it's well blended into a cohesive, heavy dough. Form the dough into an oblong about 9 inches long and place it on the baking sheet. Make a lengthwise slash in the top about 1 inch deep, put the loaf in the oven and immediately reduce the temperature to 350 degrees. Bake the stollen for 1 hour 15 minutes, or until it's nicely browned on the outside and a toothpick inserted in the center comes out clean.

While the stollen is still warm, brush it with melted butter and sprinkle it heavily with powdered sugar. Serve the bread thinly sliced (not heated or toasted), spread with unsalted butter.

---

cook's notes

⚘ If you can't find lemon oil, use 1 tablespoon grated lemon zest instead. If you can't find almond oil, use 1/4 teaspoon almond extract instead. Measuring these oils can be a little tricky. The easiest way is to use an eye dropper. Failing that, measure the drops into a spoon over the sink, then add to the dough—otherwise, it's easy to misjudge and flood the stollen with lemon or almond flavoring.

⚘ You can use 2 teaspoons rum instead of rum flavoring.

⚘ The dough will seem as if it's never going to come together, but it will. You're basically softening the butter, which is what holds it together, and that takes about 5 minutes of serious kneading.

---

hanukkah doughnuts

SOURCE

Bon Appétit

COOKS

**Selma Brown Morrow
and Reena Singh**

Israelis, say our cooks, celebrate Hanukkah not with latkes (potato pancakes), as Americans do, but with *sufganiyot*, delectable little doughnuts that are more like hush puppies or doughnut holes than the classic circles. We couldn't wait to try them. And these little morsels not only are very easy to make, they also deliver terrific crisp, crunchy texture. They're all ragged-looking, with plenty of nooks and crannies. The flavor is unusual too—unmistakably lemon, a delightful quality in a doughnut.

makes about 30 doughnuts

- 2 large eggs
- 3/4 cup sugar
- 1/4 cup heavy cream
- 1 1/2 teaspoons grated lemon zest
- 1 tablespoon fresh lemon juice
- 1 tablespoon pure vanilla extract
- 2 1/4 cups all-purpose flour
- 2 tablespoons chilled unsalted butter, diced
- 1 tablespoon baking powder
- 3/4 teaspoon salt
- Vegetable oil, for frying
- Powdered sugar

Whisk the eggs, sugar, cream, lemon zest, lemon juice and vanilla in a large bowl to blend. Blend the flour, butter, baking powder and salt in a food processor until the mixture resembles coarse meal. Stir the flour mixture into the egg mixture to form a soft dough.

Pour the oil to a depth of 1½ inches in a large heavy saucepan and heat to 340 degrees.

Working in batches, drop the dough by rounded teaspoonfuls into the hot oil. Cook, turning occasionally, until golden brown, about 3 minutes. Using a slotted spoon, transfer the doughnuts to a baking sheet lined with paper towels and drain. Reheat the oil to 340 degrees between batches. Roll the doughnuts in powdered sugar and serve as soon as possible.

cook's note

Like all doughnuts, these are best eaten within a couple of hours, though they'll still be tasty the next morning.

blueberry bannock scone

This delectable Scottish scone has a very un-Scottish layer of blueberries running through the middle. And it's completely different from the doughy, chalky scones available everywhere; this one is made with buttermilk, not cream, and it has a great crunch and nutty texture and flavor. That's because

SOURCE
Martha Stewart Living

COOK

Hannah Milman
and Susan Spungen

it has a secret ingredient: wheat germ.

Although scones are best eaten just after they're made, this one will keep overnight and makes a terrific breakfast pastry. It stays moist, and the crunch doesn't disappear.

makes one 9-inch scone; serves 8

1¼ cups all-purpose flour, plus more for dusting

½ cup finely chopped pecans

½ cup wheat germ

1 tablespoon baking powder

½ teaspoon salt

½ teaspoon ground cinnamon

5 tablespoons sugar

5⅓ tablespoons (⅓ cup) unsalted butter, chilled

½ cup buttermilk

2 large eggs

1 cup blueberries

1 teaspoon water

Preheat the oven to 400 degrees.

Lightly sprinkle a 14-x-16-inch baking sheet with flour, and set aside. In a large bowl, combine the flour, pecans, wheat germ, baking powder, salt, cinnamon and 2 tablespoons of the sugar.

Cut the butter into the flour mixture with a pastry blender or fork until it has the consistency of small crumbs.

In a small bowl, combine the buttermilk and 1 of the eggs. Add to the flour mixture and stir until just moistened. The dough will be quite wet and sticky; work it as little as possible.

Divide the dough in half and shape one piece into a 9-inch circle on the prepared baking sheet. Spread the blueberries evenly over the circle and sprinkle with 2 tablespoons of the sugar. On a lightly floured piece of parchment paper, form a 9-inch circle from the remaining dough and gently slide it onto the berries. With the backside of a knife, score the top into 8 wedges.

Beat the remaining egg with the water and lightly brush the egg wash over the top of the scone. Sprinkle with the remaining 1 tablespoon sugar.

Bake until the scone is golden brown, 20 to 25 minutes. Remove from the oven and place on a cooling rack. When cool, cut into wedges and serve.

cook's note

If the dough is sticky, it helps to flour your hands when you're forming the circle.

danish tea cake

At Bruce's Bakery in Manhattan, this pecan-topped Danish tea cake is a huge favorite with customers. The Zipes family were taught how to make it by a baker from the Netherlands named Hans, who worked in the bakery. The brown-sugar flavor is just right and

SOURCE

Bruce's Bakery Cookbook
by Bruce Zipes

COOK

Bruce Zipes

gives the cake crumb a nice pale-brown molasses color. The cake is tender and moist from the sour cream and vegetable oil and slices beautifully into thin slices. It's even better when served with a warm fruit compote.

serves 12

- ¼ cup whole pecans
- 3 cups cake flour
- 1²/₃ cups firmly packed light brown sugar
- 1 teaspoon baking powder
- ½ teaspoon baking soda
- ½ teaspoon salt
- 2 large eggs
- ³/₄ cup vegetable oil
- ½ cup water
- 1 tablespoon pure vanilla extract
- 1 cup sour cream
  Powdered sugar, for dusting

Preheat the oven to 350 degrees. Grease and flour an 8-cup Bundt pan. Place the pecans in the bottom of the pan and set aside.

In a large mixing bowl, combine the flour, brown sugar, baking powder, baking soda and salt.

In another mixing bowl, combine the eggs, oil, water and vanilla. Add the egg mixture to the flour mixture, stirring with a wooden spoon until combined. Add the sour cream and mix well. Pour the batter into the prepared pan.

Bake for 50 to 60 minutes, or until a toothpick inserted near the center comes out clean. Cool on a wire rack for 10 minutes. Remove from the pan and cool completely on a rack.

Dust with powdered sugar before serving.

cranberry butter

California chef Hans Röckenwagner developed this truly unusual cranberry butter for the people who make Butter Bell crocks, a French-inspired butter server that keeps the butter fresh without being refrigerated. This is a perfect holiday breakfast spread for toast, muffins, pancakes or waffles. The combination of sweet maple, sweet butter

SOURCE

Advertisement,
Bon Appétit

COOK

Hans Röckenwagner

and the sharp bits of cranberry is inspired.

Don't worry if the syrup doesn't blend uniformly with the butter in the same way honey does—for some reason, it just doesn't. The butter looks best scraped into ramekins. Smooth over the top and let soften a little before serving.

fills two 6-ounce ramekins

⅓ cup fresh or frozen cranberries, thawed if frozen, chopped

¼ cup maple syrup

1 cup (2 sticks) unsalted butter, at room temperature

In a mixing bowl, gently fold all the ingredients together until combined but not so much that the butter becomes uniformly pink. You should still be able to see bits of the cranberry in the butter. Refrigerate any unused cranberry butter.

---

cook's notes

❧ You'll need to roughly chop the cranberries, especially if they're the very large berries we've started seeing lately.

❧ If you don't have a sweet tooth, you might want to start by cutting the maple syrup in half, especially if you're using Grade B, which has more flavor.

---

main dishes

twice-baked spinach soufflés

Soufflé just means "puff" in French, but what a puff! For the home cook, however, the soufflé presents a certain amount of anxiety. Ever since Americans started cooking their way through Julia Child, the fallen soufflé has represented the nadir of culinary ineptitude. And because the soufflé has to be made at the last minute, the anxiety only compounds as the dramatic moment approaches.

Enter Anne Willan, who loves to solve kitchen problems, with a new/old technique that makes soufflés less intimidating.

SOURCE
From My Château Kitchen
by Anne Willan

COOK
Anne Willan

Her twice-baking trick actually requires the individual soufflés to fall—and you can make them hours ahead. Once fallen, the soufflés are tipped out of their dishes and given a coat of béchamel sauce and a bit of cheese, and on their second trip into the oven they magically puff up a bit again. In the bargain, they produce a bubbly browned cheese sauce to accompany themselves.

If there were a Nobel Prize for cooking, this recipe would send Anne Willan to the front of the pack.

serves 6

- 1 pound spinach
- 5 tablespoons unsalted butter
- 1 onion, finely chopped
- Salt and freshly ground black pepper, to taste
- 1/4 cup all-purpose flour
- 1 1/2 cups milk
- Pinch of freshly grated nutmeg
- 1 1/2 cups light cream
- 5 large egg yolks
- 6 large egg whites
- 1/2 cup grated Gruyère cheese

Pull the stems from the spinach and wash the leaves in several changes of water. Pack the wet leaves in a large saucepan, cover, and wilt the leaves over medium heat, stirring occasionally, 5 to 7 minutes. Drain and let the spinach cool. Squeeze handfuls of spinach in your fists to extract the water and then chop it.

Melt 1 tablespoon of the butter in the saucepan, add the onion and cook over medium heat until it is soft but not brown, 3 to 5 minutes. Stir in the spinach, season with salt and pepper, and continue cooking, stirring, until it is quite dry, 2 to 3 minutes. Set aside.

Melt the remaining 4 tablespoons butter in a medium saucepan, whisk in the flour, and cook until foaming but not browned, about 1 minute. Whisk in the milk, nutmeg, salt and pepper, and bring to a boil, stirring constantly, until the sauce thickens. Simmer for 2 minutes and then turn off the heat. Transfer about a third of the white sauce into a small saucepan and pour the cream on top to prevent a skin from forming. Set aside to use for the cooked soufflés.

Generously butter six 8-ounce ramekins and chill them. Stir the spinach into the sauce on the stovetop and heat until very hot. Remove the mixture from the heat and taste for seasoning; it should be well seasoned to make up for the bland eggs you are about to add. Beat in the egg yolks a bit at a time so they cook in the heat of the sauce and thicken it slightly. Press a piece of plastic wrap on the spinach mixture to prevent a skin forming.

Preheat the oven to 350 degrees. Bring a roasting pan of water to a boil on the stove for a water bath. In a large bowl, beat the egg whites until stiff, adding a pinch of salt to help stiffen them. Warm the spinach mixture gently until the pan is hot to the touch. Add about a quarter of the beaten egg whites and stir until well mixed.

---

cook's note

If you don't have individual ramekins and gratin dishes, you can bake the soufflés in muffin cups for the first baking, then turn them out into a large baking dish for the second baking.

The heat of the sauce will cook the whites slightly. Add this mixture to the remaining whites and fold them together as lightly as possible.

Fill the ramekins with the mixture, smoothing the tops with a metal spatula. Run your thumb around the edge of each dish to make a small groove so the soufflé will rise straight. Set the ramekins in the water bath, bring it back to a boil on the stove, and transfer it to the oven. Bake until the soufflés are puffed, browned and just set in the center, 20 to 25 minutes. They should rise well above the rim of the dish. Take the ramekins from the water bath and leave them to cool—the soufflés will shrink back into the ramekins, pulling away slightly from the sides.

When the soufflés are cool, run a knife around the edge of each dish and turn the soufflés out into lightly buttered gratin dishes. Whisk the cream with the reserved sauce until smooth and bring it just to a boil. Season it with salt, pepper and nutmeg and pour on top of the soufflés, letting it pool around the sides. Sprinkle with the cheese. The soufflés can be kept, covered with plastic wrap, for up to 24 hours in the refrigerator.

Preheat the oven to 425 degrees. Bake the soufflés until they are browned and slightly puffed and the sauce is bubbling, 7 to 10 minutes. Serve at once.

---

serve with

A tossed salad of tender and bitter lettuces with a mustardy vinaigrette
A crusty baguette

℮

Tart Lemon Tart (page 303)

to drink

A light red Burgundy Villages or Pinot Noir from Oregon

---

wild mushroom risotto

A *Los Angeles Times* reader wrote in to request the recipe for this terrific risotto, which she claimed was the best she'd ever tasted. At Celestino's in Beverly Hills, they use both porcini and dried morels as well as shiitakes for a wonderfully complex, powerful flavor. Because it's so intense, the risotto is best served by itself, either as a first course or as the main event, with just a simple salad.

This is another of those "backward" recipes that delivers surprising results. In-

SOURCE
Los Angeles Times

COOK
Celestino Drago

stead of adding the mushrooms at the beginning as most recipes do, you cook them separately and add them at the end. Adding the mushroom-soaking liquid to the sautéed mushrooms and then reducing it contributes a lot of the depth of flavor.

In the end, this labor-of-love recipe is a knockout—great for a special occasion, such as an intimate New Year's Eve supper or an anniversary.

serves 6

2 ounces dried porcini mushrooms
12 dried morel mushrooms
5¹/₂ cups chicken stock
4 tablespoons (¹/₂ stick) butter
1 tablespoon chopped shallots
2 garlic cloves, minced
4 medium fresh shiitake mushrooms, sliced

1 cup dry white wine
Salt and freshly ground black pepper, to taste
1³/₄ cups Arborio rice
1 tablespoon mascarpone cheese (see note)
¹/₄ cup grated Parmesan cheese
1 tablespoon chopped fresh parsley

Soak the dried mushrooms in just enough chicken stock to cover for 2 hours. Remove the mushrooms from the stock and squeeze them dry. Chop the mushrooms and set side, reserving the stock (see note below).

Melt 2 tablespoons of the butter in a medium saucepan over medium heat. Add the shallots, garlic, chopped dried mushrooms and shiitakes. Sauté for 3 minutes. Add the wine and cook until the liquid is absorbed. Add the reserved stock and cook until it is reduced by half, about 5 minutes. Add salt and pepper. Set aside.

Bring the remaining stock to a simmer in a saucepan and keep hot.

Melt 1 tablespoon of the butter in a large skillet. Add the rice and cook, stirring, for about 2 minutes to coat the grains. Add $1/2$ cup of the stock, stirring constantly with a wooden spoon. Add another $1/2$ cup of the stock and cook, stirring, until the rice becomes dry. Repeat, adding the stock in increments, cooking and stirring until the rice is tender and all the stock is used, about 25 minutes.

Stir in the mushroom mixture, mascarpone cheese, the remaining 1 tablespoon butter and the Parmesan. Add more salt and pepper if needed. Remove from the heat and mix well. Sprinkle with parsley before serving.

---

cook's notes

- You can cut the soaking time in half by soaking the mushrooms in hot stock.
- After you've soaked the mushrooms, pour off the liquid carefully and leave the sediment behind.
- Instead of mascarpone, you can use heavy cream or even cream cheese.

---

queso fundido
(melted cheese with mushrooms and smoky chipotle chiles)

This incredibly savory dish is Mexico's answer to fondue—a glorious concoction of melted cheese that falls into delectable strings as it's scooped up with hot corn tortillas. This is intimate food; everyone eats from the same dish, and it comes straight from the oven to the table.

In this version of the Northern Mexican specialty, Rick Bayless has used wild mushrooms and smoky chipotle chiles (which are smoked jalapeño peppers), along with a little red onion and thyme—nothing at all complicated, and yet there are layers of deeply satisfying flavor. It's an irresistible dish, just right for Sunday supper or a hearty snack. Add a salad with some radishes to cut the richness.

SOURCE

Mexico One Plate at a Time by Rick Bayless with JeanMarie Brownson and Deann Groen Bayless

COOK

Rick Bayless

serves 4

1½ tablespoons olive oil, preferably extra-virgin
1 medium red onion, sliced
6–8 ounces full-flavored mushrooms, such as shiitakes or oysters or wild mushrooms, stemmed and sliced (about 2 cups)
2–3 canned chipotle chiles in adobo, seeded and thinly sliced

Salt, to taste
12 corn tortillas, the fresher the better
8 ounces whole-milk mozzarella (the commercial variety, not the fresh) or Mexican quesillo, shredded (about 2 cups); see note
Generous ½ teaspoon chopped fresh thyme leaves
Freshly ground black pepper

Preheat the oven to 350 degrees.

In a large skillet, preferably nonstick, heat the oil over medium-high heat. Add the onion and cook, stirring frequently, until it is softening and beginning to brown, about 5 minutes. Add the mushrooms and stir nearly constantly until they have softened and any juice they release has evaporated, about 5 minutes longer. Stir in the sliced chiles, then taste and season with salt (about ¼ teaspoon). Transfer the mixture to a shallow baking dish, Mexican cazuela or pie plate.

Very lightly dampen a clean kitchen towel. Check the tortillas to make sure none are stuck together. Wrap them in the towel, then in foil, sealing the edges tightly. Place in the oven and set the timer for 7 minutes.

When the timer goes off, stir the shredded cheese into the warm mushroom mixture. Set in the oven alongside the tortillas and bake until the cheese is just melted, about 5 minutes more. Sprinkle with the thyme and black pepper and serve without a moment's hesitation, accompanied by the warm tortillas.

---

cook's notes

- Quesillo is a bland, fresh Mexican cheese available in Latino grocery stores.
- The mushroom mixture can be made a day ahead and refrigerated, well covered. Reheat the mixture before finishing the dish.
- A more voluptuous cheese than mozzarella for this dish is Muenster, but it may give off a little oil in the oven. If so, just blot it quickly with paper towels before serving.

pasta with asparagus-lemon sauce

SOURCE

Zanne Stewart,
Gourmet

COOK

Faith Heller Willinger

There's nothing quite so wonderful as an incredibly simple recipe—in this case, just five easy pieces that come together magically to deliver a dish that's much more than the sum of its parts. This meal-in-a-bowl dish is so easy that you'll make it long after your local asparagus season has come and gone—though it's also the perfect way to welcome the new crop.

Faith Willinger uses penne for this dish, but Zanne Stewart tried it with mafalde, a sort of skinny lasagna noodle, and liked it very much.

serves 4

1 pound fresh asparagus, tough ends trimmed
Salt
1 teaspoon finely grated lemon zest
1/4 cup extra-virgin olive oil

1 pound penne, mafalde or another pasta
1/2 cup grated Parmigiano-Reggiano cheese
Freshly ground black pepper

serve with

Antipasto of bruschetta, olives, aged provolone and sliced salami
Arugula salad

℮

Fig and Nut Torte
(page 306)

to drink

A fruity red wine, such as Dolcetta d'Alba

Cut the asparagus into 1-inch pieces, reserving the tips separately. Cook the asparagus stems in 5 to 6 quarts of boiling water with 2 tablespoons salt until very tender, 6 to 8 minutes. Transfer with a slotted spoon to a colander, reserving the cooking water in the pot, and rinse under cold water. Drain the asparagus well and transfer to a food processor or blender.

Cook the asparagus tips in the same boiling water until just tender, 3 to 5 minutes. Transfer with a slotted spoon to the colander, reserving the boiling water in the pot, and rinse under cold water. Drain the tips well.

Puree the asparagus stems with the lemon zest, oil and ½ cup of the asparagus cooking water. Transfer to a large saucepan.

Cook the pasta in the boiling asparagus cooking water until it still offers considerable resistance to the tooth, around three-fourths of the recommended cooking time on the package. Reserve 2 cups of the cooking water and drain the pasta.

Add the pasta, asparagus tips and ½ cup of the reserved water to the asparagus sauce and cook over high heat, stirring, for 3 to 5 minutes, or until the pasta is almost al dente and the sauce coats the pasta. Add more cooking water, ¼ cup at a time, until the sauce coats the pasta but is a little loose (the cheese will thicken it slightly).

Stir in the cheese and salt and pepper to taste and cook, stirring, until the cheese is melted. Serve immediately.

linguine with walnut sauce

This simple but superb pasta dish has everything going for it. You can make it in just a few minutes from ingredients you probably have on hand, and it has great texture, exceptional flavor and a lovely toasty crunch from the bread crumbs and walnuts. There's only one problem for us mortals. Unlike the irrepressible chef and TV star who created this dish, most of us are not flame-breathing chile-heads who'd love a dish with this much firepower. Try it with just a teaspoon of hot red pepper flakes and see how it goes. We know you'll make it again, and you can always up the ante next time.

As Batali points out, the pasta is so lightly sauced that it's good even at room temperature, so it doesn't have the urgency of instant serving that most pasta dishes do, although it's best hot. It makes a great first course or a light main course.

SOURCE

Holiday Food
by Mario Batali

COOK

Mario Batali

serves 4 as a main course or 6 as a starter

- 6 quarts water
- 2 tablespoons kosher salt
- 1/4 cup extra-virgin olive oil
- 3 garlic cloves, thinly sliced
- 1/2 cup toasted dry bread crumbs, preferably homemade
- 1 cup coarsely chopped walnuts
- 1 tablespoon hot red pepper flakes (or less, to taste; see note above)
- 1 pound linguine
- 1/2 cup coarsely chopped fresh Italian parsley
- 1/2 cup freshly grated caciocavallo or Pecorino Romano cheese

Bring the water to a boil and add the salt.

In a deep, wide frying pan or saucepan (12 to 14 inches wide), heat the oil over medium heat until it's very hot. Add the garlic (watch carefully, it can easily burn) and cook until light golden brown, 2 to 3 minutes, stirring constantly. Add ¼ cup of the bread crumbs, the walnuts and the pepper flakes and cook until lightly toasted, 3 to 4 minutes, stirring frequently. Remove from the heat and set aside.

Drop the pasta into the boiling water and cook according to the package directions until 1 minute short of al dente. Just before draining the pasta, add ¼ cup of the cooking water to the walnut mixture in the pan to make a sauce.

Drain the pasta in a colander and pour it back into the walnut mixture. Over medium heat, cook the pasta until it is lightly dressed with the sauce, about 1 minute. Add the parsley and cheese, stir through, pour into a heated bowl, sprinkle with the remaining ¼ cup bread crumbs and serve immediately.

serve with

Grilled or braised radicchio
Rustic bread

℘

Fresh figs and a sliver of
Gorgonzola dolce

main dishes

fettuccine with red onion, blue cheese and thyme

SOURCE

The Herbfarm Cookbook
by Jerry Traunfeld

COOK

Jerry Traunfeld

At Herbfarm, the famous restaurant and herb garden outside Seattle, chef Jerry Traunfeld performs a kind of alchemy with herbs, coaxing flavors no one has previously imagined from brilliant combinations. This pasta dish is a good example. It seems straightforward, yet the slightly crisp red onion and the intense salty blue cheese are transformed by the thyme, which is added at two different points. If you love blue cheese, this is a not-to-be-missed celebration of it.

serves 4

6 quarts water
1½ tablespoons salt
1 large red onion
2 tablespoons extra-virgin olive oil
3 tablespoons coarsely chopped fresh English thyme
⅓ cup dry white wine

¾ cup heavy cream
1 pound fresh fettuccine or 12 ounces dried
¾ cup crumbled blue cheese (3 ounces), such as Danish blue, Gorgonzola or Roquefort
Freshly ground black pepper

cook's note
Don't be thrown by the reference to "English thyme." The fresh thyme you buy in the supermarket is English.

Fill a large pot with the water, add the salt and bring to a boil over high heat.

Peel the onion and cut it in half from root to tip. Cut out the dense core at the root end and slice the onion ¼ inch thick, again from the root end to the tip. Heat the oil in a large skillet over medium heat. Add the onion and cook, stirring very often, until the slices begin to soften but still hold their shape and have some snap when you bite into a piece, about 4 minutes. Add 2 tablespoons of the thyme and the wine and let the mixture boil for a minute or two to evaporate the alcohol. Stir in the cream and remove the pan from the heat.

Stir the pasta into the boiling water and cook until tender but still firm, 3 to 4 minutes for fresh pasta, 7 to 10 minutes for dried. Bring the sauce to a simmer. Drain the pasta and add it to the skillet. Sprinkle with the cheese and toss, using tongs or two wooden spoons, until about half the cheese melts into the sauce but small pieces remain. Taste and add pepper and additional salt, depending on the saltiness of the cheese.

Transfer the pasta to warmed shallow bowls or plates and sprinkle with the remaining 1 tablespoon thyme. Serve right away.

---

serve with

Olive-studded ciabatta
Tossed salad
of mesclun greens

℮

Clementines and Italian
Shortbread with Almonds
and Jam (page 272)

---

main dishes

white lasagna

SOURCE

The Italian-American Cookbook by John and Galina Mariani

COOKS

John Mariani, after Johanne Killeen and George Germon

Lasagna has been so dumbed down in America, with its thick gummy noodles swamped in dreary tomato sauce, that only travelers to Italy have some idea of what a refined, truly celestial dish it can be. This unusual white lasagna based on onions is delicate, crammed with tremendous flavor and completely luxurious.

The recipe has its origin in northern Italy and has been developed by Johanne Killeen and George Germon, the chef-owners of the famous Al Forno in Providence, Rhode Island. Italian food buff John Mariani tinkered a bit with their recipe, and we'd say it's just about perfect now. This lasagna makes an exceptional vegetarian main dish, but it also works as a side dish, one that's particularly good with roast beef.

serves 4

WHITE SAUCE

3 tablespoons unsalted butter

3 tablespoons all-purpose flour

1 bay leaf

1²/₃ cups whole milk

1/2 teaspoon salt, preferably kosher

LASAGNA

8 tablespoons (1 stick) unsalted butter

4 large sweet onions (about 2 pounds), such as Vidalia or Spanish onions, halved vertically and thinly sliced

1 leek, white and light green parts only, well washed and thinly sliced

Salt, preferably kosher

3 sheets fresh lasagna (about 1 pound), each sheet cut into 3 lengthwise strips (see note)

1/4 cup heavy cream

1 cup freshly grated Parmigiano-Reggiano cheese

TO MAKE THE WHITE SAUCE

In a medium saucepan, melt the butter over medium heat. Add the flour and cook, stirring, for 3 minutes. Add the bay leaf and then the milk all at once. Add the salt and stir continually until the white sauce starts to thicken and comes to a boil. Reduce to a simmer and cook for 2 minutes. Set aside.

TO MAKE THE LASAGNA

In a large sauté pan, heat 7 tablespoons of the butter over medium heat. Add the onions, leek and 1 teaspoon salt. Toss to coat, and cook, stirring occasionally, until soft and lightly browned, about 25 minutes. Set aside.

Meanwhile, preheat the oven to 400 degrees.

Bring 4 quarts of water to a boil in a large stockpot. Add a heaping tablespoon of salt. Drop in 6 lasagna strips and boil for 1 minute.

---

cook's notes

❦ Although we read in about four estimable sources this year that no-boil lasagna noodles are a complete disaster and are to be avoided at all costs, we were hearing something else from chefs who specialize in authentic Italian food, the very people you'd think would be most skeptical. So we were encouraged to try them, and indeed, they're quite wonderful, especially because they're so thin and delicate. We used the Barilla brand (but also heard good things about DelVerde).

❦ An 8-x-8-inch pan works very well for this dish if you don't have the unusual 8-x-12-inch size called for here; cut the noodles to fit.

❦ You can make the white sauce up to 2 days ahead; cover the surface with plastic wrap to prevent a skin from forming on top and store in the refrigerator.

Remove the strips and let them drain, reserving the water for the next batch. Refresh the strips in cold water and drain again. Spread the strips on kitchen towels. Repeat with the remaining strips.

Remove the bay leaf from the white sauce. Spread 3 tablespoons of the sauce in an 8-x-12-inch baking dish. Drizzle the cream over the white sauce. Cover with 3 pasta strips, overlapping. Spread a few more tablespoons of the white sauce, half the onion mixture and half the cheese over the pasta. Cover with 3 more pasta strips and repeat as before, reserving 2 tablespoons of the cheese. Cover with the remaining 3 pasta strips, and spread the remaining white sauce over them. Sprinkle with the reserved cheese and dot with the re-maining tablespoon of butter.

Bake for 20 minutes, or until the top is golden brown and the lasagna is bubbling hot. Remove it from the oven and let stand for 5 minutes before cutting.

---

serve with

Steamed artichokes with vinaigrette

℘

Fig and Nut Torte (page 306)

to drink

A lively, crisp Italian Chardonnay or Sauvignon Blanc

pasta torte

SOURCE

Nancy Silverton's Pastries from the La Brea Bakery
by Nancy Silverton

COOK

Nancy Silverton

This inspired creation is somewhere between a quiche and the beloved Italian classic spaghetti carbonara. It's just bacon, eggs, pasta and potatoes, but presented as elegant comfort food. The pasta lightens the quiche and comes as a complete surprise, as does the potato crust. The small special touches here—the crème fraîche, the basil leaves, the Parmesan—bring finesse to this homey dish.

The torte works very well for a weeknight supper (make the potatoes the night before and have them ready to go) or for a terrific brunch centerpiece. Any leftovers will be delicious cold for breakfast the next day.

serves 8 to 10

CRUST

3 russet potatoes (about
   1¹/₂ pounds)
¹/₄ teaspoon kosher salt
   Freshly ground black pepper,
   to taste

CUSTARD

³/₄ cup whole milk
³/₄ cup heavy cream
¹/₈ teaspoon cayenne pepper
³/₄ teaspoon kosher salt
3 extra-large eggs
2 extra-large egg yolks

3 tablespoons crème fraîche
   or sour cream
1 cup (4 ounces) grated
   Parmesan cheese
¹/₄ cup minced fresh chives

TORTE

8 ounces angel hair pasta or
   capellini, cooked (al dente)
4–6 slices cooked bacon (chewy,
   not too crisp), pulled into
   small pieces
8–10 fresh basil leaves

TO MAKE THE CRUST

Adjust the oven rack to the middle position and preheat the oven to 400 degrees. Lightly coat a 9-to-10-inch round baking dish with melted butter.

Place the potatoes directly on the oven rack and bake until cooked all the way through, 45 minutes to 1 hour. Allow to cool. Peel the potatoes and mash them with a fork.

Using your fingers, press the mashed potatoes into the bottom and sides of the prepared pan. Sprinkle with the salt and pepper and bake for about 15 minutes, until dry.

MEANWHILE, MAKE THE CUSTARD

In a medium saucepan over medium-high heat, bring the milk, cream, cayenne and salt to a boil. Remove from the heat and allow to cool for about 15 minutes.

In a small bowl, whisk together the whole eggs and egg yolks.

---

cook's notes

❦ Chopped scallions work very well in place of the chives.

❦ The torte cooks perfectly in a 10-inch springform pan, if you have one.

Add the crème fraîche or sour cream and Parmesan to the milk mixture, whisking to incorporate. Slowly whisk in the eggs and egg yolks, and sprinkle in the chives.

TO ASSEMBLE THE TORTE

Evenly distribute the cooked pasta over the potato crust. Sprinkle in the bacon and pour in the custard. Arrange the basil leaves on the surface.

Bake for 40 to 50 minutes, or until the top is nicely browned and the custard is set. Serve hot or warm.

---

serve with

Fennel, Red Pepper
and Mushroom Salad
(page 61)

℘

Spumante–Vodka Cocktail
with Lemon Sorbet (page
328) and Italian Shortbread
with Almonds and Jam
(page 272)

to drink

A light, bright red,
such as a Bardolino,
or a sharp, fresh Soave

---

linguine with lobster, tarragon and charred yellow tomatoes

This very elegant dish is also very easy. It takes the classic (and beloved) combination of tarragon and lobster and plays with it a bit, adding flavor with shallots, garlic, sun-dried tomato paste and charred yellow tomatoes. You could use red tomatoes too, but the yellow ones are lower in acid and work better here, and their color complements the pinky-white lobster meat. Even though

SOURCE

George Foreman's Big Book of Grilling, Barbecue, and Rotisserie
by George Foreman and Barbara Witt

COOK

Barbara Witt

the charred skin gets removed, roasting the tomatoes—as Mexican cooks do—deepens their flavor.

Although this is a perfect summer evening dinner, it doesn't require balmy weather and a charcoal grill (or a George Foreman grill, for that matter). You can make everything in the kitchen, under the broiler, rain or shine.

serves 4

3/4 pound imported linguine
Salt
2 tablespoons extra-virgin olive oil
2 tablespoons unsalted butter
2 shallots, minced
3 garlic cloves, smashed and minced
Generous amounts of freshly

ground black pepper
1 tablespoon sun-dried tomato paste
2 1/2 tablespoons minced fresh tarragon
2 lobster tails, 6–8 ounces each, in shell
2 large, firm yellow tomatoes, stemmed and halved

Light the fire if you're using an outdoor charcoal grill.

Cook the pasta in a stockpot filled with rapidly boiling well-salted water for 8 to 10 minutes, or until al dente. Drain and cool slightly.

Coat your hands with olive oil and run them through the pasta to keep it from sticking (see note). Set aside.

Heat the olive oil and butter in a large skillet. Add the shallots, garlic, salt and pepper. Sauté for 2 to 3 minutes, or until the shallots soften. Stir in the tomato paste and tarragon.

Slide the sharp point of the kitchen shears under one corner of the soft shell on the underside of the lobster tail, above the flesh. Cut all the way around and pull the soft shell off in one piece. Leave the upper, hard shell in place. Cut a deep slit down the center of the exposed flesh and crack the outer shell just a bit by pushing down on each side with your thumbs (see note). This will flatten the tail slightly. Moisten the meat of each tail with a little of the tarragon mixture.

Cook the lobster tails, shell down, on a lidded electric grill for about

---

cook's notes

- Fettuccine would also be delicious as the pasta element.
- The trick of oiling the pasta to keep it from sticking is a very useful one for any pasta dish that isn't being served right away. George Foreman is a strong guy, so he can probably plunge his hands into boiling hot pasta, but you should use tongs or let it cool enough to handle before you touch it.
- If your lobster has very spiny undertails, you won't be able to crack them by just pressing down on them. Flip them over and press on the outer shell with your palm.

4 minutes, or until the meat is opaque and firm. On an outdoor charcoal grill over medium-hot coals the lobster should take 5 to 6 minutes with the lid down. Remove from the heat and cover lightly with foil to keep warm.

Char the tomato halves, skin side down, in a lidded electric grill or on the charcoal grill, for 3 to 4 minutes, or until just softened and the tomato skins have black stripes. Let them cool a little, peel off the skins and chop coarsely. Add to the remaining tarragon mixture in the skillet and toss with the cooked linguine. Reheat in the skillet.

Pull the meat from the lobster tails and cut it into chunks. Divide the pasta among 4 heated flat-rimmed bowls and arrange the lobster on top. Serve immediately.

---

serve with

Baked Greek Olives (page 4)
Sliced semolina bread or
brioche
Green salad with scallions
and toasted walnuts

℘

Santa Rosa Plum Galette
(page 300)

to drink

A toasty, rich Chardonnay

---

buttery new orleans shrimp

SOURCE
Loyno.edu

COOK
Frank Davis

Crescent City Farmers Market, in New Orleans, has a Web site, and that's where we found these succulent shrimp. It took us a little longer to track down the source: Chef Frank Davis has a TV show on WWL called Where Yat? (a typical New Orleans greeting), which features gutsy food without any uptown attitude.

Shrimp cooked this easy way come out not only buttery but also very sweet. The cayenne introduces a touch of heat and the vegetables and herbs round out the fla-vor perfectly. Chef Davis makes double this amount for a crowd, but we've cut his recipe in half to serve 6. Actually 4 people might devour this many shrimp, since it's difficult to stop eating them.

Serving the shrimp with plain rice is a good idea, but since the sauce is so spectacular, why not do as Chef Davis does and just serve the dish with French bread—the light and airy New Orleans French bread would be best of all.

serves 6

1 cup (2 sticks) unsalted butter
1 cup coarsely chopped shallots
1 cup coarsely chopped onion
1/2 cup coarsely chopped celery
1/4 cup coarsely chopped green
    bell pepper
3 garlic cloves, finely chopped
1/3 cup finely chopped fresh
    parsley

1 1/2 pounds shrimp, shells on (see
    note)
2 tablespoons paprika
1 1/2 teaspoons cayenne pepper
1 1/2 tablespoons dried basil
1 tablespoon salt
1 tablespoon freshly ground
    black pepper
1/2 cup Chablis
    Juice of 1/2 lemon

Preheat a heavy 4-quart pan, such as a Dutch oven, over medium-high heat. Toss in the butter and melt it down until it starts bubbling and foaming—don't let it burn.

Turn the heat to high and add all the chopped vegetables and the parsley, stirring them rapidly and continually into the melted butter for about 4 minutes. As they cook, the yellow tint of the butter will turn a pale green.

Drop in the shrimp along with the remaining ingredients, stirring everything immediately into the vegetable-butter mix so that every single shrimp is thoroughly coated. Keep stirring for at least 3 minutes. (The shrimp will begin to turn pink in spots.) Once the shrimp are coated, cover the Dutch oven and cook on high heat for about 3 more minutes.

cook's note

We like to use quite large shrimp for this dish—16 or 20 to the pound. Look for shrimp that have their shells on but have been deveined already, which means they've had their shells split along the back—that will allow more flavor into the shrimp and also make them easier to peel at the table.

When you take the lid off the pot, you'll notice that a sauce has begun to form as the natural shrimp juices mingle with the vegetable butter. Stir again, taste the sauce for seasoning and make any adjustments. Cover the pot once more and cook for another 3 minutes or so, until you begin to see the shrimp breaking away from their shells.

Remove the pot from the heat, put the cover back on, and let the shrimp steep for about 10 minutes in the sauce to pick up the full flavor of the seasonings before you serve them.

---

serve with

Southern-Style Spicy Pecans
(page 2), with drinks
Plain white rice
Quick Pickled French Green
Beans (page 75)

℘

Oven-Roasted Caramel
Bananas en Papillote
(page 310)

---

main dishes

shrimp braised in olive oil

SOURCE

New York Times

COOK

Mark Bittman

High-profile cook Mark Bittman is famous for his omnibus *How to Cook Everything,* for his "Minimalist" column in the *New York Times* (the source of this recipe) and for bringing the genius of chef Jean-Georges Vongerichten to home cooks via the cookbooks that Bittman writes. But possibly he should be best known as the creator of this wonderful recipe. Once you try it, you'll make it again and again.

The shrimp is cooked Spanish-style, in olive oil, with meltingly soft garlic and—the secret ingredients—cumin and paprika, the same spices that perfume North African charmoula.

It's essential to have lots of bread with the dish, since the flavored oil of the sauce is the best part. Bittman recommends using Pacific or Gulf white shrimp. Black tiger shrimp aren't as tasty, but use them if you can't find anything else.

serves 6

⅓ cup extra-virgin olive oil
3–4 big garlic cloves, peeled and cut into thin slivers
1 teaspoon ground cumin, or to taste
1 teaspoon paprika, or to taste

2 pounds shrimp (15–20 per pound); see note
Salt and freshly ground black pepper, to taste
¼ cup chopped fresh parsley

---

tip

For tastier shrimp, give them a little salt rub, says Greek cook Eva Poulos in the *Washington Post.* Just peel the shrimp and devein them, give them a rinse, then gently rub them for a few seconds with salt. Place the salted shrimp in a colander and rinse well. Don't worry, they won't taste salty.

Combine the oil and garlic in a 10- or 12-inch skillet. Turn the heat to medium, and cook until the garlic begins to sizzle, then add the cumin and paprika. Stir, raise the heat to medium-high, and add the shrimp. Season with salt and pepper.

Cook, stirring occasionally, until the shrimp are all just pink, but no more than that: Do not evaporate their liquid. Turn off the heat, add the parsley and serve with crusty bread.

---

serve with

Moroccan Tapenade with jicama sticks (page 16), with drinks
Lots of crusty bread
Mesclun and herb salad

❦

Italian Shortbread with Almonds and Jam (page 272) and red grapes

to drink

A brisk aromatic white, Pinot Grigio or Pinot Bianco

cook's notes

❦ For guests, consider peeling the shrimp first. You won't lose much flavor and unless you're serving a messy casual feast, peeling the shrimp is the kind thing to do.

❦ Two pounds of shrimp really won't fit in one skillet, so you'll need two unless you're cutting the recipe in half.

❦ To get a little crust on the peeled shrimp, run the (ovenproof) skillets under the broiler on the shelf closest to the heat just long enough to crisp the shrimp a bit on each side.

❦ For a scampi version, leave out the cumin and paprika and add lemon.

---

caramelized scallops
with smoked chile cream

For two generations now, everyone from heads of state to celebrities to just folks has been gathering at the Black Dog Tavern on Martha's Vineyard for breakfast, lunch and dinner. They eat, drink and simply hang out—and buy those black dog T-shirts you see all across America. The specialty is fish and seafood, cooked simply but memorably.

These terrific scallops are ready in just a few minutes. Don't skip the chile cream, which is also great over grilled fish or baked potatoes. Give it a little head start so the flavors mellow before you cook the almost-instant scallops.

We're glad the Black Dog is so generous with its scallops, but you really don't need more than a pound of these very rich little bivalves to serve 4 to 6 people.

SOURCE

The Black Dog Summer on the Vineyard Cookbook
by Joseph Hall
and Elaine Sullivan

COOK

Doug Hewson

serves 4 to 6

SMOKED CHILE CREAM
2 teaspoons chipotle powder (see note)
Juice of 2 fresh limes
3/4 cup sour cream
Salt, to taste

CARAMELIZED SCALLOPS
1–2 pounds large sea scallops (see note above), the larger the better

2 tablespoons chopped fresh parsley
Salt and freshly ground black pepper, to taste
Approximately 1/4 cup extra-virgin olive oil

Mixed greens for serving
Sliced lemons
Chopped fresh chives

TO MAKE THE CHILE CREAM

Mix the chipotle powder with the lime juice and let it sit for the flavors to bloom, 5 to 10 minutes. Whisk the chile-lime mixture into the sour cream and add salt. Set aside.

TO MAKE THE SCALLOPS

Sprinkle the tops of the scallops liberally with the parsley, salt and pepper. Heat enough oil to cover the bottom of a large nonstick skillet until the oil just begins to smoke.

Reduce the heat to medium-high and place the scallops seasoned side down. Cook, without disturbing, for 2 to 3 minutes, which will allow them to caramelize their sugars. Turn and sear on the opposite side for 1 to 3 minutes, depending on the size of the scallops.

Serve immediately on a bed of greens, garnished with the chile cream, lemons and chives.

---

cook's notes

♘ If you have only whole chipotle chiles, here's how to turn them into powder: Preheat the oven to 300 degrees. Pull off the stems and slit the chiles open. Remove the seeds. Lay the chiles on a baking sheet and roast for 3 to 5 minutes, or until they're completely dried out and stiff. Crumble them into a bowl, then grind in a spice grinder or coffee mill. Store tightly covered in the freezer for up to 3 months.

♘ For essential information on buying scallops, see page 49.

tip

According to *Cook's Illustrated*, if your nonstick skillet is sticking, it may be because you subject it to the dishwasher. Most nonstick skillets are not designed to undergo the typhoon in the dishwasher, and their surfaces are easily degraded by this mistreatment.

---

crisp snapper tacos with avocado and tropical fruit salsa

SOURCE
Gourmet

COOK
Lisa Ahier

It's difficult to say exactly what's so fantastic about fish tacos, but they're just sensational, with their crisp, soft and crunchy textures and their fresh, clean taste. Everyone seemed to agree with us this year and in fact, we found so many fish taco recipes we had to have a cookoff.

These terrific tacos from Texas chef Lisa Ahier were the winner, partly because they're missing the predictable toppings of tomato salsa, lettuce and sour cream. The tropical fruit salsa is not only a surprise, it's great with the fish.

serves 4 to 6

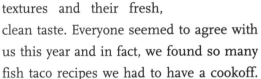

6 cups plus 6 tablespoons canola or vegetable oil
12 taco shells
Salt, to taste
1 tablespoon fresh lime juice
Freshly ground black pepper, to taste
4 skinless, boneless red snapper fillets (2 pounds), cut into 1-inch pieces

6 scallions, chopped
2 canned chipotle chiles in adobo, finely chopped
3 cups arugula or watercress, torn into bite-size pieces
3 cups Avocado and Tropical-Fruit Salsa (recipe follows)

---

serve with
Fresh Corn Soup (page 42)
℘
Coconut–Lime Cake
(page 282)

to drink
A zesty, light, dry
Alsatian Riesling

Heat 6 cups of the oil in a large deep saucepan over medium-high heat until a deep-frying thermometer registers 375 degrees. Fry the taco shells, two at a time, turning occasionally, until they are a shade darker, about 1 minute. Transfer to paper towels to drain and season with salt.

Whisk together the lime juice, 3 tablespoons of the oil, and salt and pepper for the dressing.

Season the fish with salt and pepper. Heat the remaining 3 tablespoons oil in a large nonstick skillet over medium-high heat until hot but not smoking, then sauté the scallions, stirring, for 1 minute. Add the fish and sauté, stirring occasionally, until just cooked through, about 3 minutes. Remove the skillet from the heat and gently toss the fish with the chipotles.

Toss the arugula or watercress with the dressing and adjust the salt and pepper.

Fill the taco shells with greens, the fish mixture and the salsa. Serve immediately.

Avocado and Tropical Fruit Salsa

Makes about 3 cups

2 cups finely diced tropical fruit, such as kiwi, pineapple, mango and papaya

2 California avocados, cut into ¼-inch dice

¼ cup chopped cilantro

¼ cup finely chopped red onion

1 fresh serrano or jalapeño chile, seeded and finely chopped

2 tablespoons fresh lime juice, or to taste

Salt and freshly ground black pepper

In a medium bowl, gently toss together all the ingredients. Taste and adjust the seasonings.

herbed salmon baked on rock salt

This simple-simple recipe from Portland chef Cory Schreiber delivers a lot of flavor and gives you a perfectly cooked piece of salmon. The flesh flakes off the skin with relative ease, and there is no uncooked red center. Baking the salmon on a bed of salt both tempers and

SOURCE

Wildwood: Cooking from the Source in the Pacific Northwest by Cory Schreiber

COOK

Cory Schreiber

distributes the heat, producing moist, evenly cooked fish.

The salmon is so tasty and so pretty that it doesn't really need the accompanying vinaigrette, though if you omit it, Schreiber suggests serving the salmon with a tartar sauce.

serves 8

SALMON

- 4 pounds salmon fillet, pin bones removed, with skin intact
- 2 tablespoons mixed minced fresh herbs, such as tarragon, basil, Italian parsley and thyme
- 2 tablespoons fennel seeds, cracked (see note)
- 1 teaspoon salt
- 1/2 teaspoon freshly ground black pepper
  Rock or kosher salt, for lining the pan

RED ONION–CAPER VINAIGRETTE

- 1 cup olive oil
- 1/4 cup sherry vinegar
- 1 teaspoon Dijon mustard
- 1 red onion, thinly sliced
- 2 teaspoons capers, drained
- 1 teaspoon chopped fresh basil
- 1 teaspoon salt
- 3/4 teaspoon freshly ground black pepper

Rub the fillet with the minced herbs and fennel seeds. Season with salt and pepper. (At this point the salmon can be covered and refrigerated overnight.)

Preheat the oven to 325 degrees. Cover a large jelly-roll or roasting pan with aluminum foil. Pour the rock or kosher salt into the pan, covering the surface to a depth of about ½ inch.

Place the salmon, skin side down, on the salt. Bake for 35 to 45 minutes, or until the salmon is opaque on the outside and slightly translucent in the center. Remove it from the oven, cover loosely

---

cook's notes

☙ To crack fennel seeds, place them on a cutting board and cover with the flat side of a wide chef's knife. Press down on the seeds until you hear them crack.

☙ Any leftovers are good flaked into salads or made into salmon cakes.

tip

At the Worlds of Flavor Conference (at The Culinary Institute of America at Greystone) in the Napa Valley, San Francisco food writer Niloufer Ichaporia King prepared a spice rub for fish, which she said Parsi Indian cooks use for any fish or seafood they're planning to grill, fry or roast. It would work for this salmon, in place of the herbs. Mix together equal amounts of red chile powder, turmeric and fine sea salt—that's it. Rub the mixture into the fish and let it season for 30 minutes before cooking. Use lots for a hot, intense flavor, less for a subtler effect. Serve garnished with wedges of lime, cilantro leaves and slices of avocado. The mix will keep, tightly sealed in a cool dark place, for months.

---

with foil, and let it stand for 5 minutes (the salmon will continue to cook).

TO MAKE THE VINAIGRETTE

In a small bowl, whisk together the oil, vinegar and mustard, then stir in the remaining ingredients.

To serve, use a wide spatula to remove the salmon from the salt. Remove the skin and portion the salmon onto plates. Spoon some of the vinaigrette over each portion and serve.

---

serve with

Pan-Roasted Asparagus
(page 198)
Etta's Cornbread Pudding
(page 232)
℘
Fresh berries and cream

to drink

A ripe, silky Pinot Noir from
Oregon or Santa Barbara

---

main dishes

salt-seared swordfish
with garlic and mint

This is a completely brilliant recipe in which the fish is marinated after rather than before cooking —with a minimum of ingredients. The dish is simplicity itself, so the ingredients need to be first-rate: good olive oil, very fresh garlic, good sea salt. The dish must be made with dried, not fresh, mint. Warning: If you don't love raw garlic, you won't like this recipe.

SOURCE

The Maven's Diary,
Foodmaven.com

COOK

Arthur Schwartz

It comes from the island of Ponza, not far from Naples. There's only one essential trick: Use really coarse salt and flick it off before serving the fish. Otherwise it will be too salty.

Although swordfish is off the endangered species list for the moment, it's worth checking to be sure it still is when you're thinking of making this dish. If not, try it with shark.

serves 2

6–8 large garlic cloves, minced
1 tablespoon sieved dried mint (see note)
6 tablespoons extra-virgin olive oil

2 tablespoons red wine vinegar
2 ¼-inch-thick swordfish or shark steaks
2 tablespoons coarse sea salt

---

serve with

Cantaloupe wedges wrapped
in prosciutto
Broccoli rabe
Rice with Lemon (page 228)

Clementine Cake (page 284)

to drink

Red (Valpolicella) or white
(Sauvignon Blanc)

No more than an hour before serving, combine the garlic, mint, olive oil and vinegar on a platter. Crush the garlic as you blend the raw sauce with a fork.

Cut the skin off the swordfish or shark and discard.

Just before serving, sprinkle the salt evenly over the bottom of a nonstick or cast-iron skillet and place over high heat. Don't worry if the salt pops a bit—that means the pan is hot enough.

When the pan is very hot, place the fish on top of the salt and cook for about 2 minutes. Turn the fish and cook for another 2 or 3 minutes, or until done to your taste.

When the fish is cooked, lift it off the pan with tongs or a fork and brush off any large pieces of salt that still cling to it.

Place the fish on the sauce on the platter and turn it to coat. Spoon some of the sauce on top of the fish and serve immediately.

---

cook's notes

- Rub the dried mint leaves through a fine sieve to get 1 tablespoon mint powder.
- Toss the leftover sauce with some broccoli rabe, a fine companion for this dish. Or use it as a dipping sauce for bread.

tip

Dried mint can be hard to come by, but it's very easy to dry your own, according to *The Spice Hunter*, a newsletter from Kalustyan's, a specialty foods store in Manhattan. Just dry some fresh spearmint in a single layer on some newspaper in the shade. Store the dried leaves in a tightly sealed glass jar.

cured salmon and potato gratin

SOURCE
Food Arts

COOK
Marcus Samuelsson

You might pass right by a recipe sporting this name, but don't! Samuelsson is the chef at New York's Aquavit, considered the leading Scandinavian restaurant in the country. This dish is a cross between a potato-and-salmon gratin and a quiche. The salmon is home-cured, deliciously, and the gratin is full of exhilarating dill. This makes a terrific brunch dish as well as a simple supper, in each case accompanied by a salad.

Making the cured salmon is a snap; you just need to remember to start a day ahead.

serves 6

- ½ cup salt
- ½ cup sugar
- 1 teaspoon white peppercorns, cracked
- 1 pound salmon fillet, skinned
  Freshly ground black pepper
- 2½ pounds potatoes, boiled, peeled and cut into ¼-inch-thick slices

- 1 onion, diced
- 2 bunches of dill, chopped (about 3 cups)
- 3 large eggs
- 2½ cups half-and-half
- ⅓ cup chopped fresh dill
- 8 tablespoons (1 stick) unsalted butter, melted
- 1 cup freshly grated horseradish

---

serve with

Romaine lettuce salad with oranges, toasted almonds and paper-thin slices of red onion

℮

Peppery Ginger Cookies (page 270)

to drink

A dry, softly perfumed Pinot Gris

Mix the salt, sugar and peppercorns in a bowl. Place the salmon in a nonreactive container. Rub the salt-sugar mixture into the salmon, cover and refrigerate overnight.

Preheat the oven to 350 degrees.

Remove the salmon from the refrigerator, wipe off the salt and sugar with a damp towel and thinly slice the salmon, seasoning each side with black pepper.

Grease an ovenproof baking dish (about 3 quarts) with butter. Starting and ending with potatoes, make alternate layers of potatoes and salmon, sprinkling onion and dill over each layer, saving a little dill for the final garnish.

Whisk together the eggs and half-and-half and pour the mixture over the layers. Bake for 45 minutes (see note).

To serve, cut the gratin into serving portions, Place a portion on each plate, sprinkle with dill, and serve the hot melted butter and horseradish in separate dishes on the side.

---

cook's notes

- Don't overcook the potatoes. They should have some bite left, or they'll crumble when you cut the gratin.
- The dish is done when the custard is firm. If you wait for the potatoes to brown, it will be overcooked.
- Don't be tempted to skip the melted butter and horseradish—they really make the dish. You'll want a good inch of horseradish and a little drizzled butter on each portion. Fresh horseradish is available in many supermarkets.

olive oil–poached cod
with roasted tomatoes and broccoli rabe

There are a couple of surprises here. One of them is that Trotter, a master chef acclaimed for his highly complex restaurant food, has come up with such a simple, useful recipe for the home cook. Even more surprising is this technique of cooking fish in olive oil at a very low temperature—an Italian idea that appeared in several magazines and newspapers this year. Although it may seem impossible, fish—especially firm fish such as cod, salmon and swordfish—emerge from a luxurious oil bath not the slightest

SOURCE
Charlie Trotter Cooks at Home by Charlie Trotter

COOK
Charlie Trotter

bit oily. Instead, the oil seals in the juices and produces a piece of fish that's tender, moist and perfectly cooked. It's a particularly good way to cook cod, which easily loses its moisture if it's not served slightly underdone.

With the cooking temperature this low, you may think the fish isn't cooking at all. But once you turn the fillets, you'll see the telltale bubbles in the oil. You do need a cooking thermometer to test the oil temperature, however, because it's the key to success with this technique.

serves 4

ROASTED TOMATOES
- 3 large tomatoes (see note)
- 3 garlic cloves
- 1/2 cup extra-virgin olive oil
- 1/4 cup balsamic vinegar
- 2 sprigs of fresh thyme
  Salt and freshly ground black pepper, to taste

BROCCOLI RABE AND COD
- 1 bunch of broccoli rabe, cleaned and blanched
- 2 tablespoons unsalted butter
  Salt and freshly ground black pepper
- 2 cups extra-virgin olive oil
- 4 5-ounce cod fillets, skinned

TO PREPARE THE TOMATOES

Preheat the oven to 375 degrees. Bring a large pot of water to a boil.

Blanch the tomatoes in the boiling water for 30 seconds, or just until the skins pucker, and then peel off the skins. Cut each tomato into 8 wedges, place in a small roasting pan and toss lightly with the garlic cloves, olive oil, balsamic vinegar and thyme. Bake for 20 to 25 minutes, or until the tomatoes are soft. Remove the tomatoes from the pan, season with salt and pepper and keep warm. Strain the cooking liquid through a fine-mesh sieve and season with salt and pepper. Keep warm.

TO PREPARE THE BROCCOLI RABE AND THE COD

Cook the broccoli rabe in the butter in a small sauté pan over medium heat for 5 minutes, or until warm. Season with salt and pepper.

In a medium saucepan over very low heat, warm the olive oil to 120

---

cook's notes

- If tomatoes aren't in season, you can roast a couple of baskets of cherry or grape tomatoes. Don't bother peeling them, but you might want to cut them in half and squeeze out the seeds before roasting.
- It seems extravagant to pitch out so much olive oil, and you shouldn't; strain it through a coffee filter and store in the refrigerator, tightly sealed, for up to a week. The flavored oil won't taste fishy and will be delicious over salad, vegetables, potatoes or rice.

degrees. Season both sides of the fish with salt and pepper and place in the warm oil. The oil should cover the fish and should stay at a steady 110 to 115 degrees—don't let it get hotter. Cook the fish for 9 minutes, turn the fillets over and cook for an additional 9 minutes, or until just done.

Place some of the roasted tomatoes in the center of each plate and top with a piece of fish. Arrange the broccoli rabe around the plate, drizzle the tomato cooking liquid over the fish and around the plate and serve.

serve with

Gorgonzola Mascarpone
Torta (page 20),
with drinks

Cashew Coffee Biscotti
(page 274) and nectarines
or pears

to drink

Medium-bodied white
Côtes du Rhône or
California Pinot Blanc

david's famous fried chicken

SOURCE

Staff Meals from Chanterelle
by David Waltuck
and Melicia Phillips

COOK

David Waltuck

At Chanterelle, one of New York City's most prestigious restaurants, the guests dining on fine French food have nothing on the staff, for whom Chef Waltuck cooks a down-home meal every afternoon. This is a time for Waltuck to put his own spin on some classic dishes as well as nurture his devoted staff as an adoring parent might. In fact, the staff meals have become so legendary they got their own cookbook this year.

What does the staff love best? David's fried chicken, which is quite different from anyone else's. It has a deeply crisp, shattering crust which conceals perfectly moist meat that has absorbed the spicy flavors in its long buttermilk bath. The crust is double-dipped in flour for extra crunch, and there's not a speck of black pepper here —heresy for Southern fried-chicken cooks.

Get the chicken soaking in the morning and you can make great fried chicken on a weeknight. All you need is an hour for the second flour dip to dry out in the fridge and you're set to fry. Serve hot or at room temperature.

serves 6 to 8

2 chickens, 3–3½ pounds each
1 quart buttermilk
¼ cup Tabasco sauce

2 tablespoons Doctored Harissa (see note, page 147)
All-purpose flour, for coating
Oil, for frying
Kosher salt, to taste

Rinse the chickens well inside and out, removing any excess fat, and cut each chicken into 8 serving pieces. Pat dry with paper towels.

Combine the buttermilk, Tabasco and harissa in a bowl or roasting pan large enough to hold the chicken pieces, whisking to combine.

main dishes

Add the chicken pieces and coat well with the seasoned buttermilk. Cover and let season in the refrigerator for at least 8 hours or up to 16 hours, turning occasionally.

When you're ready to proceed, put 1½ cups flour into a shallow bowl or plate and coat each chicken piece heavily, replacing flour as necessary. Let the chicken pieces rest, not touching, on a baking sheet or large platter in the refrigerator, letting the flour absorb most of the buttermilk coating, about 1 hour.

If you're planning to serve the chicken hot, preheat the oven to its lowest setting and have ready a platter lined with paper towels.

Pour oil to a depth of ½ inch in a large, wide, deep heavy skillet—or two skillets. Heat over medium-high heat until it's almost smoking at 350 degrees on a deep-frying thermometer (the surface will be trembling and giving off a faint haze). Just before you add each piece to the skillet, dip it again in the flour, lightly this time, shaking off any excess. Add only enough pieces to fit into the skillet without touching; don't crowd the pan. Fry the chicken, turning as

---

serve with

Garlicky Fried Peanuts (page 67), with drinks
Indian Ratatouille (page 214)
Big green salad with cilantro, mint and scallions
Warmed pita wedges

℘

Coconut–Lime Cake (page 282)

to drink

Beer or Sauvignon Blanc

---

needed, until all sides are golden brown and the pieces are cooked through, 10 to 15 minutes per side. Using a slotted spatula, remove the pieces of chicken to the lined serving platter and keep warm while you fry the remaining chicken, replenishing and reheating the oil as necessary. Keep the cooked chicken pieces warm in the oven.

When you're ready to serve, salt the chicken pieces and serve warm or at room temperature.

---

cook's notes

- To make **Doctored Harissa:** Get a can (4.7 ounces) of North African harissa, the spicy chile condiment that's most often used in making couscous, and add 2 tablespoons extra-virgin olive oil, 1 teaspoon tomato paste and the juice of a lemon, mixing well. You can store the Doctored Harissa in the refrigerator for months and months, using a bit to stir into scrambled eggs, rice and beans, mayonnaise or olives. Add a little minced cilantro to the mixture before using. If you're going to use the entire amount (about $^3/_4$ cup) at once, mix in 2 tablespoons finely chopped cilantro leaves — but with the cilantro already added, you won't be able to keep the harissa more than a couple of days.

- If there's no harissa to be had, you can use a couple of tablespoons of pureed chipotle peppers in adobo sauce, the kind that come in a can. And if there's none of that, mix up some tomato paste, cumin, paprika, hot pepper flakes, minced garlic and a little olive oil until it tastes good and use that instead.

- Cut-up chicken pieces are a convenience here, and if you use all the same kind, thighs or breasts, they'll all cook in roughly the same time period. If you're using two skillets, put the breasts in one, thighs in the other.

- We like fried chicken best when it's fried in peanut oil or (gasp) lard. A big enameled cast-iron pot works very well if you don't have the right skillet.

- To drain off the most fat, set the cooked chicken pieces on a rack over the platter, not on paper towels.

---

main dishes

quick and easy chicken breasts
with fresh mozzarella

If you think you can't bear to cook yet another boneless skinless chicken breast, you ought to try this recipe. It's everything the title promises, plus it's elegant, with the refined touch of white wine and fresh tarragon. The chicken obligingly makes its own sauce as it cooks. Paula Lambert, founder of the Mozzarella Company and maker of fine hand-crafted cheeses, has been teaching this dish for years now, and it's become a favorite in the family

SOURCE

The Cheese Lover's Cookbook and Guide by Paula Lambert

COOK

Paula Lambert

repertoires of her former students.

It's easy to see why: Making this dish from scratch takes no more than about 20 minutes, and it does wonders for the pallid chicken breast.

There's one secret, Lambert says: Cook the mozzarella only long enough to barely melt it, just until it's soft. We'd add: This will be even better if you use an excellent mozzarella, which Lambert just assumes you will.

serves 4

4 boneless skinless chicken
    breasts (about 1½ pounds)
  Salt and freshly ground black
    pepper, to taste
2 tablespoons unsalted butter

1 garlic clove
½ cup dry white wine
8 ounces fresh mozzarella,
    cut into 8 slices
4 sprigs of fresh tarragon

Rinse the chicken and pat dry. Season with salt and pepper. Melt the butter in a large skillet over medium heat and add the garlic. Add the chicken breasts and cook for 6 to 10 minutes, or until golden brown on both sides and almost cooked through, turning as necessary. Transfer to a plate and keep warm.

Add the wine to the pan, scraping to release any browned bits on the bottom, and simmer briefly to reduce the sauce by half. Return the chicken to the pan and cook for 1 minute. Place 2 slices of fresh mozzarella and a sprig of tarragon on top of each chicken breast. Cover the pan, remove it from the heat, and set aside for a few minutes to let the mozzarella soften and begin to melt. Sprinkle the chicken with additional salt or pepper as desired. Remove the garlic clove from the pan and discard. Serve the chicken on heated serving plates and spoon some of the sauce over it.

---

serve with

Scallion and Mushroom Soup (page 34), to start
Buttered Sugar Snap Peas with Fresh Mint (page 201)
Crusty baguette

℮

Caramelized Pineapple Clafoutis (page 296)

to drink

A crisp, lively Chablis

tip

What to do with the remains of the wine? Since conventional wisdom says it deteriorates almost immediately, you should either turn it into vinegar, as a thrifty French person would; preserve it using a fancy gizmo from the wine store; or just dump it down the drain. But when Karen MacNeil-Fife did an exhaustive experiment for *Sunset* magazine with three different wines using every possible preservation method, she made an amazing discovery. No preserving system worked better than just recorking the bottle, and in some cases the opened wine actually tasted better than its freshly uncorked self, even several days later.

port-and-black-currant-glazed chicken thighs

SOURCE

Susan Westmoreland,
Good Housekeeping

COOK

Susan Westmoreland

Port and black currant jelly don't usually make an appearance at American barbecues. But these quintessentially British ingredients bring a lot to the party, especially when they're combined as they are here with Dijon mustard and fresh tarragon. It's a robust combination that goes very well with the dark meat of chicken thighs, which happens to be our favorite part of the bird. And unlike most marinated grilled chicken recipes, this one asks you to marinate for only 15 minutes.

If it rains, as it very well might at a British barbecue, you can cook the chicken indoors in a 400-degree oven on a rack in a shallow pan for 40 to 45 minutes, turning it frequently.

serves 4

1/3 cup ruby port
1/4 cup Dijon mustard
1/2 teaspoon salt
1/4 teaspoon coarsely ground black pepper

2 tablespoons chopped fresh tarragon leaves
8 medium bone-in chicken thighs (about 2 1/2 pounds), skin removed
1/4 cup black currant jelly

---

serve with

Southern-Style Spicy Pecans (page 2), with drinks
Quick Pickled French Green Beans (page 75)
Warm potato salad

℘

Plum Crumb Cake (page 278)

to drink

A light red with plenty of fruit, a Gamay or Chinon

Preheat the grill.

In a large bowl, whisk the port, mustard, salt, pepper and 1 table-spoon of the tarragon until blended. Transfer 3 tablespoons of this marinade to a small bowl.

Add the chicken to the marinade remaining in the large bowl. Toss until evenly coated. Cover the bowl and let the chicken stand for 15 minutes at room temperature or 30 minutes in the refrigerator.

Meanwhile, whisk the black currant jelly into the marinade in the small bowl until blended, and set aside.

Place the chicken on the grill over medium heat and cook for 25 minutes, or until the juices run clear when the thickest part of the thigh is pierced with a knife, turning once. Brush the jelly mixture all over the chicken and cook for 1 to 2 minutes or longer until glazed, turning once. Place the chicken on a serving platter and sprinkle with the remaining tablespoon of tarragon.

butterflied chicken with crisp potatoes

SOURCE

Cook's Illustrated

COOK

Dawn Yanigahara

Make this hot-roasted chicken once and it will become your standard roast chicken. Not only can you now produce a delicious, perfectly roasted bird in under an hour, you'll also have wonderfully crisp, flavorful potatoes to serve on the side because they've cooked directly underneath the bird and absorbed all its great juices.

There are a couple of tricks to this recipe. One is that the chicken is butterflied — that is, the backbone is removed (a butcher can do this for you) and the chicken is squashed out flat, sort of like a sprawling frog, so that the dark meat cooks much faster and the bird is easier to carve. Butterflying the chicken also means you don't have to worry about turning it or flipping it over at any point in the cooking and the skin gets crisp all over.

The other trick is brining, but if you don't have time for that, you can either just do a quick rub with coarse salt and let the chicken air-dry in the fridge for a couple of hours for a crisp skin or use a kosher chicken, which is prebrined.

You can make the chicken alone without the potatoes, you can skip the under-skin seasoning (chipotle butter with lime and honey) and you can also use other vegetables alongside the potatoes, such as carrots, parsnips, leeks, turnips, shallots — anything that roasts well.

serves 4

- 1 cup kosher salt for brining, plus $3/4$ teaspoon for potatoes
- $1/2$ cup sugar
- 2 quarts cold water
- 1 whole chicken, $3^1/2$–4 pounds, giblets and fat around cavity removed

- 1 recipe Chipotle Butter with Lime and Honey (recipe follows; optional)
- $2^1/2$ pounds (4–5 medium) russet or Yukon Gold potatoes, peeled and sliced $1/4$–$1/8$ inch thick
- $1^1/2$ tablespoons olive oil
  Freshly ground black pepper, to taste

About 1 hour before you plan to cook the chicken, dissolve the 1 cup salt and the sugar in the water in a large container. Immerse the chicken and refrigerate for 1 hour. Meanwhile, adjust the oven rack to the lower-middle position and heat the oven to 500 degrees. Line the bottom of a broiler pan with foil and spray with nonstick vegetable cooking spray (or grease the foil with some olive oil).

Remove the chicken from the brine and rinse thoroughly under cold running water. To butterfly the chicken, cut through the bones on either side of the backbone and remove it. Flip the chicken over and use the heel of your hand to flatten the breastbone. If you're using the seasoned butter, slip your fingers between the skin and the chicken breast, loosening the membrane and working some of the butter evenly all over the flesh. Repeat the procedure with the drumsticks and thighs. Transfer the chicken to the rack and push the legs up to rest between the thighs and the breast. Thoroughly pat the chicken dry with paper towels.

Toss the potatoes in a bowl with 1 tablespoon of the oil, the 3/4 tablespoon salt and pepper. Spread the potatoes in an even layer in the foil-lined broiler pan. Place the roasting rack with the chicken on top. Rub the chicken with the remaining 1/2 tablespoon oil and sprinkle with pepper.

Roast the chicken until spotty brown, about 20 minutes. Rotate the pan and continue to roast for 20 to 25 minutes, or until the skin

---

cook's note

You can also butterfly-roast a turkey. Choose an 8-pound turkey, remove its back and pound it flat with your fist. It should be done in about 1 1/2 hours or a little longer—check with an instant-read thermometer to be sure the leg temperature is about 170 degrees in the thickest part.

---

crisps and turns a deep brown and an instant-read thermometer registers 170 degrees in the thickest part of the thigh.

Remove the chicken to a cutting board or serving platter. Scrape the potatoes into a serving bowl. Keep warm and blot any excess grease with paper towels. Cut the chicken into serving pieces and serve the potatoes alongside.

Chipotle Butter with Lime and Honey

2 tablespoons unsalted butter, softened

1 medium garlic clove, pressed

1 teaspoon honey

1 teaspoon very finely grated lime zest

1 medium canned chipotle in adobo, seeded and minced to a paste

1 teaspoon adobo sauce

Combine all the ingredients and season the chicken under its skin before roasting.

---

serve with

Big green salad with sourdough croutons and a lemony-dill dressing

℮

Double-Baked Chocolate Cake (page 276)

to drink

A dry Chenin Blanc or earthy Pinot Noir

---

chicken cooked under a brick

We've been checking out versions of this traditional Italian dish for a couple of years now and finally we've found a sensationally good one that works every time. Joseph Verde developed this recipe when he was the chef at Oscar's in the Waldorf-Astoria, and once the word went out, it became his best-seller. It's easy to see why. The thigh and breast cook together so that the breast doesn't dry out, the meat is juicy and the crusty skin is divinely crisp and crackling. Verde also treats his birds to a little Tuscan marinade (olive oil, garlic, thyme, rosemary) overnight to make them even tastier.

SOURCE

Joseph Verde,
Fine Cooking

COOK

Joseph Verde

You do, of course, need a couple of bricks to make this dish, though stones also work. For urbanites with no access to bricks or stones, another heavy skillet weighted with a can or two can stand in. You (or your butcher) also need to do a little surgery on the chicken to make it lie flat in the pan, which needs to be a heavy cast-iron or enameled cast-iron one. But nothing here is difficult, and once you make this "chicken bricken," as we can't help calling it, it can become your signature dish too. Everyone will beg you for it.

serves 2

- 1 3-to-4-pound chicken, preferably free-range
- 2½ tablespoons fresh thyme leaves, coarsely chopped
- 2 tablespoons fresh rosemary leaves, coarsely chopped

- 6 garlic cloves, peeled and smashed
- 1 cup extra-virgin olive oil
  Salt and freshly ground black pepper, to taste
  Vegetable or olive oil, as needed

Rinse the chicken in cold water and pat dry. Cut off the first two wing joints with a chef's knife. Turn the chicken breast side down and remove the backbone by cutting along it on both sides with poultry shears or a sharp chef's knife. Flatten the chicken and split it completely in half by cutting through the breastbone. With a cleaver or the heel of a chef's knife, hack off the knuckle end of the drumsticks. To make the chicken easier to eat, you may want to trim away the keel bone (that flat white soft piece that runs down the center) and cut away the rib bones. Now you have two pieces of mostly boned chicken; save the trimmings for stock.

Rinse and dry the chicken halves again. Combine the thyme, rosemary, garlic and olive oil in a large resealable plastic bag or mixing bowl. Add the chicken halves, cover and refrigerate overnight or for at least 4 hours.

Preheat the oven to 450 degrees. Wrap 2 bricks in a couple of layers of foil. Remove the chicken from the refrigerator, let the excess marinade drain off, and sprinkle with salt and pepper.

---

serve with

Roasted Bell Pepper Salad
with Pine Nuts (page 70)
The Best Grated Potato
Pancakes (page 220)

℘

Burnt Caramel Ice Cream
(page 314)

to drink

A lighter-style Merlot

Set a large cast-iron pan over medium-high heat. When hot, add just enough vegetable oil to lightly film the pan. Put the chicken halves, skin side down, in the pan and instantly put a brick on top of each half. Turn the heat to medium and cook without moving the chicken until the skin is a deep golden brown and the chicken is cooked about halfway through, 20 to 25 minutes. Remove the bricks, turn the chicken halves over, and put the pan in the hot oven to finish roasting the chicken until a meat thermometer registers at least 165 degrees, another 20 to 25 minutes. Serve.

hot-roasted turkey with sausage, black olive and walnut dressing

SOURCE

Jonathan Reynolds,
New York Times Magazine

COOK

Karen Hess

This heretical way of roasting turkey—at a very high temperature for a very short time—made its debut in the *New York Times* in 1974, and it's just as startling today as it was then. The plan here is to solve the eternal problem of keeping the white meat moist while cooking the dark meat long enough—and getting a crisp skin in the bargain. The turkey is also brined for better flavor, texture and moisture.

If you're alone in the kitchen and unsure about hoisting a giant bird out of a blistering oven every 20 minutes to turn it and baste it, you can do the next best thing: Don't turn it, just baste it and cover it loosely with heavy-duty foil when it starts to look done, about halfway through the cooking time. It won't be as perfectly browned all over, but if you perch it on a bed of curly kale —much sturdier and prettier than parsley or watercress—no one will notice.

The recipe is for a 12-pound turkey, but you can use a larger one if you like, adjusting the temperature: A 16-pounder will be done in 2^1/2 hours and a 20-pounder in 3 hours.

The stuffing is unusual because of the olives and walnuts. We asked culinary historian Karen Hess about using the green ripe California olives instead of the black ones, and she said she'd tried that once and didn't like it. She also volunteered that these days she doesn't usually bother with the olives, just adds more celery, and has no complaints from the family. As she says, this is one of those stuffings that you make your own, adjusting it until it's just the way you like it.

Start a day ahead to brine the turkey.

TURKEY

1   12-pound turkey, preferably
      free-range
2   cups kosher salt
2–3 gallons cold water

STOCK

Neck, gizzard and heart from
   the turkey
1   carrot, scrubbed and sliced
1   celery rib, sliced
1   large onion, quartered
Handful of fresh parsley

Sausage, Black Olive and
   Walnut Dressing (page 163)

2   tablespoons vegetable oil
8   tablespoons (1 stick) butter, at
      room temperature

GRAVY

1   cup turkey stock
½   cup cognac, white wine or dry
      sherry

---

cook's notes

℘ A contemporary turkey may be loaded with plastic: buttons on its breast,
   strange bondage contraptions in its intimate parts. Remove these if possible. If you truss the legs together, the bird will take much longer to
   cook. Let it loll around on the rack "like a ravished hooker," as Reynolds
   says, and it will roast perfectly.

℘ Or forget the brine and just salt the bird very well inside and out with
   kosher salt and leave it in the refrigerator for 12 hours. Rinse thoroughly
   and pat dry before proceeding.

---

main dishes

TO BRINE THE TURKEY

About 20 hours before you plan to cook the bird, remove its giblets and cut off the wing tips (save them for the stock). Swish the salt around in the water until it's dissolved—don't bother heating it. Submerge the turkey in the brine and be sure it's completely covered. You can do this in a heavy-duty garbage bag inside a basin, a picnic cooler or a giant stockpot. You need to keep the turkey cold, though, either in the refrigerator or outdoors if the temperature is in the thirties, or in a picnic cooler with blue ice packs and/or plastic bags filled with ice cubes. You may need to weight the turkey to be sure it's entirely covered by the brine.

After 12 hours of brining, rinse the turkey thoroughly inside and out and pat dry. Leave it uncovered in the refrigerator for 7 hours to help the skin crisp when it's roasted.

---

tip

We're crazy about this tip from *Fine Cooking* reader Debra Rich in Sarasota, Florida—and we'll never roast a turkey or a chicken again without taking her advice. Remove the wishbone before roasting, which makes carving a cinch, almost like carving a boneless roast beef. Here's how (or try to talk your butcher into doing this for you). The wishbone is the bird's collarbone; feel for the V-shaped bone under the top of the breast. Once you've found it, take the tip of a sharp paring knife and cut through the flesh just deep enough to free the bone on both sides, leaving it attached in three places (at the ends and in the middle). Hook your finger underneath and pull out the bone; don't worry if it breaks, just pull out the broken piece too.

MEANWHILE, START MAKING THE STOCK

Deeply score the turkey parts (except the liver, which can be finely diced and added to the stuffing) and add to a saucepan along with the carrot, celery, onion and parsley and the reserved wing tips. Cover with water. Simmer for 3 hours, adding more liquid as necessary. Strain the stock and reserve.

Prepare the dressing.

An hour before roasting the turkey, take it out of the refrigerator to come to room temperature. Oil a V-shaped nonadjustable rack and put it in the roasting pan. Add the 2 tablespoons oil to the bottom of the roasting pan.

---

serve with some or all of these dishes

Southern-Style Spicy Pecans (page 2), with drinks
Crimped Shrimp (page 22), to start
Beet Soup in Roasted Acorn Squash (page 36), to start
Roasted Green and Yellow Wax Beans with Hazelnut Oil (page 204)
Sweet Potatoes with Southern Comfort (page 222)
Potato–Green Chile Gratin (page 238)
Etta's Corn Bread Pudding (page 232)
Orange-Ginger Cranberries (page 224)
Thomas Jefferson's Sweet Potato Biscuits (page 246)
Parker House Rolls (page 248)
℘
Rummy Pumpkin Cheesecake (page 292) or Pumpkin Caramel Pudding (page 298)
Caramelized Orange Chips (page 316), with after-dinner drinks

to drink

Zinfandel, Pinot Noir or a big, buttery Napa Valley Chardonnay

---

main dishes

TO ROAST THE TURKEY

Preheat the oven to 450 degrees.

Stuff the turkey and rub it all over with the soft butter. Set it on its side on the rack in the pan and roast for 30 minutes. Smoke may pour out of the oven (especially if it's not clean), but ignore it unless the pan juices or the turkey itself start to turn black—in which case, turn down the heat to 400 degrees or even 375.

Baste the turkey and, using two huge wads of wet paper towels on either end of the bird, turn it on its other side. Let it roast for 20 more minutes and repeat the turning and basting. After another 20 minutes, turn the turkey and baste again; roast for another 20 minutes. Repeat the turning and basting and roast for a final 20 minutes. Your total cooking time should be about 1 hour 50 minutes. The turkey is done when the thickest part of its thigh registers 135 to 145 degrees—it will finish cooking after it comes out of the oven. Let it sit on its serving platter, covered loosely with foil, for 20 minutes for the juices to settle.

MEANWHILE, MAKE THE GRAVY

Pour off all but a couple of tablespoons of the fat and set the roasting pan over two burners. Add the stock and, over high heat, scrape up all the delicious little bits that have stuck to the pan. Add the cognac, wine or sherry and bring to a boil or set it afire to burn off the alcohol. Taste for salt and reduce further, or add more stock if necessary.

Carve the turkey and serve with the dressing. Pass the gravy separately.

Sausage, Black Olive and Walnut Dressing

1 pound bulk pork sausage
1 turkey liver, minced
1 cup chopped onion
1/2 cup very thinly sliced celery
1 teaspoon chopped fresh thyme
1 loaf of good bread, sliced
1 cup mild pitted California-style
    black olives, sliced
1 cup walnut pieces

1/2 cup chopped fresh Italian
    parsley
2 tablespoons cognac or 4
    tablespoons Madeira, port
    or dry sherry
Kosher salt and freshly ground
    black pepper, to taste
1/2–1 cup stock

Cook the sausage and the turkey liver in a large, heavy pan over medium heat, stirring until cooked and making sure the sausage meat is well broken up, about 12 minutes.

Add the onion, celery and thyme and cook, stirring frequently, until the onion is tender and pale yellow, about 10 minutes.

Toast the bread slices and dice; you should have about 3 cups. Place the sausage mixture in a large bowl and add the bread. Add the olives, walnut pieces, parsley, spirits, salt and pepper. Add enough stock so the stuffing will hold together in the bird. Refrigerate if not using within 1 hour.

turkey in a bag

SOURCE
Jeanne McManus,
Washington Post

COOK
The Reynolds Kitchens

A 90-year-old matriarch we know reacted in horror to the idea of roasting a turkey inside a giant plastic bag, even though she'd seen it with her own eyes on TV and the turkey looked just fine. We were just about as skeptical, but this speeded-up, sanitized version of roasting turns out a tasty bird that's extremely juicy with almost no work and no mess. It doesn't look like a Norman Rockwell painting because it doesn't have the deeply browned crackling skin. On the other hand, those gorgeous birds are the ones with the dry breast meat.

Does it produce the makings of good gravy? Absolutely; in fact there's plenty of juice in the bottom of the bag. Does it smell good while it's roasting? It smells great. Can you stuff it? Yes . . . and best of all, there's almost no cleanup—just toss the bag. Here are the details. You can find Reynolds brand turkey-size roasting bags in the supermarket.

serves 12 to 14

- 1 12-to-14-pound turkey, at room temperature
- 1 tablespoon all-purpose flour
- 2 celery ribs, diced
- 1 medium onion, sliced
  Vegetable oil or melted butter

Salt and freshly ground black pepper, to taste
Herbs and seasonings of choice (see note)

- 1 Reynolds Oven Bag, turkey size

Preheat the oven to 350 degrees.

Remove the giblets and neck from the body and neck cavities of the

---

serve with
See the menu for Hot-
Roasted Turkey (page 161)

---

turkey. Rinse the turkey in cold water, drain it and pat it dry with paper towels. If desired, you may stuff the turkey.

Add the flour to the bag (be sure it's a turkey-size bag specially made for roasting turkeys) and shake to coat. Place the bag in a roasting pan at least 2 inches deep. Scatter the celery and onion in the bottom of the bag.

Brush the turkey with the oil or melted butter. Season with salt and pepper and any favorite herbs or seasonings. Place the turkey in the bag on top of the celery and onion and close with the nylon tie that comes with the bag. Cut 6 slits, each about ½ inch long, in the top of the bag.

Roast the turkey until a thermometer registers 180 degrees in the thigh or 170 degrees in the breast—about 2 hours or less for a 12-pound unstuffed bird, 2½ hours for a 16-pounder.

---

cook's notes

- You might want to add thyme, garlic, sage—whatever you enjoy with your turkey.
- Simmer the neck and giblets in chicken stock as in the recipe for Hot-Roasted Turkey (page 158) to make stock.
- It can be difficult to maneuver the turkey out of the bag. The easiest way is to perform a "cesarean": Just slit open the bag and haul it out. The juices can then spill into the roasting pan, ready to be made into gravy.

skirt steak with shallot-thyme butter

SOURCE

Mark Bittman,
New York Times

COOK

Steve Johnson

Next to a perfectly aged, marbled porterhouse or strip steak, our favorites are the chewy streaked-with-fat skirt steak and hanger steak. These steaks tend to have the beefiest taste, and although they've become more expensive as cooks have learned to prize them, they're still a relative bargain.

Steve Johnson of the Blue Room in Cambridge, Massachusetts, came up with this classic French treatment of good old skirt steak, and it's sensationally good. It's especially tasty grilled, but even if you don't have access to an outdoor grill, you can broil the steak with excellent results.

serves 4

8 tablespoons (1 stick) unsalted butter, softened slightly
10 chives, minced
1 shallot, minced
¼ teaspoon fresh thyme leaves

Salt and freshly ground black pepper
½ teaspoon red wine vinegar or fresh lemon juice
About 1½ pounds skirt steak, cut into 4 pieces

serve with

Crimped Shrimp
(page 22) with cocktail
sauce to start
Blasted Broccoli (page 200)
Rice pilaf
℘
Cherry-Almond Pound Cake
(page 289)

to drink

Australian Shiraz

Prepare a gas grill or charcoal fire; it should be so hot you can hold your hand over it for only a couple of seconds.

Meanwhile, cream the butter with a fork, adding the chives, shallot, thyme, ½ teaspoon each of salt and pepper and the vinegar or lemon juice.

Grill the steak, 2 minutes per side for rare, about a minute longer per side for medium-rare. As it cooks, season with salt and pepper.

Spread each steak with about a tablespoon of the flavored butter and serve. The remaining butter can be wrapped and refrigerated or frozen.

---

cook's notes

𝕃 Use a high-fat butter (such as Plugra or Land O' Lakes Creamy) for an especially delicious flavored butter.

𝕃 As Mark Bittman points out, you can experiment with the flavored butter, making roasted garlic the base, or putting together a southwestern butter by adding a minced jalapeño along with a tablespoon of minced cilantro and a teaspoon of fresh lime juice.

𝕃 Whatever you do, don't overcook the steak; it needs to be cooked at very high heat and briefly or it can turn into shoe leather.

beef fillets
with stilton-portobello sauce

This prize-winning recipe comes from a cook in Osage, Iowa, where they're serious about their beef. The challenge was to come up with a holiday main dish using eight ingredients or fewer. This simple, straightforward recipe delivers the goods. It's elegant and rich, and it makes the most of the great combination of beef, blue cheese and red wine.

Although its richness is part of the celebratory point, you can cut it back a bit by searing the fillets in just a very thin film of vegetable oil in a nonstick pan. Then add just 3 tablespoons butter when you sauté the mushrooms.

SOURCE

Southern Living
holiday contest

COOK

**Diane Sparrow,
Grand Prize Winner**

serves 6

6 beef tenderloin fillets, 6 ounces each

2 teaspoons chopped fresh tarragon, plus sprigs for optional garnish

1/2 teaspoon freshly ground black pepper

5 tablespoons butter

8 ounces portobello mushroom caps, sliced

1/3 cup dry red wine

1/2 cup sour cream

3 ounces Stilton or other blue cheese, crumbled (1/4 cup plus 2 tablespoons)

---

cook's notes

❧ Look for center-cut fillets, which will be nicely shaped and thick. We'd also add a little salt to the pepper when seasoning the fillets.

❧ Instead of Stilton, you could use a creamy Danish blue cheese or Iowa's Maytag blue.

❧ Heavy cream or crème fraîche can substitute for the sour cream.

Rub the fillets with the tarragon and pepper. Melt 2 tablespoons of the butter in a large skillet over medium-high heat. Cook the fillets for 4 to 5 minutes on each side, or to the desired degree of doneness. Remove from the skillet and keep warm.

Melt the remaining 3 tablespoons butter in the skillet. Add the mushrooms and sauté for 3 to 4 minutes, or until tender. Add the wine and cook for 1 to 2 minutes, stirring to loosen browned bits from the bottom of the skillet. Stir in the sour cream. Sprinkle 1/4 cup of the cheese into the sauce, stirring until melted.

Arrange the fillets on a serving platter and drizzle with the sauce. Sprinkle with the remaining cheese and garnish with tarragon sprigs, if desired.

---

serve with

Southern-Style Spicy Pecans (page 2), with drinks
The Best Grated Potato Pancakes (page 220)
Watercress and endive salad

℘

Tart Lemon Tart (page 303)

to drink

A peppery full-bodied Cabernet Sauvignon

---

beef tenderloin with garlic

SOURCE

Advertisement for Stew Leonard's markets in *Harper's Bazaar*

COOK

Stew Leonard family

For a spectacular dinner party or holiday feast, nothing else is quite as impressive as a perfectly roasted beef tenderloin (known as filet mignon once it's trimmed). This expensive cut is lean but buttery and filled with extraordinary beefy flavor. It's also one of the easiest main courses ever devised and makes wonderful leftovers.

When we saw this recipe in a Stew Leonard's ad, we took notice, because Stew is noted for his well-priced and especially delectable tenderloins, which he features in huge bins at his cow-themed supermarkets in Connecticut and New York. And we were a little nervous since the recipe is so simple, without so much as an herb. But fear not: This is a recipe designed to showcase the meat itself, with sweet garlic flavor and a great aroma as it roasts.

serves 8 to 10

1 whole beef tenderloin, 7–8 pounds, trimmed, at room temperature
Handful of garlic, finely chopped

Olive oil, to taste
Salt and freshly ground black pepper, to taste

---

serve with

Spinach Dip with Jicama and Sweet White Onions (page 18)
Mashed Potatoes with Toasted Coriander (page 218)
Blasted Broccoli (page 200)
Parker House Rolls (page 248)

℘

Blum's Coffee Crunch Cake (page 286)

to drink

A big, intense Merlot

Preheat the oven to 450 degrees.

Place the fillet on a rack in a roasting pan. In a small bowl, mix the garlic with some olive oil and brush generously all over the tenderloin. Season with salt and pepper.

Roast the fillet for 35 to 40 minutes, or until it reaches an internal temperature of 140 degrees. Remove it from the oven and let it sit, loosely covered in foil, for at least 10 minutes for the juices to redistribute, before slicing and serving.

cook's notes

✿ Stew Leonard says finding the best tenderloin is easy: Just squeeze the vacuum-sealed package and look for the softest tenderloin. If it's hard, you'll be buying more fat and less meat. Count on 1 pound for each person.

✿ Usually you have to buy a whole tenderloin to get a good price, but if you're serving just 4 people, you can simply cut the tenderloin in half and freeze the half you don't roast for another time. Defrost it in the refrigerator for a day or two for best flavor. The cooking time is actually the same, since it's a long thin roast. For rare, pull the roast from the oven before it hits an internal temperature of 120 degrees—at 116 degrees, ours was perfect.

✿ If you're lucky enough to have a butcher, he or she will probably trim almost all of the fat away and toss it. But it's delicious for roasting potatoes or making Yorkshire pudding or just feeding to the birds. And since you're paying for it anyway, you might as well use it.

beef and onion stew

SOURCE

Williams-Sonoma Taste

COOK

Andy Harris

The birth of a new food magazine is an exciting event in itself—and how gratifying to realize that the editor-in-chief of the spanking-new *Williams-Sonoma Taste*, Andy Harris, is as skilled at cooking as he is at editing. This deeply flavored stew is full of baking spices: allspice, cloves, nutmeg and cinnamon. Since it's best marinated overnight, you can prepare everything ahead of time and brown the meat and vegetables, and then cook them shortly before you serve the dish. Or do it all 2 days ahead; like all other stews, this one only improves with a long rest in the refrigerator before being reheated and served.

The stew is classically made with rabbit instead of beef. If rabbit is an option in your kitchen, try it this especially savory way.

serves 6

MARINADE AND BEEF

- 1 cup dry red wine
- ¼ cup red wine vinegar
- 2 bay leaves
- 2 cinnamon sticks
- 4 whole cloves
- 3 whole allspice berries
- ½ teaspoon ground allspice
  Pinch of freshly grated nutmeg
  Salt and freshly ground black pepper
- 3 pounds boneless well-marbled stew beef, cubed (see note)

- 4 tablespoons (½ stick) butter
- 2 tablespoons olive oil
- 1½ pounds pearl onions or shallots, peeled
- 3 celery ribs, peeled and sliced
- 1 14½-ounce can diced tomatoes, including their juice
- 1 tablespoon tomato paste

TO MARINATE THE BEEF

Combine the marinade ingredients in a large bowl. Add the beef and toss to coat. Cover and refrigerate for at least 6 hours or preferably overnight.

Drain the beef, reserving the marinade. Melt the butter with 1 tablespoon of the olive oil in a large saucepan over medium heat and sauté the onions or shallots and celery until softened, about 10 minutes. Using a slotted spoon, transfer to a bowl.

Add the remaining 1 tablespoon olive oil to the pan. Dry the beef cubes well and sauté the beef in batches until browned, about 10 minutes. Return the onions and celery to the pan. Add the reserved marinade, tomatoes, tomato paste, salt and pepper and enough water to just cover the beef.

Bring to a boil, reduce the heat to low and simmer, partially covered, until the meat is tender and the sauce has thickened, $1\frac{1}{2}$ to 2 hours. Serve hot.

---

cook's notes

- You'll be best off buying a hunk of meat and cutting it into 2-inch cubes yourself. A chuck roast will be particularly well marbled and flavorful.
- An enameled cast-iron pot is perfect for cooking this stew, which can also be cooked in the oven at 325 degrees if you'd rather.

serve with

Buttered egg noodles
Big green salad

Upside-Down Cranberry Cake (page 280)

to drink

A spicy Syrah

---

kuala lumpur lamb

Josh Parsons is a young chef who owns Culinary Capers, a take-out shop and eat-in restaurant in Mystic, Connecticut. Before settling in the Northeast, he cooked in the Caribbean, and he has a taste for intense, tropical flavors. These fragrant, very tender meat skewers are from the great Asian tradition of street food.

SOURCE

Connecticut Chefs 2000
by Lee White

COOK

Josh Parsons

You can marinate the lamb a day ahead and just bring it to room temperature before setting the skewers on the grill. The sauce is made in a flash while the skewers are grilling. Parsons suggests some vegetable skewers as well—keep them separate from the meat and just brush them with peanut oil and add a little salt and pepper.

serves 8

1 3-pound leg of lamb, boned and cut into 1½-inch cubes
½ cup dark soy sauce (or regular soy plus 1 teaspoon molasses)
¼ cup hot water
⅓ cup smooth peanut butter
½ cup chopped peanuts
1 garlic clove, minced
2 lemons, juiced

1 teaspoon cayenne pepper
4 ounces tomato sauce
1 teaspoon Tabasco
¼ cup unsweetened coconut milk
Salt and freshly ground black pepper
Assorted skewered vegetables (bell peppers, cherry tomatoes, patty pan squash, baby onions)

Skewer the lamb. If you're using wooden skewers, soak them in water for half an hour so they won't burn.

In a small saucepan, combine the soy sauce, water, peanut butter, chopped peanuts, garlic, half the lemon juice and cayenne. Bring to a boil and stir until smooth. Remove from the heat and let cool. Pour half of the marinade over the lamb, reserving the remaining marinade for the sauce.

Let the lamb marinate for 2 hours at room temperature or overnight in the refrigerator.

Bring the lamb to room temperature before grilling. When you're ready to cook the skewers, get the fire going.

Grill the lamb skewers over medium-high coals for 4 to 6 minutes on each side for medium-rare, or until done to your liking.

Meanwhile, make the dipping sauce. Combine the reserved marinade with the remaining lemon juice, tomato sauce, Tabasco and salt and pepper to taste in a small saucepan and bring to a boil. Remove from the heat and stir in the coconut milk. Pour into a serving bowl. Serve the lamb hot, with the dipping sauce.

---

serve with

Garlicky Fried Peanuts (page 67), with drinks
Jasmine rice

℮

Toasted Coconut Ice Cream (page 312) and Lime Sugar Cookies
(page 266)

to drink

Gewürztraminer or cold beer

---

algerian lamb shanks

Although we've never to our knowledge eaten Algerian food before, this dish has a very familiar taste. Almost everything in the spice cabinet goes into it, along with wine, tomatoes, orange and fennel. This fragrant, deeply satisfying dish is perfect for a cold winter's night.

SOURCE

Williams-Sonoma Catalogue

COOK

**Greg Cole,
Celadon Restaurant,
Napa, California**

It's also perfect for company, since it's even better the next day. Just heat it up, add some plain rice or couscous and a salad, and you've got a sensationally good dinner. Some clementines and cookies are a simple, clean finish to this sumptuous meal.

serves 4

4 lamb shanks, external fat trimmed
Salt and freshly ground black pepper, to taste
1/4 cup olive oil
1 pound onions, diced
1/4 cup garlic cloves (from about 1 head of garlic)
1 tablespoon finely chopped fresh ginger
2 tablespoons curry powder
2 teaspoons fennel seeds
1 teaspoon chile flakes
1 teaspoon ground cloves
1 teaspoon caraway seeds
2 cardamom pods, papery skins removed

1/2 cinnamon stick
Pinch of saffron
1/2 cup blanched slivered almonds
1/2 cup golden raisins
2 10-ounce cans diced plum tomatoes, drained
1 bottle of dry white wine (750 ml)
Zest and juice of 1 orange
1 pound carrots, peeled and coarsely diced
1 large fennel bulb, coarsely diced
Orange-infused olive oil, to taste (see note)

Preheat the oven to 350 degrees.

Season the lamb shanks with salt and pepper. In a Dutch oven over high heat, warm 2 tablespoons of the olive oil. Add the lamb shanks and brown them all over, turning occasionally, 4 to 5 minutes per side. Transfer the meat to a platter.

Add the remaining 2 tablespoons oil, the onions and the garlic. Sauté the vegetables, stirring, until the onions are soft, 3 to 5 minutes. Add 1 tablespoon salt, the ginger, curry, fennel seeds, chile flakes, cloves, caraway seeds, cardamom pods, cinnamon, saffron, almonds and raisins. Sauté, stirring, for 5 minutes.

Add the tomatoes, wine, orange zest and juice, and stir to mix. Return the lamb shanks to the pan, cover, transfer to the oven and braise until the meat nearly falls off the bone, about 2 hours. Add the carrots and fennel; cover and bake about 15 minutes more. Remove the cinnamon stick from the pot. If you'd prefer, you can also pull the meat off the lamb shank bones and discard them, returning the meat to the pot. In that case, you can easily serve 6 with this recipe.

As each plate is served, drizzle a little orange-infused oil over the top.

cook's notes

🌿 If after 2 hours there's too much liquid in the pan, uncover and return it to the oven for 30 minutes. Or strain the liquid and boil it down to a thick sauce, which can be returned to the pot.

🌿 If you have no orange-infused olive oil (which is delicious and available at specialty markets or from Williams-Sonoma), you can warm a little olive oil with a strip of orange zest to improvise. Or just skip this step; the dish is perfect without it.

seven-hour leg of lamb

SOURCE

Paula Wolfert,
Food & Wine

COOK

Paula Wolfert,
after La Mazille

Slow cooking produces tender, juicy, melt-in-your-mouth dishes that are bursting with flavor. Paula Wolfert's extraordinary leg of lamb is delicate, perfumed with dozens of cloves of garlic that are soft and sweet by the time the dish is cooked.

This is a wonderful choice for a dinner party, since the work is all done early in the day and your kitchen will be filled with delectable aromas. There's lots of delicious juice to serve with the lamb, which is so tender you serve it with a spoon. The succulent garlic cloves can either be mashed into the juices along with the meat or spread on bread.

serves 6

3¹/₂ quarts water

1 5-pound whole New Zealand leg of lamb, without the shank

2 tablespoons vegetable oil, goose fat or duck fat

5 dozen plump garlic cloves, peeled

3 tablespoons cognac

1¹/₄ cups sweet wine, such as orange Muscat (see note)

Salt and freshly ground black pepper, to taste

---

cook's notes

❧ Get the butcher to trim the shank off the leg of lamb, which otherwise won't fit in your casserole.

❧ Purists wouldn't, but you can of course use store-bought peeled garlic cloves if you have a source for them.

❧ You don't need to use an expensive wine or even an orange-flavored one; if you add a strip of orange peel to the pot along with 1¹/₄ cups Riesling you'll get the same effect.

About 8 hours before serving, fill a 6- or 7-quart enameled cast-iron casserole with the water and bring to a rolling boil. Carefully add the leg of lamb and boil for 15 minutes.

Preheat the oven to 200 degrees.

Remove the lamb and drain on kitchen towels. Discard the water. Heat the oil or fat in the casserole over medium heat until sizzling. Add the lamb and cook until golden brown on all sides. Tilt the casserole and use a bulb baster to remove some of the fat. Add the garlic and cognac and, when heated, ignite. (Be sure to avert your face.) When the flames die out, add the wine, salt and pepper and bring to a boil. Cover the pot with crumpled wet parchment paper or foil and a tight-fitting lid and set in the oven to cook for 6 or 7 hours, turning the leg once midway.

Remove the casserole from the oven and let it stand, uncovered, for 30 minutes. Skim off all the fat and reheat gently just before serving.

serve with

Beet and Spinach Salad with Lemon, Cilantro and Mint (page 68)
French bread
Green beans with toasted almonds
Mashed Potatoes with Toasted Coriander (page 218)

℮

Clementine Cake (page 284)

to drink

A fine, mature Spanish Rioja

pork chile verde with posole

Sheryl Julian and Julie Riven have performed a huge public service by reprinting this recipe from TV's *Two Hot Tamales*. It's a great party dish, made a day ahead and served with just plain rice and tortillas (see page 109 for heating directions), and the leftovers are especially good with poached eggs for breakfast.

If you live in posole country, you know that the dried corn takes a lot of fussing to cook in this sort of dish. Milliken and Feniger have wisely used canned hominy here. And if you've ever wondered what to do with those strange little tomatillos, the golf-ball-size green tomatoes with a papery husk in supermarkets all across the land, this is your dish. They work as a sort of secret ingredient here, contributing a piquant accent to the pork.

SOURCE

Sheryl Julian and Julie Riven, *Boston Globe*

COOKS

Mary Sue Milliken and Susan Feniger

serves 6

PORK CHILE VERDE

- 1 pound tomatillos, husked and washed, or green tomatoes
- 2 pounds boneless pork, cut into 1 1/2-inch pieces
- 1 teaspoon salt, or to taste
- 1/2 teaspoon freshly ground black pepper, or to taste
  All-purpose flour, for dredging
- 2 tablespoons canola oil
- 1 onion, chopped
- 2 Anaheim or poblano chiles, cored, seeded and chopped

- 2 jalapeño peppers, cored, seeded and chopped
- 2 green bell peppers, cored, seeded and chopped
- 3 garlic cloves, chopped
- 1 1/2 cups canned hominy (posole), drained
- 1/2 cup chopped cilantro leaves
- 1 tablespoon dried oregano
- 2 teaspoons ground cumin
- 3 cups chicken stock or water

SALSA

2 plum tomatoes, cored and diced

1/2 small red onion, chopped

1 jalapeño pepper, cored, seeded and chopped

1/4 red bell pepper, cored, seeded and chopped

1 tablespoon chopped fresh cilantro

1 tablespoon fresh lime juice

Salt and freshly ground black pepper, to taste

Liquid hot sauce (optional)

TO MAKE THE CHILE VERDE

Preheat the broiler. Set the tomatillos or green tomatoes on a rimmed baking sheet and slide them under the broiler. Cook, turning often, for 5 to 8 minutes, or until they are charred. Set them aside to cool.

Chop the tomatillos or tomatoes, reserving all the juices.

Sprinkle the pork with the salt and pepper. Dust it with flour.

In a large skillet, heat the oil over medium-high heat. Add the pork in batches and brown it on all sides. Remove the pork from the skillet and transfer to a soup pot.

Using the same skillet, turn the heat to medium and add the onion. Cook it for 10 minutes, stirring often, until it is soft. Add the Anaheim or poblano chiles and jalapeño and bell peppers. Cook, stirring often, for about 4 minutes. Add the garlic and cook for 1 minute more. Transfer to the soup pot.

Stir in the hominy, cilantro, oregano, cumin, stock or water and the tomatillos or tomatoes and their juices. Bring to a boil, lower the heat, and simmer, partially covered, for 1½ hours, or until the pork is tender. Serve hot in deep bowls, with the salsa.

MEANWHILE, MAKE THE SALSA

In a medium bowl, combine the tomatoes, onion, jalapeño, bell pepper, cilantro and lime juice. Add salt, pepper and hot sauce to taste. Set aside.

When ready to serve, pass the salsa to accompany the pork chile verde.

---

serve with

Charred Tomatillo Guacamole with Seeded Tortilla Triangles (page 10), with drinks

Steamed rice

Warm tortillas

℮

Roasted Apricots with Sugared Pecans and Dulce de Leche (page 308)

to drink

Mexican beer is the only choice

---

aromatic lemongrass and pork patties

If you haven't worked with lemongrass before, this is a great recipe to cut your teeth on, since it's so simple and so accommodating. The lemongrass has a delicate perfume that's not quite like lemon, but a bit like lemon zest with an herbal element.

SOURCE

Hot Sour Salty Sweet
by Jeffrey Alford
and Naomi Duguid

COOKS

Jeffrey Alford
and Naomi Duguid

In southeast Asia, these pork patties are served as part of a rice meal, with a vegetable dish and a salsa. They're also great as mini-patties with cocktails; serve with toothpicks. See page 184 for a tasty salsa to serve with them.

serves 4

¹/₂ pound boneless lean pork, butt or shoulder
¹/₄ cup sliced shallots
 1 lemongrass spear, trimmed and minced (see tip, page 185)

¹/₄ teaspoon salt
¹/₄ teaspoon freshly ground black pepper

serve with

Singapore Salad (page 66)
Walla Walla Onion Rings
(page 212)
℘
Christmas Morning Melon
Wedges (page 77)

to drink

Bonny Doon Pacific Rim
Riesling

main dishes

Thinly slice the pork and transfer to a food processor. Add the remaining ingredients and process for about 30 seconds, or until the mixture forms an even-textured ball. Turn out into a bowl.

Set out several plates. Working with wet hands, pick up a scant 2 tablespoons of the pork mixture and shape it into a flat patty 2 to 3 inches in diameter. Place on a plate and repeat with the remaining mixture to make 7 or 8 patties. Do not stack them.

Heat a large, heavy skillet over medium-high heat. Rub lightly with an oiled paper towel and add the patties. Lower the heat to medium and cook until golden on the first side, then turn over and cook for

---

Cilantro Pesto

The pork patties are especially delicious with this easy salsa. (It's also good with grilled shrimp.) You can make it earlier on the day you plan to serve it —or, in a pinch, the night before, though it won't be quite as fresh-tasting. The recipe is from Molly Stevens and was published in *Fine Cooking*.

SALSA
- 2 cups loosely packed fresh cilantro leaves and tender stems
- 1/3 cup unsalted roasted peanuts
- 1 garlic clove
- 1 jalapeño pepper, seeded and minced
- 3 scallions, trimmed and coarsely chopped
- 1 tablespoon fish sauce
- 1/3 cup fresh lime juice
- 1/4 cup peanut oil

In a food processor, combine the cilantro, peanuts, garlic, jalapeño and scallions. Process to a rough paste. Add the fish sauce and lime juice; process until the mixture becomes creamy. With the motor running, slowly pour in the oil and process until combined.

---

another 3 to 4 minutes, until golden and cooked through. As the patties cook, use a spatula to flatten them against the hot surface. (You can also grill or broil the patties until golden and cooked through, turning them over part way through the cooking.)

Serve hot.

tip

As Jeffrey Alford and Naomi Duguid explained in a *Food & Wine* Web chat, lemongrass is great to keep on hand because it lasts a very long time in the refrigerator. To use it, just cut off the hard root tips about ½ inch up and remove the top leafy dry parts, which leaves you with 2 to 3 inches of stem and the bulb. Peel off the dry outer layer and smash what's left with the side of a knife or a cleaver. Toss the lemongrass into soup broths or mince it fine and use it in recipes like this one.

tuscan pork roast with herbed salt

SOURCE

Sally Schneider,
Food & Wine

COOK

Sally Schneider, after
Piero Ferrini

A Tuscan chef produced this sensationally good roast pork from what appears to be an ancient recipe. It's based on herbs —rosemary and sage, though you can also use thyme and oregano—a little garlic and salt, but these are applied to the roast in an unusual way. The roast loin of pork is first liberated from its bones, which then form a rack on which to roast it. Next, a long-handled wooden spoon is used to bore a hole through the center of the roast, which is then filled with the herbed salt and stuffed at either end with a branch of rosemary. The whole roast is then rubbed with more herbed salt, a thick coat of pancetta is added and more rosemary sprigs go on top.

As the roast cooks, white wine bastes it, giving a wonderful caramelization as well as producing the base for a delicious sauce to serve with the pork. This dish will happily sit on a buffet for hours. It's one of the best pork dishes we've ever tasted.

serves 8 to 10

1 7-pound pork loin roast, rack
   bones removed in one piece
   and reserved
   Tuscan Herbed Salt (recipe
   follows)
4 sturdy rosemary branches, 10
   inches long

Coarse salt
4 ounces thinly sliced meaty
   pancetta
1 teaspoon extra-virgin olive oil
2 cups dry white wine
   Freshly ground black pepper

Pat the pork loin thoroughly dry. Using a long-handled wooden spoon, pierce a hole lengthwise through the center of the roast. Using your fingers and the wooden spoon handle, stuff 3 tablespoons of the Tuscan Herbed Salt into the hole in the roast. Insert a rosemary branch in each end of the hole. Mix the remaining tablespoon of the herbed salt with 1½ teaspoons coarse salt and rub it all over the roast. Cover the pork roast with the pancetta and top with the two remaining rosemary branches. Tie the roast at 1-inch intervals to give it a neat shape. Transfer to a platter, cover with plastic wrap, and refrigerate for at least 2 hours and up to 24 hours. Bring to room temperature before cooking.

Preheat the oven to 450 degrees.

Set the rack of rib bones in a large roasting pan. Unwrap the roast, pat it dry, and rub with the olive oil. Place the roast on the rack and roast for 15 minutes. Remove the pan from the oven, turn the roast over and baste it with a few tablespoons of the wine. Return the roast to the oven, reduce the temperature to 350 degrees, and cook for about 1½ hours, turning the roast and basting it with wine every 20 minutes. Reserve ½ cup of the wine for the sauce. The roast is done when an instant-read thermometer inserted in the center reads 145 degrees.

Transfer the roast and rack to a platter and pour the pan juices into

serve with

Fennel, Red Pepper and Mushroom Salad (page 61), to start
Fresh Corn Polenta (page 230)
Roasted Green and Yellow Wax Beans with Hazelnut Oil (page 204)
Focaccia

℘

Pears and Gorgonzola

to drink

A sharp red wine with good fruit, such as Sangiovese or Merlot

a glass measuring cup. Skim off as much fat as possible. Set the roasting pan over two burners on moderate heat. When it starts to sizzle, add the reserved ½ cup wine and cook for 2 minutes, scraping up the drippings from the bottom of the pan. Pour the pan juices into the measuring cup and let the fat rise to the surface. Skim off the fat again and season the sauce with salt and pepper. Remove the strings and carve the roast into thin slices. Serve the pork roast with the pan sauce.

Tuscan Herbed Salt

This salt is delicious as a seasoning for pork, veal or vegetables such as potatoes and green beans.

makes ¼ cup

1 garlic clove
1 tablespoon sea salt

30 fresh sage leaves
Leaves from 2 sprigs of fresh rosemary

Chop the garlic with the salt. Chop the herbs together, then chop again with the salt. Use the salt right away or let it dry and store for up to 1 month in an airtight container.

---

cook's note
If you have trouble turning the roast, don't bother—it will be fine.

---

miami black beans

These beans are actually Cuban, a tribute to the huge Cuban population in Miami, which has contributed so much good food to the city's repertoire. This wonderfully savory stew is crammed with three kinds of pig meat, black beans and cabbage, all made lively with rum, spices and tomato.

It's a rustic, festive dish that's good for serving a crowd. Not only does it make a lot, but it's best made a couple of days ahead, so

SOURCE

Bruce Aidells' Complete Sausage Book by Bruce Aidells and Denis Kelly

COOK

Bruce Aidells

all you have to do is reheat it the day you serve it.

It's also a forgiving dish; it can be a main dish or a side dish, you can leave out the pigs' feet, you can use any kind of cabbage, smoked or unsmoked ham hocks, fresh or canned tomatoes . . . You can even use only half as much sausage as the recipe specifies. The one thing you do need is a butcher to saw the ham hock and pigs' feet into pieces, or they won't cook through.

serves 8 to 12

- 1 pound dried black beans (2½ cups), picked over, soaked overnight and drained
- 4–6 cups chicken or beef stock
- 1 ham hock, sawed into 3 or 4 pieces
- 2 pigs' feet (about 2 pounds), sawed into 3 or 4 pieces (optional)
- 2 pounds garlicky sausage, such as Cajun-style andouille, Portuguese chouriço, linguiça or pepperoni
- 2 bay leaves
- 2 teaspoons ground cumin

- 2 large onions, chopped
- 1 tablespoon chopped garlic
- 1 tablespoon annatto oil, if available, or a pinch of saffron and 1 tablespoon olive oil
- 1 small head of cabbage, quartered, cored and shredded (about 4 cups)
- 1 cup fresh or canned tomatoes, peeled, seeded and chopped
- ¼ cup dark rum
  Salt and freshly ground black pepper
  Malt vinegar

GARNISHES

Lime wedges   Chopped cilantro
Chopped red onion   Tabasco sauce

Rinse the beans well. In a heavy 5-to-6-quart pot or Dutch oven, combine the beans with enough stock to cover them by 2 inches and bring to a boil. Add the ham hock, pigs' feet (if using), a ½-pound piece of the sausage, the bay leaves, cumin, and half of the chopped onions and half of the garlic. Decrease the heat and simmer, partially covered, for 1 to 2 hours, or until the ham hocks and pigs' feet are tender and the beans are soft enough to mash against the side of the pot with a spoon. Add more stock if needed while cooking.

Heat the oil in a heavy skillet over medium heat. Slice the remaining sausage into ½-inch rounds, and fry them until lightly browned. Remove the sausage with a slotted spoon and add to the beans. In the same fat, cook the remaining onions until they are

cook's notes

❧ A wide pot will be much easier to use than a tall skinny pot.

❧ If you don't have any malt vinegar, use cider vinegar.

soft but not brown, about 5 minutes. Add the rest of the garlic and the cabbage. Sauté, stirring frequently, until the cabbage has wilted. Add the tomatoes and rum, along with a few grindings of pepper. Bring to a boil and cook, stirring often, for 3 to 5 minutes. Stir this tomato-vegetable mixture into the bean pot.

Cook everything over medium heat for 5 to 10 more minutes. Taste for salt and pepper, and add malt vinegar to taste. Remove the whole piece of sausage, the ham hocks, and pigs' feet. Slice the sausage into ½-inch pieces, bone the hocks and pigs' feet, chop the meat coarsely, and add to the beans.

Pass the garnishes at the table. This dish is even better made ahead and reheated.

serve with

Steamed medium-grain
white rice
Romaine salad with oranges,
avocado and red onion

℘

Coconut sorbet with Potato
Chip Cookies (page 261)

to drink

Mexican beer

main dishes

slow-roasted chipotle pork

As Michele Anna Jordan says, chipotle pepper and pork is one of the best flavor combinations on the planet. Here she uses chipotle powder for its rich, complex flavor, but if you can't find either the powder or the whole chiles, make this dish anyway using canned chipotles in adobo.

This dish is a Mexican equivalent of pulled pork, and it's just the sort of mindlessly easy but sensationally flavored recipe we're always looking for, with that soul-food quality that's universally appealing.

SOURCE

*The New Cook's
Tour of Sonoma*
by Michele Anna Jordan

COOK

Michele Anna Jordan

serves 4 to 6

3 tablespoons kosher salt
1 tablespoon chipotle powder
  (see note)
1 pork shoulder roast, about
  3½ pounds

2 dozen small corn tortillas
2 limes, cut into wedges
¼ cup minced fresh cilantro

In a small bowl, mix together the kosher salt and chipotle powder and rub it into the pork, being sure to cover the entire surface of the meat with the mixture. Put the pork in a clay roaster or other deep

---

cook's notes

℞ To heat tortillas ahead of serving time, see the directions on page 109.

℞ To make chipotle powder, see the note on page 131. Jordan especially likes the (very expensive) chipotle powder sold by Tierra (1-888-7-TIERRA or tierravegetables.com).

roasting pan with a lid, place the covered roaster in the oven, and turn the heat to 275 degrees. Cook until the pork falls apart when you press it with the back of a fork, 3½ to 4 hours. Remove it from the oven and let it rest, covered, for 15 minutes.

Heat the tortillas on a medium-hot griddle, turning them frequently, until they are warmed through and soft. Wrap them in a tea towel and place in a basket. Transfer the pork to a large serving platter and use two forks to pull it into chunks. Add the lime wedges to the platter, place the cilantro in a small serving bowl and serve immediately, with the tortillas on the side.

To fill the tortillas, double them up: Set one on top of another on a plate, spoon some of the pork on top, squeeze a little lime juice over the pork, sprinkle some cilantro on top and fold in half.

serve with

Mesa Grits (page 225)

℘

Cherry-Almond Pound Cake (page 289)

to drink

Mexican beer or a dry Riesling

pulled pork

SOURCES

Saveur and *How to Cook Meat* by Chris Schlesinger and John Willoughby

COOKS

Chris Schlesinger and John Willoughby

When *Saveur* was trying to imagine how to get the spectacular effects of spit-roasting a whole pig without actually going to those lengths, they called on the barbecue guys, Chris Schlesinger and John Willoughby, who of course knew the answer. The answer is: Brine a skin-on, bone-in pork shoulder using equal parts of salt and sugar. Then just roast away for either 5 hours or, for falling-off-the-bone meat, 8 hours. We like it cooked for the longer time, and we also like to serve it with this spicy, vinegary barbecue sauce from their book *How to Cook Meat*.

Your reward is a delectable dish with crackling, crispy skin; succulent, tender meat; and a wonderful rich slow-cooked flavor. It's worth going to a little trouble to get the right cut of meat and fussing with the brine. Pork shoulder (also called pork butt and Boston butt) probably isn't just sitting there in the meat case waiting for you to pick it up. You may have to order it, especially if you want the skin on, or go to an ethnic butcher (Italian, Chinese, Mexican, Polish), where they know a thing or two about pork.

serves 10 to 12

PORK
- 4 gallons cold water
- 4 cups kosher salt
- 4 cups sugar
- 1 8-to-10-pound skin-on, bone-in pork shoulder

BARBECUE SAUCE
- 1/2 cup white vinegar
- 2 tablespoons Tabasco sauce
- 2 tablespoons sugar
- 1 tablespoon kosher salt
- 1 tablespoon freshly ground black pepper

TO MAKE THE PORK

Pour the water into a large stockpot or plastic bucket. Add the salt and sugar and stir until dissolved. Place the pork in the brine and set it aside in a cool place to soak for 8 to 12 hours or overnight.

Drain the pork, rinse, then pat dry with paper towels.

Preheat the oven to 350 degrees.

Place the pork on a rack set in a roasting pan. Pierce the skin (avoid piercing the meat) all over with the tip of a sharp knife. Roast the pork for 5 hours, then reduce the temperature to 300 degrees and roast for another 3 hours. Allow the pork to rest for 20 minutes. Carve, pull apart or chop the meat and serve with the sauce.

TO MAKE THE BARBECUE SAUCE

Mix all the ingredients in a small bowl and serve with the pork.

---

cook's notes

- If you have a relatively small container for brining, you can use just 3 gallons of water, 3 cups of salt and 3 cups of sugar. That will still be enough to cover the meat.
- Pray for leftovers, which make great sandwiches. Serve the pulled pork on soft white buns with the barbecue sauce and some coleslaw on top or on the side.
- If you can't find the pork shoulder with skin on no matter how hard you beg, just make the pork anyway. Don't let the butcher cut off the layer of fat all around the shoulder, though; it will caramelize into a lovely crisp golden brown crust as the fat drains off.

serve with

Spicy Mustard Greens with Cumin (page 206)
Angel Biscuits (page 244)

Toasted Coconut Ice Cream (page 312) and Lime Sugar Cookies (page 266)

---

side dishes

pan-roasted asparagus

You know you can steam asparagus, you know you can grill it, you know you can hot-roast it in the oven —but we bet you didn't know you can roast it right on top of the stove. We didn't. And we know one person who swears she'll never cook asparagus any other way, it's so good.

This sophisticated asparagus doesn't

SOURCE

Think Like a Chef
by Tom Colicchio

COOK

Tom Colicchio

have the pure, grassy, spring asparagus flavor, but a much more mature taste that brings out a new dimension of this favorite vegetable's personality. The technique works best with thin asparagus, even pencil-thin, but thicker spears can also take this treatment, though they'll need to cook longer.

serves 4

2 tablespoons peanut oil
2 pounds thin asparagus, trimmed
Kosher salt and freshly ground black pepper, to taste

About 3 tablespoons unsalted butter
1 teaspoon fresh thyme leaves
Coarse sea salt (optional)

Heat the oil in a large skillet (or two if the asparagus won't fit in your skillet) over medium-high heat until it shimmers. Add the asparagus, a handful at a time, making sure the pan is always sizzling but never smoking.

Add kosher salt and pepper and reduce the heat to medium. Cook the asparagus, turning the stalks occasionally. When the pan begins to look dry, begin adding the butter, a tablespoon at a time.

Cook the asparagus, continuing to turn the stalks, for about 10 minutes. Add the thyme and a little more salt and cook until the asparagus is tender, about 5 minutes more. Serve immediately, sprinkled with sea salt if desired.

cook's notes

❦ When you get your asparagus home, remove its corseting so it can breathe and store it loose in a plastic bag in the vegetable bin of the fridge.

❦ To trim, snap off pencil-thin asparagus at the bottom, where it naturally breaks. Cut thicker spears at the point where the color changes and then peel them about two thirds of the way up with a vegetable peeler.

blasted broccoli

SOURCE

Food & Wine

COOK

**Tina Ujlaki,
after Brooke Dojny and
Melanie Barnard**

When a reader wrote in to ask *Food & Wine* for a healthful vegetable dish for a special dinner, editor Tina Ujlaki came up with several interesting ones. But the one we find ourselves making all the time is this "blasted" one. Maybe it's just the name we like, but there's something about the crisp broccoli that ensures every last bite will disappear. It's also the easiest broccoli recipe we know, which doesn't hurt.

As with all dishes depending on balsamic vinegar, the better the vinegar, the tastier the dish. You don't need the best vinegar here, but a good one will be much appreciated.

serves 4

4 cups broccoli florets, rinsed
  and slightly drained
Olive oil, to taste

Sea salt, to taste
Balsamic vinegar, to taste

Preheat the oven to 500 degrees.

Arrange the broccoli florets in a single layer on a baking sheet. Toss them with olive oil and salt and roast until they are cooked through and crispy brown at the edges, just a few minutes.

Remove the broccoli to a bowl and toss with balsamic vinegar to taste. Serve immediately.

buttered sugar snap peas
with fresh mint

This insouciant recipe from the chef at Manhattan's Grange Hall seems to embody spring itself. We've seen peas with mint everywhere this year, especially in delicate purees. But this extremely simple version has become a favorite. The sugar snaps are cooked minimally, so they retain their crunch. After a quick blanching, they're stirred in a skillet with melted butter and treated to some fresh mint —spring mint, a more delicate version of summer's stronger herb. This is a delightful, heady dish, perfect with spring lamb or roast chicken.

If you get your sugar snaps at the farmer's market, you'll be amazed at how long they keep when they're truly fresh. But of course they're best of all cooked right away.

SOURCE

The Greenmarket Cookbook
by Joel Patraker
and Joan Schwartz

COOK

Kevin Johnson

serves 6

1 pound sugar snap peas, ends snapped to remove stems and strings
Salt

2 tablespoons unsalted butter
Freshly ground black pepper
1/4 cup coarsely chopped fresh mint

Blanch the peas for 1 minute in a pot of boiling salted water. Melt the butter in a large skillet over medium-high heat. Add the peas and stir until bright green and crisp-tender, about 3 minutes. Season with salt and pepper to taste, toss with the mint, and serve hot.

stir-fried spinach with pine nuts

SOURCE

Big Bowl Noodles and Rice
by Bruce Cost
and Matt McMillin

COOK

Bruce Cost

Much as we love the Italian way with spinach and pine nuts, the Chinese technique used in this version is a real eye-opener. "There's no greater test," say the authors, "of one's ability to stir-fry than to cook fresh spinach so that it's just wilted and soft but hasn't gone one second beyond that point to where it 'breaks' and gives up its juices in an unattractive pool." The secret is to toss the spinach rapidly in the wok to thoroughly coat the leaves with oil. Try it; spinach cooked this way is unbelievably succulent. There are just a few seasonings, so that the pure flavor of the greens comes through.

serves 2 to 4

- 1 cup peanut oil
- ¼ cup pine nuts
- 1 teaspoon kosher salt
- 2 teaspoons sugar
- 2 tablespoons Shaoxing rice wine
- 1 tablespoon very fine julienne of fresh ginger
- 1 pound very fresh spinach, washed and thoroughly dried
- A few drops of toasted sesame oil

Heat the oil in a small saucepan over high heat to hot but not smoking. Add the pine nuts, stir and turn off the heat. Allow to sit for 5 minutes, or until the nuts are a light golden brown. Remove the pine nuts to a paper towel to drain, reserving the oil.

Combine the salt, sugar and rice wine and set aside.

Heat a large wok, preferably 16 inches or larger, over high heat and add 3 to 4 tablespoons of the reserved oil. When it is hot, add the ginger, sizzle it very briefly, then add the spinach. Cook, stirring and tossing rapidly as you would a salad, for about 20 seconds, or until all the spinach leaves are coated with the oil. Add the rice wine mixture and continue to toss just until the spinach is beginning to wilt. Remove it from the heat, toss a few more times, and transfer it to a serving plate.

Sprinkle with the pine nuts and sesame oil and serve.

tip

We learned another great no-fuss spinach treatment from Irish chef James O'Shea. Use baby organic spinach (which is expensive but saves a lot of work) and rinse it briefly in a colander. Put the spinach in a large pot with a trickle of olive oil and some sea salt. Cover and cook over medium heat just until the spinach is wilted, turning several times. Drain and proceed with your recipe or enjoy it all by itself, served in a little bowl.

roasted green and yellow wax beans with hazelnut oil

Although you can use all green beans or all yellow beans, mixing the two colors makes this dish visually exciting as well as exciting to the palate. If you've never tasted a roasted bean before, you'll be surprised, and we hope de-

SOURCE

The Tribeca Grill Cookbook
by Don Pintabona

COOK

Don Pintabona

lighted, by this dish. It couldn't be simpler, unless you blanch the beans 2 days ahead and keep them in the refrigerator. Then all you have to do is roast them with the hazelnut oil and toss with the almonds.

serves 6

¹/₂ pound fresh green beans, trimmed

¹/₂ pound fresh yellow wax beans, trimmed

Coarse salt, to taste

2 tablespoons unsalted butter

¹/₄ cup hazelnut oil (see note)

Freshly ground black pepper, to taste

3 tablespoons toasted slivered almonds (optional)

Preheat the oven to 350 degrees.

Bring a medium saucepan of salted water to a boil over high heat. Add the beans and butter. Return to a boil and boil for 2 minutes. Drain the beans well and refresh them under cold running water in a colander. Dry the beans well. (At this point you can keep the beans, well covered and refrigerated, for up to 2 days before proceeding.)

Place the beans in a shallow roasting pan and drizzle with the hazelnut oil, tossing to coat well. Season with salt and pepper. Place the beans in the oven and roast for 8 minutes, or until they are very tender with a touch of color. One minute before the beans are ready, add the toasted almonds, if using, and toss with the beans. Roast for 1 more minute and serve hot.

cook's note

If you don't have hazelnut oil, use any delicious oil that would be good with beans, such as almond, peanut or olive.

spicy mustard greens with cumin

The jacket of Peter Berley's vegetarian book is clinically modern, all gray and didn't seem to promise voluptuous food inside. Wrong: This is glorious vegetarian fare, and our only problem was choosing a single recipe to represent the book. This mouth-watering dish of greens is the one. We couldn't stop eating it, and neither could our guests. The mustardy greens are slow-cooked, which renders them almost sweet, but the cumin seeds are the real standout in this dish. For the moment, we can't imagine cooking mustard greens any other way.

SOURCE
The Modern Vegetarian Kitchen by Peter Berley

COOK
Peter Berley

serves 4

- 2 tablespoons extra-virgin olive oil
- 1 onion, coarsely chopped (about 1 cup)
- 3 garlic cloves, chopped
- 1 red jalapeño pepper, seeded and chopped, or 1/2 teaspoon hot red pepper flakes
- 1 1/2 teaspoons cumin seeds
- 1 large bunch of mustard greens (about 2 pounds), chopped into bite-size pieces
- Cider vinegar
- Coarse sea salt and freshly ground black pepper, to taste

In a large pot over medium heat, warm the oil. Add the onion and sauté until softened, about 5 minutes. Add the garlic, jalapeño or pepper flakes and cumin seeds and sauté for 2 to 3 minutes more. Add the greens and increase the heat. Stir until wilted. Reduce the heat to low and simmer, covered, for 25 to 30 minutes, or until the greens are tender.

Season with vinegar, salt and pepper. Serve hot or at room temperature.

asparagus baked with roncal cheese

SOURCE

Florence Fabricant,
New York Times

COOK

Florence Fabricant

In trying her wings with the newly available Spanish cheeses in America, Florence Fabricant came up with this absolutely wonderful baked asparagus dish. She uses Roncal, a somewhat salty but also slightly sweet sheep cheese from Navarre, in much the same way you'd use Parmesan. But there are other small Spanish touches here—the almonds, most surprisingly, and the ham—that make this dish really sing.

You might think a pound and a half of asparagus is too much for 2 to 3 people, but every scrap will be happily devoured.

Don't be deterred by the ingredients; if there's no Roncal, you can use an aged Manchego, and prosciutto can take the place of the serrano ham.

serves 2 to 3

1½ pounds medium-thick asparagus
2½ tablespoons extra-virgin olive oil, preferably Spanish
Salt and freshly ground black pepper

2 ounces serrano ham or prosciutto, finely chopped (optional)
2 ounces Roncal, Mahon or aged Manchego cheese, shredded
2 tablespoons finely ground unblanched almonds

Preheat the oven to 425 degrees.

Snap off the woody ends of the asparagus, and peel the stalks. Place the spears in a baking dish, add 2 tablespoons of the oil and roll the asparagus to coat well. Arrange in one layer and season with salt and pepper. Scatter the ham (if using), cheese and almonds over the asparagus. Drizzle with the remaining ½ tablespoon oil and bake for 15 to 20 minutes, or until the spears are tender and the cheese melts. Serve hot.

side dishes

cauliflower with garlic and paprika

SOURCE

*Savoring Spain
and Portugal*
by Joyce Goldstein

COOK

Joyce Goldstein

We found this recipe reprinted in the *Houston Post* and immediately got all excited. Cauliflower's been a wallflower vegetable for so long in America that its day was bound to come; it's so delicious when it's treated properly. This recipe from the Murcia region in Spain is our favorite to date, a sensationally good dish that's hard to stop eating. The cauliflower takes on a deep, rusty color from the paprika, and the nutty, garlicky sauce with its crisp bread crumbs is perfect. The cauliflower offers itself as a sweet, delicate background for these gutsy flavors. Though it's meant to be served hot, the cauliflower is just as good at room temperature.

If you think you don't like cauliflower, you owe it to yourself to try it this way.

serves 6

- 2 pounds cauliflower, cut into florets
- 2 teaspoons fresh lemon juice
- 1/3 cup olive oil
- 2–3 slices coarse country bread, crusts removed
- 1 tablespoon paprika
- 2 cups water

- Salt to taste
- 3 garlic cloves, coarsely chopped
- 3 tablespoons chopped fresh Italian parsley
- 2 tablespoons pine nuts, toasted (see note)
- Freshly ground black pepper, to taste

Fill a bowl with water and add the cauliflower florets and lemon juice. Set aside until needed.

In a large frying pan over medium heat, warm the olive oil. Add the bread slices and fry, turning once, until crisp and golden on both sides, 3 to 5 minutes total. Remove from the pan, break into pieces, and place in a blender or food processor.

Add the paprika to the oil remaining in the pan and reduce the heat to low. Cook for a minute or two to release the paprika's fragrance. Add the water and bring to a boil. Drain the cauliflower and add to the pan. Season with a little salt and cook, uncovered, until the cauliflower is tender, 10 to 15 minutes.

Meanwhile, add the garlic, parsley and pine nuts to the bread in the blender or food processor and pulse until well crushed. When the cauliflower is tender, add about $1/4$ cup of the cauliflower cooking water to the bread crumb mixture, pulse once, and then transfer the mixture to the frying pan. Stir to mix; cook for 5 minutes over low heat to blend the flavors.

Season the cauliflower with salt and pepper, transfer to a warmed serving bowl, and serve.

---

cook's notes

- If at all possible, use real Spanish paprika.
- If you think pine nuts taste soapy and unpleasant, you may have been using Chinese pine nuts (the usual supermarket variety), which are not nearly as nice as European ones, more likely to be found at specialty markets. To toast pine nuts, see the note on page 227.

roasted red onions
with thyme and butter

Part of the very impressive British invasion this year is the Naked Chef—alas, he's not really naked on his new television show. It's just that Jamie Oliver likes to strip food down to its bare essentials and make it really sing. This compulsively watchable young chef is always asking questions of the people who actually grow and raise the food we eat, getting to the heart of the matter.

SOURCE

The Naked Chef
by Jamie Oliver

COOK

Jamie Oliver

It's difficult to imagine a simpler dish than these roasted onions, and yet they're amazingly complex-tasting; all the harsh onion flavor mellows into sweetness. Whether they're nestled up against a roasting chicken or leg of lamb or simply roasting away on their own, they smell delicious in the oven and delight all diners with their succulence.

serves 6

6 equal-size medium to large red
    onions
Chopped fresh thyme

Salt
Butter

Preheat the oven to 400 degrees.

Remove the outer layer of each onion's skin and cut off the base a bit so the onion can sit up straight. Make two cuts in the top of the onion down to its ample waist, but don't go so far as to cut the onion into quarters. Put some chopped thyme and some salt right down into the gaps in the onion (see note). Add a generous knob of butter.

Set the onions on a layer of salt in an earthenware baking dish — or just set them on a piece of foil on a baking sheet or arrange them around a roast. Roast the onions for 35 to 40 minutes, or until they are completely tender. Serve hot or warm.

cook's note

If you want to gild the lily, you can drizzle some balsamic vinegar into the gaps in the onion as well.

side dishes

211

walla walla onion rings

There are two very smart elements to this recipe, which is not at all your usual onion rings. One is using the Japanese crumbs called *panko* for an extra-crunchy, light coating. Second, and even better, you can cook the onion rings ahead and just reheat them in the oven to recrisp before serving. The other little trick is flavoring the onion rings with lime zest and cilantro and serving them with lime wedges. Not only are they

SOURCE

The Pacific Northwest Cookbook by Jean Galton

COOK

Jean Galton

unusually delicious, they also go well with ethnic foods, such as Asian and Mexican.

Several kinds of sweet onions have come onto the market now and sometimes they're available year-round. If you can't find them, use Spanish onions instead. And pick up some panko when you see it—it's a good thing to have on hand any time you need dry bread crumbs, especially for frying.

serves 4

Vegetable oil, for frying
1 large Walla Walla or other sweet onion, sliced ¼ inch thick
⅔ cup water
⅔ cup all-purpose flour

1½ cups panko
Grated zest of 1 lime
1 teaspoon coarse salt
2 tablespoons chopped fresh cilantro
Lime wedges, for serving

Pour the vegetable oil into a deep, heavy saucepan to a depth of 2 inches and heat to 375 degrees on a deep-frying thermometer. Preheat the oven to 250 degrees. Line a baking sheet with paper towels.

Separate the onion slices into rings. In a bowl, whisk together the water and flour until smooth. Spread the panko on a plate.

When the oil reaches the correct temperature, dip the onion rings, 4 or 5 at a time, into the batter. Lift them out, let the excess batter drip off, and then dip the rings in the panko crumbs, coating evenly. Slip the rings into the oil and fry, flipping them once to brown evenly, until golden brown, 1 to 2 minutes. Transfer to the baking sheet and place in the oven. Repeat until all the rings are cooked.

Transfer the rings to a platter and sprinkle with the lime zest, salt and cilantro. Serve immediately with lime wedges.

---

cook's notes

❦ To reheat the cooked onion rings and recrisp them, place them on a baking sheet in a 350-degree oven for 10 minutes just before serving. The crispness will magically return.

❦ You can use less oil if you fry the onion rings in a wok.

tip

John Martin Taylor passed on a great tip about eliminating the odors of frying food in a letter to *Fine Cooking* magazine: Place a shallow dish of bleach near the cooking area. For some reason, the bleach attracts the particles of whatever it is that creates the odor, and they deposit on the surface as a cloudy film. This works even if you're frying fish or other pungent foods. If you're not alone in the kitchen, it's a good idea, as gourmet.com suggests, to label the dish of bleach so no one mistakenly adds it to the food.

indian ratatouille

SOURCE

Bon Appétit

COOK

Floyd Cardoz

At Tabla, an upscale Indian restaurant in Manhattan, Floyd Cardoz is always coming up with surprising juxtapositions of flavors and textures. His Indian ratatouille makes perfect sense and yet it's a total surprise. It's both spicy and subtle; only the mustard seeds and the ginger take it off in the direction of India. If you want a more direct hit of Indian flavors, add more ginger and a tablespoon of cumin seeds and substitute cilantro for the mint. Yellow mustard seeds look very pretty in the dish and add a good crunch to the otherwise soft vegetables.

Make this side dish at the height of summer, when the eggplants are least bitter and tomatoes are at their peak. But it also works as a winter dish, with a can of diced organic tomatoes instead of the fresh ones. It's delicious with any roasted meat.

serves 6

¹/₄ cup vegetable oil
1 tablespoon mustard seeds
1 red onion (about 8 ounces), cut into ¹/₂-inch pieces
1 large jalapeño chile, chopped
1 tablespoon chopped fresh ginger
2 ³/₄-pound eggplants, quartered lengthwise, cut crosswise into ¹/₃-inch-thick slices

2 medium zucchini, halved lengthwise, cut crosswise into ¹/₃-inch-thick slices
³/₄ pound plum tomatoes, chopped
3 large garlic cloves, chopped
2 tablespoons chopped fresh mint
1 tablespoon fresh lemon juice
Salt and freshly ground black pepper, to taste

Heat the oil in a large, heavy pot over medium-high heat. Add the mustard seeds, and cook until the seeds darken and begin to pop, about 2 minutes. Add the onion, chile and ginger, and cook, stirring, for 1 minute. Add the eggplant and zucchini slices and cook, stirring, for 5 minutes. Cover and cook for 5 more minutes. Mix in the tomatoes and garlic. Reduce the heat to medium, cover again, and cook until the vegetables are tender, stirring occasionally, about 25 minutes. Mix in the mint and lemon juice and season with salt and pepper.

Serve warm or at room temperature.

---

cook's note

For maximum firepower, include the jalapeño seeds in the dish.

---

roasted potatoes
with garlic, lemon and oregano

This very simple roasted potato dish packs so much flavor that it is, as Aglaia Kremezi points out, irresistible, one of those side dishes that can steal the show from any food they accompany. So you should plan to make plenty, because

SOURCE

The Foods of the Greek Islands
by Aglaia Kremezi

COOK

Aglaia Kremezi

your guests will want seconds. In Greece, when a leg of lamb or a chicken is roasted for the main dish, the potatoes are cooked in its juices, so as the roast sits on a rack in the oven, the potatoes below it absorb all the drippings.

serves 4 to 6

3 pounds baking potatoes, peeled and cut into 1¹/₂-inch cubes

¹/₂ cup olive oil

4 garlic cloves, minced

1¹/₂ teaspoons dried oregano, crumbled

1 teaspoon salt
Freshly ground black pepper

¹/₂ cup meat stock or chicken stock

¹/₃ cup fresh lemon juice

2–3 tablespoons chopped fresh oregano (see note)

Preheat the oven to 400 degrees.

Place the potatoes in a single layer in a 9-x-13-inch baking dish. Add the oil, garlic, dried oregano, salt and pepper and toss well to coat with the oil.

Bake the potatoes for 15 minutes, add the stock, then toss and bake for 10 minutes more. Add the lemon juice, toss and bake for 10 to 15 minutes more, or until the potatoes are cooked through. If you like, preheat the broiler and brown the potatoes for 2 to 3 minutes, or until golden brown.

Sprinkle with the fresh oregano and serve at once.

---

cook's notes

- If you have no fresh oregano, don't worry; because the dish already contains dried, you won't miss it.
- If you're using very small potatoes, you don't need to peel them, but do cut them in half so they absorb more of the juices.

mashed potatoes with toasted coriander

When we first heard about this recipe, we could not quite believe it: Who would think of combining the fragrant, nutty toasted coriander seeds with good old American mashed potatoes? A gardener, as it turns out; Ron Zimmerman is the co-owner of the Herbfarm, a legendary gardening center near Seattle. These are frankly unusual mashed potatoes, heavily speckled with bits of coriander

SOURCE

The Herbfarm Cookbook
by Jerry Traunfeld

COOK

Ron Zimmerman

seed. The roasted garlic paste adds a slightly sweet depth of flavor that doesn't register as garlicky at all.

There's much less butter and cream here than in most over-the-top mashed potato recipes, and yet the potatoes taste very buttery. They're delicious with everything from turkey to roast beef to Indian-flavored dishes.

serves 6

3 tablespoons dried coriander seeds

2 pounds russet (Idaho), Yellow Finn or Yukon Gold potatoes

1/4 cup whole milk

1/4 cup heavy cream

4 tablespoons (1/2 stick) unsalted butter

1 1/2 tablespoons roasted garlic paste (see notes)

3/4 teaspoon salt

Freshly ground black pepper

Toast the coriander seeds in a small dry skillet over medium heat, shaking the pan constantly, until the seeds darken and smell wonderfully fragrant and toasty; be careful not to overcook them. Pour them out onto a paper towel to stop the cooking. Using the paper towel as a funnel, transfer them to a spice mill (or a clean coffee mill reserved for that purpose or a mini food processor) and grind very fine.

Peel the potatoes and cut them into quarters. Put them in a large (4-quart) saucepan and fill the pan with cold water to cover the potatoes by 1½ inches. Bring the potatoes to a boil over medium-high heat and cook until they are easily pierced with a fork, about 20 minutes.

When the potatoes are done, drain them in a colander. Using the same saucepan, bring the milk and cream to a simmer over medium heat. Remove the pan from the heat. Press the potatoes through a ricer, letting them fall into the hot cream. Whip the potatoes with a sturdy wire whisk or a portable electric mixer. Add the coriander, butter, garlic paste and salt and continue to whip until the butter is melted and thoroughly incorporated. Taste and season with pepper and additional salt if needed.

Serve right away or keep the potatoes warm in a covered metal bowl set over a pan of simmering water for up to 1 hour.

---

cook's notes

❧ For the roasted garlic paste, preheat the oven to 400 degrees. Cut the top quarter off a whole head of garlic (or several of them, if you'd like extra roasted garlic paste) and place the head of garlic on a square of heavy-duty aluminum foil. Drizzle a little olive oil over the cut top of the garlic head and enclose the garlic with the foil, leaving the top covered loosely. Roast for about 1 hour, or until the cloves are soft and the garlic at the top is a nutty brown.

Let the garlic cool enough to handle, then squeeze out the garlic cloves; they'll pop out easily. Mash them to a paste with a fork and store covered tightly in the refrigerator for up to 1 week.

❧ If you forget to make the roasted garlic paste, you can just cook about 10 peeled garlic cloves along with the potatoes and rice them as well.

❧ Ricing potatoes is the best way to make mashed potatoes. If you don't have a ricer, get one; they're less than $15 and they guarantee perfect mashed potatoes with a minimum of effort. The most useful ricers have a hook so that you can attach them to the pot while you're ricing directly into cream.

---

the best grated potato pancakes

SOURCE

Julia's Kitchen Wisdom
by Julia Child

COOK

Julia Child,
after Sally Darr

We've seen dozens of potato-pancake recipes, but these very simple ones really *are* the best. They have lots of crisp edges and a moist, almost creamy center. And they're wonderfully useful because you have to cook the potatoes themselves ahead, so the final preparation is quick. If you don't want to serve them right away, they'll hold for several hours (but no longer) and easily reheat for serving. These good little kitchen soldiers get even crisper on reheating.

They make a great side dish but they're also sturdy enough to hold up as a base for roast chicken, sautéed salmon or grilled scallops.

serves 6

3 large baking potatoes, unpeeled	Salt and freshly ground black pepper
	Clarified butter (see note)

Several hours before you plan to serve the pancakes, steam the potatoes for 15 to 20 minutes, or until almost but not quite tender. Set aside for several hours, until completely cold.

Peel the potatoes and rub through the large holes of a hand grater. Toss with a sprinkling of salt and pepper and divide loosely into mounds.

Film a frying pan with ⅛ inch clarified butter and set the pan over

Meanwhile, place the unpeeled sweet potatoes in a large baking pan, add about 2 inches of water and cover tightly with foil. Bake on the lower shelf of the oven until tender, about $1^1/2$ hours. (If the water evaporates, replace it with a bit more.)

Remove the potatoes from the oven and let them cool enough to be handled. Peel them and add them to a food processor in batches, along with the remaining ingredients (except the nuts), processing until smooth. Transfer the pureed sweet potatoes to a mixing bowl and beat with a wooden spoon to combine thoroughly.

Serve the puree hot, garnished with the glazed nuts.

---

cook's note

You can make the sweet potatoes and the pecans a day ahead. When you are ready to serve, reheat the potato puree and add the nuts at the last minute.

---

orange-ginger cranberries

SOURCE

Parade

COOK

Sheila Lukins

Lukins, who's half of the famous Silver Palate team, swears she could live on these berries. We feel the same way and wish we'd made a double recipe so we'd have more to spoon over our breakfast yogurt. You couldn't make too much, really, since the berries keep for a good 2 months in the refrigerator and even longer if frozen. So they also qualify as a first-rate hostess present.

They're a wonderful combination of sweet, tart and zesty. You won't want to spend another Thanksgiving without them.

serves 10

1 pound fresh cranberries

2 cups sugar

1 tablespoon grated orange zest

1 cup fresh orange juice

1 tablespoon finely minced fresh ginger

Combine all the ingredients in a saucepan and cook over medium heat until the berries pop open, about 10 minutes. Skim any foam that rises to the top.

Let the cranberries cool and then refrigerate, covered well.

---

cook's note

Cranberries now come in 12-ounce packages, so if you don't want to have any left over, just use one package and cut back on the sugar by $1/2$ cup and the orange juice by $1/4$ cup. Use slightly less ginger and orange zest.

---

mesa grits

SOURCE

Time Out New York

COOK

Bobby Flay

These aren't true grits in the southern sense — ground dried corn — but rather shortcut grits that are made after the fact, ground from good old canned hominy. What you get is great big hominy flavor and a creamy, thick, rich dish that's pure comfort food. Given that it's Bobby Flay, the southwestern chef, cooking here, it's surprising to find not a chile in sight. But of course you could add some yourself, as well as some ham or cheese. But try this Flay's way first for its purity.

This is also good served for breakfast alongside ham or sausage.

serves 4

2 tablespoons butter
1 Spanish onion, finely chopped
2 garlic cloves, finely chopped
2 cans hominy, rinsed and
    drained

2 cups heavy cream
  Salt and freshly ground black
    pepper, to taste

Heat the butter in a medium saucepan over medium heat. Add the onion and garlic and cook until translucent. Add the hominy and cook for 10 minutes.

Transfer the mixture to a food processor and process until almost smooth (the grits should have some texture).

Return the mixture to the pan and stir in the cream. Cook over low heat until the mixture thickens, about 10 minutes. Season with salt and pepper and serve.

---

cook's note
There's a lot of variation in canned hominy. Goya is a reliable brand.

---

side dishes

225

almond-currant couscous

SOURCE

Secrets of Success Cookbook
by Michael Bauer

COOK

Annie Somerville

A new way of cooking instant couscous gives it a distinctive character. Annie Somerville, the chef at the legendary Greens vegetarian restaurant in San Francisco, toasts the couscous in butter to bring out its nutty flavor and keep the grains separate—no gummy clumps of couscous here. She also uses the water that plumps the couscous as a flavoring agent in its own right, adding cinnamon and currants to the water rather than stirring them in at the end.

This is a simple, delicious side dish and could even make an appearance at breakfast. It's also accommodating: You could add cumin or use 1/4 cup chopped dried apricots in place of the currants.

serves 4 to 6

2 tablespoons unsalted butter
1 1/2 cups instant couscous
1/4 cup whole blanched almonds, toasted (see note) and chopped
1 1/2 cups water

1/4 cup dried currants
1/2 teaspoon cinnamon, preferably freshly ground
1/4 teaspoon (or more) salt

In a medium skillet with a tight-fitting lid, melt the butter over medium heat. Add the couscous and almonds and stir until the grains are fragrant and heated through, 4 to 5 minutes. Remove from the heat.

Bring the water to a boil in a small saucepan. Stir in the remaining ingredients. Pour over the couscous. Cover the skillet and let it stand for 20 minutes.

Fluff the couscous with a fork and season with additional salt if needed. Serve immediately.

---

tips

❦ Instead of toasting nuts in the oven at 300 degrees for 10 minutes, or until they smell toasty, Denise Landis (in the *New York Times*) recommends toasting them in the microwave. Spread a small amount of nuts evenly in a single layer in a 10-inch glass pie plate and stir every 30 seconds. They'll be done in a few minutes. This method works especially well for delicate nuts, such as pine nuts, which can so easily burn in the oven or on top of the stove.

❦ Claudia Roden, the Middle Eastern food expert, suggests another way of making quick-cooking couscous that brings out its full flavor. For $2^3/4$ cups couscous (a 1-pound package) or 3 cups (a 500-gram package), put the couscous in a wide ovenproof dish and pour over it an equal amount of warm salted ($1/2$ to 1 teaspoon salt) water, stirring continually so the water is absorbed evenly. Leave for 10 to 15 minutes, or until the grain is plump and tender. From time to time, fluff it with a fork so the grains don't stick together. Mix in 3 tablespoons vegetable oil and rub the grains between your hands above the bowl to break up any lumps and air them. Put the couscous in a preheated 400-degree oven and heat through for 15 to 20 minutes, or until very hot. Halfway through the heating, fluff the grains again with a fork.

Before serving, work in 3 tablespoons butter and break up any lumps very thoroughly.

rice with lemon from the piedmont

John Thorne's Web site is outlawcook.com, and he prides himself on being a sort of cheerful curmudgeon of a food critic. Above all else he's curious, tracking down fascinating recipes and food tales and information you'll find nowhere else. Certainly we've never seen a recipe like this one, for a superb lemony rice rich with cheese and eggs.

SOURCE

Pot on the Fire
by John Thorne

COOK

John Thorne

As Thorne says, the delicate creaminess of the way the rice is cooked tempers the acidity of the lemon without crowding its bright citrus flavor.

The rice is free-boiled here, cooked like pasta in a large amount of boiling water. Purist that he is, Thorne always uses pure water, not tap water, for cooking the rice to produce the best taste.

serves 4 as a side dish, 2 as a main dish

3–4 quarts water
    Pure sea salt
½ pound (1 cup) Italian rice, such as Arborio or carnaroli
2 large egg yolks
2 tablespoons fresh lemon juice

1 cup freshly grated Parmesan, plus more for the table
2–3 tablespoons unsalted butter, in one piece
    Salt and freshly ground black pepper, to taste

Bring the water to a boil in a large pot and salt it as you would to cook pasta. Pour the rice into a pitcher (see note) and sprinkle it steadily into the pot, stirring once with a big wooden spoon. When the water returns to a rolling boil, lower the heat and simmer the rice until it is just al dente, 15 to 18 minutes.

Meanwhile, beat the egg yolks in a small bowl with a fork until frothy and well blended. Beat in the lemon juice and then stir in the

Parmesan. When the rice is done, pour it into a sieve or colander and gently shake out any remaining liquid. Immediately return it to the pot and, with a large cooking spoon, stir in the egg-cheese mixture. Put the lump of butter on top and press it into the rice with the spoon.

Put the pot on the burner over the lowest possible flame and let it sit there for 2 or at the most 3 minutes—just long enough for the butter to melt completely. Mix it gently all through the rice, taste for salt, and grind a generous amount of pepper on top. Serve at once in a warmed bowl with the additional Parmesan.

cook's notes

- A glass measuring cup with a spout is ideal for pouring the rice into the water.
- The rice doesn't have to be lemony. If you leave out the lemon, you have rice with eggs, which is almost as good.

fresh corn polenta

This is one of those double-take recipes: fresh corn polenta? But as Scotto, the chef and co-owner of Manhattan's Italian restaurant Scopa, says, "If the Italians had sweet corn, they'd know what to do with it." Scotto certainly does; he grates it and squeezes out every last bit of the delicious creamy juice, then cooks it gently in the best olive oil he can lay his hands on. It comes out a delicate, delectable mush that's so stunning you'll feel compelled to make it several times each corn season. Taking the polenta approach to our national vegetable really seems to bring out corn's secret Italian soul.

SOURCE

Macy's De Gustibus recipe handout

COOK

Vincent Scotto

serves 4

4 ears of fresh corn
½ cup water
2 tablespoons best-quality extra-virgin olive oil
Salt, to taste

Grated Parmigiano-Reggiano cheese, to taste
Freshly ground black pepper, to taste

Stand the shucked ears of corn upright in a shallow bowl and cut off the kernels as close to the cob as you can. Go around again and scrape out the remaining milk in the cobs.

Grind the corn kernels in a food processor in batches until you have a slurry.

Put the corn in a large saucepan along with the water and the olive oil. Bring to a simmer and cook for 20 minutes, stirring every few minutes; don't let the corn scorch.

Add salt, cheese and pepper, along with a drizzle of olive oil if you like. Serve immediately.

---

tip

In the *Farm Chronicle of Virginia, Maryland and Delaware*, we found Pete Ferretti, professor of vegetable crops at Penn State, explaining how best to cook corn on the cob. For very fresh corn, you'll get the best flavor, aroma, sweetness and tenderness if you microwave it. Remove the outer husks so only the clean, thin inner husks remain. Wash a single ear in cold water and wrap it in a paper towel dipped in cold water. Microwave on high for 2 to 3 minutes, depending on your microwave oven. Using gloves or mitts (the cooked corn is very hot), shuck the husks downward in one easy motion to remove them completely.

For older corn, boil without salt but adding a few tablespoons of sugar and a teaspoon of skim milk (to help remove some minerals). Boil, uncovered, for about 7 minutes.

etta's corn bread pudding

Though savory bread puddings have become popular recently, we haven't seen one based on corn bread before. But it's a terrific idea. The corn bread has a more interesting texture than ordinary bread; here it's surrounded by a rich, smooth, eggy custard, so it makes a good contrast.

The pudding goes very well with roasted

SOURCE

*Tom Douglas'
Seattle Kitchen*
by Tom Douglas

COOK

Tom Douglas

meats, poultry and salmon. Vegetarians may find it's plenty as a main course.

You have to make more corn bread than you need, but you can either eat it warm with butter and honey, as Douglas's staff does, or just freeze it to make another pudding later.

serves 8

CORN BREAD

- 1 cup all-purpose flour
- 3/4 cup medium-ground yellow cornmeal
- 1/2 cup grated pepper Jack cheese (1 1/2 ounces)
- 1 teaspoon baking powder
- 1 teaspoon salt
- 2 large eggs
- 1 cup milk
- 3 tablespoons honey
- 4 tablespoons (1/2 stick) unsalted butter, melted

PUDDING

- 1 tablespoon unsalted butter, plus a little more for the pan
- 1 cup thinly sliced onion (about 1/2 large onion)
- 1/4 cup grated dry Jack cheese (see note)
- 2 teaspoons chopped fresh Italian parsley
- 1/2 teaspoon chopped fresh rosemary
- 1/2 teaspoon chopped fresh thyme
- 2 1/4 cups heavy cream
- 4 large eggs
- 1 teaspoon kosher salt
- 1/2 teaspoon freshly ground black pepper

TO MAKE THE CORN BREAD

Preheat the oven to 425 degrees. Butter an 8-inch square baking dish. Combine the flour, cornmeal, cheese, baking powder and salt in a large bowl. In a medium bowl, whisk together the eggs, milk and honey. Add the wet ingredients to the dry ingredients, stirring until just combined. Add the melted butter and stir into the mixture. Pour into the prepared pan and bake until a toothpick comes out clean, 15 to 20 minutes. When the corn bread is cool enough to handle, cut it into 1-inch cubes. You should have about 8 cups corn bread cubes, but you need only one-third of them ($2^2/_3$ cups) for this recipe.

TO MAKE THE PUDDING

Reduce the oven temperature to 350 degrees. Put the $2^2/_3$ cups of the corn bread cubes in a buttered 8-inch square baking dish and set aside.

Heat the 1 tablespoon butter in a sauté pan over low heat and cook the onion very slowly until soft and golden brown, at least 20 minutes, stirring occasionally. Remove from the heat.

---

cook's note

The dry Jack made by the Vella company in northern California is the one Tom Douglas prefers. It's a great cheese, the closest American cheese ever gets to Parmesan. If you can't find it, substitute Parmesan.

Scatter the onion, cheese and herbs over the corn bread cubes. Whisk together the heavy cream and eggs with salt and pepper in a mixing bowl and pour over the corn bread cubes. Let sit for 10 minutes so the corn bread absorbs some of the custard. Set the pudding dish in a larger roasting pan filled with hot water to come two-thirds of the way up the sides of the dish. Bake until the top is golden and the center is just lightly set, about 40 minutes. Don't wait for it to be too firm, or the whole thing will curdle. Remove from the water bath immediately or the pudding will keep cooking and possibly curdle. Serve hot.

tip

The pudding reheats very well, so you can make it a day ahead, cover it well and refrigerate it. Before serving, cover it with foil and reheat it at 375 degrees until warmed through, 35 to 40 minutes.

gratin of summer squash with leeks and rice

This summer gratin is an all-in-one dish, including vegetables and starch, that's baked and served in a skillet. For vegetarians, it can be a meal in itself, along with some sliced tomatoes and bread.

The delicacy of the summer squash, which so often seems bland, is captured here and highlighted by the sweet earthy leeks and the creamy rice. Worthing-

SOURCE

The Taste of Summer
by Diane Rossen
Worthington

COOK

Diane Rossen
Worthington

ton first removes the excess liquid from the squash so it will cook perfectly, then re-serves the liquid to use in flavoring the finished dish.

You can make the gratin in the morning up to the point of baking it, and bring it to room tempera-ture before proceeding with the baking. It will also travel well, so it's a good contribu-tion to a potluck dinner.

serves 6

2½ pounds mixed yellow crookneck and green zucchini squash
1 teaspoon salt
1½ cups water
½ cup long-grain white rice
¼ cup olive oil
3 medium leeks, white and light green parts only, finely chopped (about 3 cups)

2 medium garlic cloves, minced
2 tablespoons finely chopped fresh Italian parsley
2 tablespoons all-purpose flour
2 cups half-and-half
¾ cup freshly grated Parmesan cheese
Salt and freshly ground black pepper

Using a food processor fitted with the shredder blade, shred the squash and place in a colander. Add the salt and mix thoroughly with your hands. Place the colander over a bowl and let the squash drain thoroughly, capturing the juices in the bowl, for 15 to 30 minutes.

Wrap the shredded squash in a kitchen towel and wring it over the bowl to collect any additional juices. Set the juices aside and dry the squash well with a dry towel.

In a medium saucepan, bring the water to a boil. Add the rice, reduce the heat to a simmer, and cook for 5 minutes. Drain and reserve.

Preheat the oven to 425 degrees.

In a large ovenproof skillet over medium-high heat, warm 3 tablespoons of the oil. Add the leeks and sauté until slightly softened, about 5 minutes. Add the remaining tablespoon of olive oil and the squash, and sauté until almost tender, about 3 minutes. Add the garlic and parsley and sauté for another minute.

Sprinkle in the flour and stir over medium heat (a pasta fork works well) for 2 minutes. Remove from the heat and add the half-and-half and the squash liquid. Return to medium heat and continue to cook, stirring constantly, until slightly thickened, about 3 minutes.

---

tip

French chef Roger Vergé tops off his gratins with a gleaming golden glaze. According to *À La Carte*, a cook's newsletter published by La Cuisine in Alexandria, Virginia, here's how to do it: Whip 2 tablespoons cold heavy cream. When it forms soft peaks, whisk in an egg yolk and season with salt and pepper. Spread a thin, even layer of this mixture on top of your baked gratin and broil for a few moments, watching constantly, until it is perfectly browned. You can also stir in a tablespoon of grated Parmesan or Swiss Gruyère.

Add the reserved rice and all but 2 tablespoons of the Parmesan cheese and mix well. Season with salt and pepper. Sprinkle the remaining cheese on top.

Bake until the gratin is browned and bubbling, or until all the liquid has been absorbed by the rice. Serve hot.

potato–green chile gratin

The Santa Fe–based vegetarian cook Deborah Madison has always produced the most exquisite vegetable dishes imaginable, but this time she's really outdone herself. There are just a few ingredients in this dish—chiles, potatoes, cream, a solitary clove of garlic, no cheese—and yet it has a complex flavor that's memorable. There's never any left, no matter how few people are at the table.

You can make the gratin a day ahead, cool it completely before chilling it and simply reheat (covered, in a 350-degree oven) after it has come to room temperature. This flexibility makes it a great candidate for a potluck supper.

SOURCE

Zanne Stewart,
Gourmet

COOK

Deborah Madison

serves 6

6 fresh green Anaheim or poblano chiles, roasted and peeled (see note)
2 cups heavy cream or half-and-half

1 large garlic clove
2½ pounds russet potatoes (about 5 medium)
Salt, to taste

Preheat the oven to 375 degrees.

Discard the chile seeds (and the ribs if you'd like less heat) and finely chop the chiles. Set aside.

In a medium saucepan, bring the cream with the garlic just to a simmer, then remove it from the heat. Set aside to steep. Peel the potatoes and cut them crosswise into ⅛-inch-thick slices using a mandoline or a sharp knife.

Arrange one-fourth of the potatoes evenly in the bottom of a well-buttered 2-quart shallow baking dish, overlapping them slightly, and sprinkle with salt and one-fourth of the chiles. Make 3 more layers in the same manner. Remove the garlic from the cream and pour the cream over the potatoes.

Cover the dish with foil and bake in the lower third of the oven for 45 minutes. Remove the foil and bake until the gratin is golden brown on top and bubbling, about 30 minutes more. Cool slightly before serving.

---

cook's note

To roast the chiles, place them on the rack of a broiler pan about 2 inches from the heat. Roast them, turning often with tongs, until the skins are blackened, 5 to 8 minutes. Put the chiles in a bowl and cover with a plate. Let them steam for about 15 minutes. Peel off the skins with your fingers or rub them off with paper towels. Don't try to rinse the skins off or you'll lose a lot of flavor down the drain. Remove and discard the stems and seeds.

dad's baked beans

Caprial Pence is a busy woman. She's the chef at Caprial's Bistro, her restaurant in Portland, Oregon, she has a television show, and she has two children— but she wouldn't dream of not entertaining. Although sometimes she likes to pull out all the stops, usually it's a casual affair with simple great food that everyone loves.

These baked beans are always a hit at

SOURCE

Caprial Cooks for Friends
by Caprial Pence

COOK

Caprial Pence

Caprial's. Actually, most baked beans are a big hit, but these have something extra going for them: A smokiness from two sources (ham hock and chipotle chiles), two kinds of beans, fresh ginger and soy sauce, along with the more traditional bean flavorings, such as molasses, dry mustard and onion. Maybe Caprial's talent is genetic: These really are her dad's beans.

serves 8

- 1 pound dried pinto beans, rinsed
- 1 cup dried black beans
- 2 smoked ham hocks
- 1 onion, diced
- 2 tablespoons peeled, chopped fresh ginger
- 2 garlic cloves, chopped

- 1 canned chipotle chile in adobo sauce, chopped
- 1 packed cup light brown sugar
- 2/3 cup molasses
- 1 tablespoon soy sauce
- 1 teaspoon dry mustard
- 1 teaspoon ground cumin
  Salt and freshly ground black pepper, to taste

Place both kinds of beans in a large stockpot and add cold water to cover. Bring to a boil over medium heat and cook until the beans are tender, about 1½ hours. Drain the beans and place them in a Dutch oven or roasting pan. Add the chipotle, ham hocks, onion, ginger, garlic, brown sugar, molasses, soy sauce, dry mustard and cumin and mix well. Season with salt and pepper.

Preheat the oven to 275 degrees. Cover and bake for 4 hours, or until thick and flavorful. Serve warm.

cook's note

After the beans are baked, pull out the ham hocks and pick off any meat. Stir it back into the beans, discarding the bone, fat and skin. There's not a lot of meat on these bones, but it has great flavor.

breads

skillet corn bread

Southerners are passionate about their corn bread, and perhaps the noisiest of them all is Hoppin' John, who has broadcast this recipe far and wide in hopes of converting those who add sugar to

SOURCE

Hoppin' John's Lowcountry Cooking
by John Martin Taylor

COOK

John Martin Taylor

their recipes. This one is pure and sensationally good, a foolproof recipe baked in an old-fashioned cast-iron skillet ("well seasoned, never washed," cautions Hoppin').

serves 8

1   large egg
2   cups buttermilk
1³/₄ cups cornmeal, preferably stone-ground

1¹/₂–2 teaspoons strained bacon grease
1   scant teaspoon baking powder
1   scant teaspoon baking soda
1   scant teaspoon salt

In a medium bowl, mix the egg into the buttermilk. Add the cornmeal and beat it well; the batter should be thin.

Put enough bacon grease into a 9- or 10-inch cast-iron skillet to coat the bottom and sides with a thin film, then set the skillet in a cold oven. Preheat the oven to 450 degrees. When it reaches the right temperature, the bacon grease will be just at the point of smoking. Add the baking powder, baking soda and salt to the batter, beat in well and pour the batter all at once into the hot pan.

Return the pan to the oven to bake for 15 to 20 minutes, or until the top of the corn bread just begins to brown. Turn the loaf out onto a plate and serve hot with lots of the freshest butter you can get your hands on.

angel biscuits

SOURCE

The Baking Sheet,
King Arthur Flour

COOK

Cathy Case Emerson

Angel biscuits are also called bride's biscuits, and they're a traditional favorite in the South, where they're likely to appear with a paper-thin slice of country ham tucked inside. They're crunchy on the outside and fluffy and light inside—angelic indeed. They may be called bride's biscuits because they're easy. They have both yeast and baking powder, so you're guaranteed a light biscuit (a great boon for the novice baker), and they can be made ahead and either kept overnight or frozen once they've risen.

We think they're best served hot, with butter and jam, but they're also good at room temperature, as mini-sandwiches.

Their creator, Cathy Case Emerson, of Charleston, South Carolina, notes that you can also cut the biscuits smaller than the usual 2 inches, using a champagne flute to make the smaller rounds, and serve them for brunch.

makes 15 biscuits

- 1/2 cup lukewarm water
- 1 teaspoon active dry yeast
- 2 1/2 cups unbleached all-purpose flour
- 2 tablespoons sugar
- 2 teaspoons baking powder
- 1 teaspoon salt
- 1/4 cup vegetable shortening
- 4 tablespoons (1/2 stick) butter, chilled
- 3/4 cup milk or buttermilk

In a small mixing bowl, whisk together the warm water, yeast and 1/4 cup of the flour. Set the mixture aside for 30 minutes. In a medium bowl, whisk together the remaining 2 1/4 cups flour, the sugar, baking powder and salt. Cut in the shortening and the butter, mixing until everything's rough and crumbly.

Add the milk or buttermilk to the yeast mixture, and pour this all at once into the dry ingredients. Fold together gently until the mixture leaves the sides of the bowl and becomes cohesive. Sprinkle with an additional tablespoon of water only if necessary to make the dough hold together.

Turn the dough out onto a lightly floured work surface. Pat it gently into an 8-x-10-inch rectangle about ¾ inch thick. Cut the dough into fifteen 2-inch round biscuits. Gather, reroll and cut the scraps, if desired; the resulting biscuits will probably be a bit tougher.

Place the biscuits on an ungreased or parchment-lined baking sheet. Cover lightly and allow them to rise for 1 hour, or until they've increased in size by about a third. (You can refrigerate the biscuits for several hours or overnight at this point, or freeze them to use later.)

Preheat the oven to 450 degrees.

Bake the biscuits in the top third of the oven for 6 minutes. Turn the oven off, but don't open the door for an additional 5 minutes. The biscuits will be golden brown on the top and bottom. Serve hot, with butter and jam or ham and eggs.

---

cook's note

To bake frozen biscuits, bake for 8 minutes before turning off the oven.

---

thomas jefferson's sweet potato biscuits

Sweet and aromatic, tender and tall, these are over-the-top biscuits, full of brown sugar, spices, cream and pecans—just the thing for Thanksgiving or an-

SOURCE

Los Angeles Times

COOK

City Tavern, Philadelphia

other feast. Did Thomas Jefferson really love them? We don't know, but we love them, and we think you will too.

makes 24 biscuits

5 cups all-purpose flour, plus more for rolling
1 cup packed light brown sugar
2 tablespoons baking powder
1 1/2 teaspoons ground cinnamon
1 teaspoon salt
1 teaspoon ground ginger

1/2 teaspoon ground allspice
1 cup shortening
2 cups cooked and cooled mashed sweet potatoes (see note)
1 cup whipping cream
1/2 cup coarsely chopped pecans

Preheat the oven to 350 degrees.

Stir together the 5 cups flour, brown sugar, baking powder, cinnamon, salt, ginger and allspice in a large mixing bowl.

Cut in the shortening with two knives or a dough cutter until crumbly. Add the sweet potatoes and mix well with a wooden spoon. Add the cream and pecans and stir just until moistened.

Turn the dough out onto a lightly floured surface. Roll it out to a thickness of 1 1/2 inches. Cut out biscuits with a floured 2-inch biscuit cutter. Place the biscuits 1 inch apart on ungreased baking sheets.

Bake until golden brown, 25 to 30 minutes. Serve hot, or cool on a wire rack to room temperature.

cook's note

To cook the sweet potatoes, bake them whole in a 400-degree oven on a sheet of aluminum foil to catch the drips. They should be done in about 1 hour, depending on their size. They're ready when they're very tender. To get 2 cups, you'll need to bake 1½ pounds of sweet potatoes.

parker house rolls

We've seen more ersatz recipes for Parker House rolls than for any other American classic, and we see more of them every year. These most buttery of American rolls are so good because they're tender, soft, a bit sweet and, as chef Jasper White says, elegant. Because White spent over a year in the original Parker House kitchen in Boston, he knows the real recipe.

The Parker House was an innovative hotel that opened in 1856. Along with the rolls, it's the source of Boston Scrod and Boston Cream Pie. As with so many great American dishes, the rolls are reputed to have their source in an accident, in this case an angry baker outraged that his lover, a

SOURCE

50 Chowders
by Jasper White

COOK

Jasper White,
after The Parker House

chambermaid, had been falsely accused of stealing a guest's jewelry. The baker supposedly smashed all the unbaked rolls he could find with his fist. But the show had to go on, and once he calmed down, he brushed them with butter, folded them back together and baked them. The dinner guests raved, and the rolls have been buttered and folded ever since.

The rolls aren't at all difficult to make, but they do require some time for the three rises. They don't need as much kneading as other rolls because they're supposed to be soft, not chewy. The only hazard of serving these for a holiday meal is that they may become an unbreakable tradition.

makes 24 rolls

- 1 cup whole milk
- 1 1/2 teaspoons kosher salt or 1 teaspoon table salt or fine sea salt
- 1 tablespoon unsalted butter, plus 5–6 tablespoons more, melted
- 1 envelope (1/4 ounce) active dry yeast
- 1 tablespoon sugar
- 1/4 cup warm water (110–115 degrees)
- 3 cups all-purpose flour, or a little more if needed
- 2 teaspoons vegetable oil

In a small saucepan, combine the milk, salt and the 1 tablespoon butter. Scald (heat just until a few bubbles appear around the edges) over medium heat. Immediately remove from the heat. Let the milk cool slightly—it should be warm, not hot, when you add it to the dough.

Combine the yeast, sugar and warm water in the bowl of a standing mixer or in a large bowl and give it a stir. Let it sit for about 10 minutes while the yeast "blooms." When the yeast is frothy, add the warm milk mixture and the 3 cups flour. Using the dough hook, jog the mixer (turn it on and off quickly) to prevent the flour from flying out of the bowl, and mix until the dough comes together and the sides of the bowl are clean. Alternatively, mix it with a wooden spoon. If the dough is sticky, add another tablespoon of flour. Knead the dough by machine for about 5 minutes, or by hand for 8 to 10 minutes, until smooth and elastic.

Grease a large bowl with the vegetable oil. Shape the dough into a ball, place it in the bowl, and turn it once so it is lightly greased all over. Cover with plastic wrap or a damp cloth and place in a warm, draft-free spot, such as an oven that has been heated to 200 degrees and then turned off. Let the dough rise for about 30 minutes, until it doubles in size.

Punch down the dough. Divide it into 24 equal pieces, weighing about 1 ounce each (it's easiest to shape the dough into a rectangle, cut it lengthwise into 4 strips, then cut each strip crosswise into 6 pieces). Using a pastry brush, generously brush melted butter on the baking sheet (use at least 1½ tablespoons). Roll each piece of dough into a ball and arrange about 1 inch apart on the baking sheet. Place the pan back in the warm, draft-free spot and let the balls rise for about 20 minutes, until they double in size. (There is no need to cover them for this step.)

After the balls have doubled in size, press the handle of a wooden spoon down across the center of each ball, without cutting the balls in half. The balls will deflate a little. Generously brush one side of each ball with melted butter, using about $1^{1}/_{2}$ tablespoons in all. Fold the unbuttered side of each roll over the buttered side and press together. The rolls will look like half-moon-shaped pillows. Place the pan back in the warm spot and let the rolls rise until they have doubled in size.

While the dough is rising for the last time, preheat the oven to 400 degrees.

Place the rolls in the oven and bake for 15 minutes, or until the tops are evenly browned, turning the pan front to back halfway through the baking. Remove the rolls from the oven and, while they are still piping hot, brush the tops generously with the remaining melted butter. Serve warm.

---

cook's notes

♉ When you fold the rolls, you may find that they want to unfold them-selves—just be firm and press down on them and they'll behave.

♉ If 24 rolls is too many, you can freeze any leftovers, well wrapped, and warm them up to serve.

basic artisan bread

SOURCE

Recipe Collection,
Cuisinart Power Prep
Plus Food Processor

COOK

Charles Van Over

You just can't improve on this incredibly easy food-processor French bread, which also appeared this year in the revised *Cook's Catalogue* in slightly different form. In fact, you'd be happy to find a bread this good in Paris these days. You can shape the dough in a variety of ways: two long loaves, two round loaves or the particularly charming *épi*, in which pieces of dough are twisted off the long loaf on either side to form a sort of sheaf-of-wheat design.

makes 2 loaves

1 pound (3¹/₃–4 cups) unbleached bread flour (see note on page 252)

2 teaspoons fine sea salt

1 teaspoon instant (rapid-rise) yeast

1¹/₄ cups water

Cornmeal, for the baking sheet

Place the flour, salt and yeast in a food processor fitted with the metal blade or the dough blade. Using an instant-read thermometer, test the temperature of the flour. Adjust the temperature of the water so that the flour and the water together have a combined temperature of 145 degrees. (If the flour is 70 degrees, for instance, the water should be 75 degrees.) With the machine running (on dough speed, if your machine has it), pour in all the water through the small feed tube and process for 45 seconds.

Place the dough in a large ungreased bowl and cover with plastic wrap. Let the dough rise at room temperature for 1¹/₂ to 2 hours.

Scrape the dough onto a lightly floured work surface and divide into 2 equal pieces. Shape the dough into rough balls and let it rest, covered, for 15 to 20 minutes.

Roll each ball of dough into the desired loaf shape. Place the loaves on a cornmeal-dusted baking sheet. Cover with plastic wrap and let rise for 30 to 45 minutes, or until the dough increases by half its size. It should feel soft but still spring back slightly when poked with your finger.

Adjust the oven rack to the second shelf so that it's about 8 inches from the top of the oven. Dust the back of a baking sheet with cornmeal. Place a baking stone on the rack if you have one (see the tip on the facing page). Preheat the oven to 475 degrees and place a small cast-iron skillet (for water) on the oven floor or the bottom shelf.

Just before baking, dust each loaf lightly with flour. Gently transfer the loaves onto the back of the baking sheet, taking care not to deflate them. Score each round loaf with 4 slashes in a tic-tac-toe pat-

---

cook's notes

- The reason for the variation in the flour measurement is humidity, which is why it's a good idea to weigh the flour. On a damp day, it will probably be $3^1/_3$ cups of flour. If in doubt, spread 4 cups of the flour out on a baking sheet and dry it in a slow (200-degree) oven for about 20 minutes, and then measure 4 cups.
- Once you're used to taking the temperature of flour, it may not seem such a stretch to take the bread's temperature as well. The round loaves are done when their temperature is between 205 and 210 degrees, tested with an instant-read thermometer.

tern or an X. (For long loaves, make several diagonal slashes on top.) Carefully pour about 1 cup warm water into the skillet in the oven. Slide the baking sheet directly onto the baking stone, if using. Reduce the heat to 450 degrees.

Bake the loaves for 25 to 30 minutes (for long loaves), 30 to 40 minutes (for round ones), or until the crust is a deep mahogany brown and the loaves sound hollow when tapped on the bottom. (For a crisper crust, transfer the loaves directly onto the baking stone halfway through the baking.)

Remove the bread from the oven and place it on a rack to cool completely before storing or serving.

---

tip

Peter Berley (author of *The Modern Vegetarian Kitchen*) learned this tip from Jim Lahey of the Sullivan Street Bakery in Manhattan. To approximate the great crusts you find in traditional brick-oven bakery breads, bake the bread —a single round one in this case, slashed with an X just before baking—in a covered cast-iron pot (enameled cast-iron is fine) that's been heated in the oven for about 45 minutes. Remove the cover for the last quarter of the baking time (30 to 40 minutes). You get to skip the baking stone and the pan of water in the bottom of the oven this way.

hi-rise's boston brown bread

SOURCE

*Artisan Baking
Across America*
by Maggie Glezer

COOK

René Becker

This Boston brown bread really does come from Boston—or rather Cambridge, where baker-owner René Becker holds forth at the Hi-Rise Bread Company. Becker's version of the classic is completely unlike the stodgy, soggy, super-sweet brown breads of yore. Instead of being steamed, it's baked, so it's crisp and light while retaining the moistness of the original. There's also a secret ingredient: cornmeal, which gives this bread a nice bite.

Fast (about 10 minutes of prep) and easy, this quick bread is born to be served with Dad's Baked Beans, page 240. Or just serve with a smear of cream cheese or a slice of sharp Cheddar.

makes 2 loaves

Unsalted butter, at room temperature, for buttering the cans
2 cups whole rye flour
1¹/₂ cups unbleached all-purpose flour
1 cup whole wheat flour
²/₃ cup stone-ground white cornmeal

1 tablespoon baking soda
1¹/₂ teaspoons baking powder
1¹/₄ teaspoons salt
2 cups milk
¹/₂ cup light molasses
1 cup dried blueberries, currants or raisins

Preheat the oven to 300 degrees and set the rack on the bottom shelf of the oven, removing all other racks. Generously butter two clean 14-to-16-ounce empty coffee cans (or any cylindrical metal container that's 4 inches in diameter and 5¹/₂ inches tall).

Combine the rye flour, white flour, wheat flour, cornmeal, baking soda, baking powder, and salt in a large bowl. Combine the milk and molasses in a pitcher. Stir enough of the milk mixture into the dry ingredients to make a thick paste, then beat until the batter is smooth. Mix in the remaining milk mixture, then fold in the dried fruit. Spoon the batter into the coffee cans, which should be about three-fourths full.

Put the cans immediately into the oven and bake for $1\frac{1}{2}$ hours, rotating halfway through the baking. (The breads may overflow their edges, but that's fine.) When they're done, the breads should be well domed, brown and crusty. Remove from the oven and run a knife around the inner edge to remove them from the cans. Let cool on a rack.

---

cook's notes

- Like all quick breads, these are best eaten the day they're made, though they make good toast the next morning.
- Make sure your coffee cans will hold 16 ounces (read the label); some cans hold only 12 ounces, which will be too small for these breads.

---

b r e a d s

ethiopian honey-spice bread

SOURCE

Honey
by Gene Opton

COOK

Gene Opton

The dominant note in this intriguing bread is a lost-and-found spice, ground coriander—the dried seeds of the herb most commonly known as cilantro in this country. Although it used to be the favorite cookie spice of Colonial American cooks, few modern Americans, says Opton, can even identify the flavor. This lovely bread is reason enough to put coriander back on your spice shelf.

Here it's partnered with other sweet and warming spices and a touch of honey. This is a very good bread on its own with everything from chicken salad to ham, but Ethiopians usually spread it with butter and honey. It keeps very well and toasts brilliantly.

makes 1 loaf

1 tablespoon active dry yeast
¹/₄ cup warm water
1 teaspoon sugar or honey
¹/₈ teaspoon ground ginger
1 large egg
¹/₂ cup mild honey
1 tablespoon ground coriander
¹/₂ teaspoon ground cinnamon

¹/₄ teaspoon ground cloves
1¹/₂ teaspoons salt
1 cup whole milk, warmed
4 tablespoons (¹/₂ stick)
   unsalted butter, melted and
   cooled
About 4¹/₂ cups unbleached
   all-purpose flour

Combine the yeast, water, sugar or honey and ginger in a small ceramic bowl and set in a warm, draft-free place until it bubbles vigorously.

Combine the egg, honey, spices and salt in a large mixing bowl or the bowl of a heavy-duty mixer. Add the milk and the butter. Mix in 1 cup of the flour.

Add the yeast mixture and beat until all the ingredients are well blended. Add more flour, $1/2$ cup at a time, using only enough to make a soft dough. Use your hands, if needed, to work in the last bit of flour.

Turn out onto a lightly floured surface and knead the bread by folding it end to end, pressing down and pushing forward several times with the heel of your hand. (The dough will be sticky. Use a dough scraper to clear the board and turn the mass of dough. Avoid adding more flour.)

In about 5 minutes the dough will become smoother and more elastic. Shape into a rough ball and place in a large oiled bowl, cover with a tea towel, and let rise until doubled in bulk.

Heavily butter a 3-quart round baking dish that is 3 inches deep, such as a casserole or enameled Dutch oven. Punch down the dough with a single blow of your fist. Knead the dough for a few minutes, shape into a rough ball, and place in the prepared pan. (Press the dough down so that the bottom of the pan is covered completely.) Cover and let rise again until the dough has doubled and reaches the top of the pan.

At least 20 minutes before baking, preheat the oven to 300 degrees.

Bake for 50 to 60 minutes, or until the bread is nicely rounded on top and a light golden brown. Leave in the pan for 5 minutes, then remove and transfer to a rack to cool before slicing.

rhubarb bread

SOURCE

Los Angeles Times Modern California Cooking

COOK

Terrie Snell

You may never have thought of putting rhubarb in bread, and you may not even think it sounds very good. But this midwestern specialty is one of those great vanishing breads: Once you bake it, it's gone. It's a moist, falling-apart-tender bread with a crackly, crinkly sugar topping that both looks pretty and adds great texture, with a caramel flavor to balance out the tart taste of the rhubarb

This is a great companion for tea or coffee, and it's also excellent for breakfast—or just for snacking, for that matter.

makes 2 loaves

1½ cups packed light brown sugar
⅔ cup vegetable oil
1 large egg
1 cup buttermilk
2½ cups all-purpose flour
1 teaspoon baking soda
1 teaspoon salt

1 teaspoon pure vanilla extract
2 cups diced rhubarb
½ cup chopped walnuts or pecans
1 tablespoon butter, at room temperature
¼ cup sugar

Preheat the oven to 350 degrees.

Combine the brown sugar and oil in a large bowl. Stir well until smooth. Stir in the egg, buttermilk, flour, baking soda, salt and vanilla. Blend until moist. Fold in the rhubarb and nuts. Turn the batter into two greased 8-x-4-inch loaf pans.

Combine the butter and sugar until crumbly. Sprinkle over the batter.

Bake until a toothpick inserted in the center comes out dry, 50 to 55 minutes. Turn out onto wire racks and cool before slicing.

desserts

potato chip cookies

When New York's *Newsday* sent out a call for recipes for great homemade cookies for the holidays, Rita Cayea's coworkers at United Parcel Service in Farmingville, Long Island, started an E-

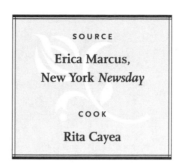

SOURCE

Erica Marcus,
New York *Newsday*

COOK

Rita Cayea

mail blitz to get the word out about her cookies. It's Cayea's firm belief that "there's no good cookie without nuts in it." She also has a fondness for the offbeat cookie, like this one.

makes about 40 cookies

½ cup crushed potato chips
½ cup finely ground pecans
1½ cups all-purpose flour
½ cup sugar

1 cup (2 sticks) butter, at room temperature
1 large egg yolk
1 teaspoon pure vanilla extract
Powdered sugar

Preheat the oven to 350 degrees.

In a medium bowl, combine the crushed potato chips, ground pecans and flour. In a large bowl, cream together the sugar and butter until fluffy, then beat in the egg yolk and vanilla. Beat in the dry ingredients until the mixture is well integrated.

With damp hands, form the dough into 1-inch balls and place 1½ inches apart on ungreased cookie sheets. Bake until the cookies just start to color, 15 to 18 minutes. Cool slightly and roll in powdered sugar.

Store the cookies in an airtight container, separating layers of cookies with sheets of wax paper.

mayan mystery cookies

At New Rivers restaurant in Providence, Rhode Island, these cookies first appeared in a lunchtime cookie basket and quickly rocketed to local fame. Clearly there's a mystery ingredient here that makes them so good, and their creator offered a free cookie basket to whoever guessed it. But only two people ever did (one of them Julia Child's associ-

SOURCE

Postcard mailing, Fleet Bank

COOK

Pat Tillinghast

ate, Nancy Verde Barr). As you can see, it's cayenne pepper, partnered with its alluring Mexican companion, chocolate.

As Chef Bruce Tillinghast explains, every other item on the menu changes from time to time—but not these cookies created by his late wife.

makes about 60 cookies

³/₄ cup (1¹/₂ sticks) unsalted butter, at room temperature
³/₄ cup sugar, plus more for rolling
1¹/₂ cups all-purpose flour
1¹/₂ teaspoons baking powder
¹/₄ teaspoon salt
1 teaspoon ground cinnamon

¹/₂ teaspoon finely (and freshly) ground black pepper
¹/₄ teaspoon ground allspice
¹/₈ teaspoon cayenne pepper
³/₄ cup cocoa
1 large egg
1¹/₂ teaspoons pure vanilla extract
Semisweet chocolate morsels

Preheat the oven to 350 degrees.

Cream the butter and the ³/₄ cup sugar in a food processor. Sift the flour, baking powder, salt, spices and cocoa in a medium bowl and add to the butter mixture. Add the egg and vanilla and mix until the batter is uniform.

Chill the dough for at least 1 hour.

Using your hands, roll the dough into balls about the width of a quarter and tuck about 5 chocolate morsels into the center of each one. Put some sugar on a flat plate and roll the balls in the sugar to cover lightly.

Line 2 cookie sheets with parchment paper and place the balls on the sheets. Bake for 8 minutes, being careful not to overbake; the cookies should be delicate and soft in the center. Let cool on the cookie sheets.

Store the cookies in an airtight container, separating the layers with sheets of wax paper.

pecan wafers

These easy cookies deliver great flavor as well as a crisp texture. The brown sugar gives them a bit of a caramel taste. They also

SOURCE

Cookies Unlimited
by Nick Malgieri

COOK

Nick Malgieri

make great sandwich cookies: Just melt a little milk chocolate and smear it between two cookies.

makes about 50 cookies

8 tablespoons (1 stick) unsalted butter, at room temperature
1 cup firmly packed light brown sugar
½ cup sugar
1 large egg

1 teaspoon pure vanilla extract
1½ cups all-purpose flour
4 ounces (about 1 cup) pecan pieces, finely chopped but not ground

Set the oven racks in the upper and lower thirds of the oven and preheat to 375 degrees. Line two or three cookie sheets or jelly-roll pans with parchment paper or foil.

In the bowl of a standing electric mixer fitted with the paddle attachment, beat together the butter, brown sugar and sugar until combined, then beat in the egg and vanilla. (Or do this in a large bowl by hand — it will just take a little longer.) Beat until smooth without overbeating.

Remove the bowl from the mixer and, with a large rubber spatula, stir in the flour and pecans. Roll rounded teaspoonfuls of the dough into balls, then place them 2 or 3 inches apart on the prepared pans, and press them slightly to flatten.

Bake the cookies for 12 to 15 minutes, or until they have spread and are deep gold around the edges but are still fairly pale on top.

Slide the papers off the pans onto wire racks. After the cookies have cooled, detach them from the paper and store them between sheets of parchment or wax paper in a tin or plastic container with a tight-fitting cover.

---

cook's notes

𝔠 Lightly spoon the flour into the measuring cups so that it's not too packed. Otherwise you'll have little mounds of cookies, not wafers, and you won't be able to sandwich them.

𝔠 Although pecans seem just about perfect in this cookie dough, you can also use hazelnuts or macadamia nuts. If you use hazelnuts and you want a sandwich cookie, try a little Nutella instead of the milk chocolate to hold the cookies together.

---

lime sugar cookies

SOURCE

Gourmet

COOK

Lori Walther Powell

What could be better than a crisp, thin, buttery sugar cookie? One that has a zingy bite of lime, as these cookies do. The lime flavor comes from grinding lime zest with sugar in the food processor, which produces a lovely green sugar with flecks of zest. The flavored sugar is beaten right into the cookie dough but also decorates the tops of the cookies and provides a nice crunch.

The cookies are great with almost any food or drink companion you can imagine, but they are especially good with Mexican and Indian flavors. The lime sugar keeps for about 3 days in the refrigerator, fortunately, since the leftovers will be delicious over cut fruit, such as watermelon, or stirred into iced tea. You can easily increase the proportions for the lime sugar if you think you'll use more.

makes about 36 cookies

LIME SUGAR
- 2 limes
- 3/4 cup sugar

COOKIES
- 6 tablespoons (3/4 stick) unsalted butter, at room temperature
- 2 tablespoons cold vegetable shortening

- 1 cup sugar
- 1/2 cup lime sugar
- 1 large egg
- 1 teaspoon pure vanilla extract
- 1 1/4 cups all-purpose flour
- 1 teaspoon baking powder
- 1/2 teaspoon salt

TO MAKE THE LIME SUGAR

Remove the zest from the limes in strips with a vegetable peeler and cut away any white pith from the zest. Chop the zest fine, then grind it in a food processor with the sugar until the mixture is pale green with flecks of zest. Store any leftovers tightly covered in the refrigerator.

TO MAKE THE COOKIES

Beat together the butter, shortening, sugar and 2 tablespoons of the lime sugar with an electric mixer until light and fluffy. Beat in the egg and vanilla. Sift the flour, baking powder and salt together over the egg mixture, then beat on low speed until just combined.

Form the dough into a 10-inch log about 2 inches in diameter, then wrap in wax paper. Chill the dough until firm, at least 4 hours.

Preheat the oven to 375 degrees and set the rack on the middle level.

Remove the wax paper and cut the log into ¼-inch-thick rounds. Place the cookies at least ½ inch apart on ungreased baking sheets. Bake in batches for 10 to 12 minutes, or until pale golden.

Transfer immediately with a metal spatula to a rack set over a sheet of wax paper and sprinkle the tops with the remaining lime sugar. Let the cookies cool before storing in an airtight container for up to 2 days.

---

cook's notes

❦ You can make the dough 2 days ahead and chill it, wrapped well in plastic.

❦ It's easiest to remove the lime zest with a Microplane grater, which will leave all the pith behind. And the lime sugar will adhere to the cookie tops much more reliably if you sprinkle it on before the cookies go into the oven. The lime color won't be quite as bright, but it looks fine.

---

desserts

skinny peanut wafers

Halfway between candy and cookies, these crunchy tidbits are jam-packed with peanuts. We like them best in small bites (a rounded teaspoon of dough), but they also make great giant cookies: Just be generous with the rounded tablespoon the recipe specifies.

SOURCE
Food & Wine

COOK
Maida Heatter

The cookies keep for several days in a tightly sealed tin, or they'll freeze for up to a month. If you keep honey-roasted peanuts on hand, everything else here is a staple so you can rustle up these cookies in just moments.

makes about 24 cookies

1 pound honey-roasted peanuts
   (about 3 cups)
1 cup sugar
1 cup sifted all-purpose flour
½ teaspoon baking soda

1 large egg
2 tablespoons milk
2 tablespoons unsalted butter,
   melted and cooled

Preheat the oven to 400 degrees. Line several cookie sheets with foil, shiny side up.

In a food processor, pulse 1 cup of the peanuts with ¼ cup of the sugar several times, until some of the nuts are finely chopped and some are coarsely chopped. In a small bowl, whisk the flour with the baking soda.

In a large bowl, beat the egg with the milk, butter and the remaining ¾ cup sugar until blended. Beat in the flour and the chopped peanuts. Spoon slightly rounded tablespoons of the dough about 3 inches apart on the prepared baking sheets. Press 1 tablespoon of the remaining peanuts onto each cookie, flattening the cookies slightly.

Bake the cookies in the middle of the oven, one sheet at a time, for about 15 minutes, or until golden brown. Turn the sheet from front to back halfway through the baking. Slide the foil onto a wire rack and let the cookies cool completely. Bake the remaining cookies. When they are cool, invert the cookies and peel off the foil. Store the cookies in an airtight tin between sheets of wax paper.

cook's note

The peanuts will roll all over the cookie sheet as you top the cookies with them. Just pick them up again and press them onto every available cookie surface .

peppery ginger cookies

These prize-winning cookies are chewy, spicy and slightly peppery, with a nice textural crunch. As their inventor points out, they bite back, thanks to the pepper, but in a very pleasant way. The little bits of

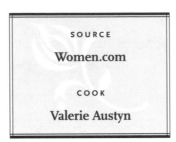

SOURCE
Women.com

COOK
Valerie Austyn

candied ginger are a great idea too.

The cookies keep well, and they're even better on the second day. They're fun for kids to make, since they don't require rolling out.

makes 3½ to 4 dozen cookies

¾ cup (1½ sticks) unsalted butter
¼ cup molasses
1 teaspoon pure vanilla extract
2 cups all-purpose flour
1 packed cup light brown sugar
2 teaspoons baking soda
1 tablespoon ground ginger
2 teaspoons ground cinnamon
½ teaspoon ground nutmeg

¼ teaspoon ground cloves
¼ teaspoon ground cardamom
½ teaspoon freshly ground black pepper
¼ teaspoon salt
1 large egg, beaten
½ cup chopped candied ginger
Turbinado (raw) sugar, for rolling

Melt the butter in a medium saucepan, stir in the molasses and vanilla and let cool. In a separate bowl, mix the flour, sugar, baking soda, all the spices, pepper and salt.

Add the beaten egg to the cooled butter mixture. Fold into the bowl with the flour and spices and add the candied ginger. Cover and refrigerate for at least 15 minutes to make the dough firm.

Preheat the oven to 375 degrees.

Put the turbinado sugar in a shallow dish. Using a cookie scoop, make balls of the dough and roll the balls in the turbinado sugar. Place on ungreased baking sheets, 2 inches apart.

Bake for 10 minutes, or until the cookies are starting to brown on the bottom and the tops start to crack. Let the cookies cool on a rack for 5 minutes — they will firm up a bit at this point. Important: Do not overbake, or the cookies will be brittle and bitter. Store the cookies in an airtight tin.

---

cook's notes

❧ If you have a nutmeg grater, using freshly grated nutmeg makes these cookies even better.

❧ It's easiest to snip the candied ginger into small pieces with kitchen shears.

❧ Turbinado sugar is unrefined "raw" sugar, found in some supermarkets and specialty stores.

---

italian shortbread
with almonds and jam

SOURCE

*Mediterranean Flavors,
California Style*
by Cindy Mushet

COOK

Cindy Mushet

We've completely fallen in love with this recipe. Not only is the almond shortbread delicious, it's made in about 5 minutes from staples (so it's a great emergency dessert), it smells heavenly as it bakes, and it's so gorgeous it makes you look like a genius pastry chef. And you don't even have to grease the pan!

The shortbread tastes best the day after it's baked —if there's any left by the next day—and leftovers will keep well wrapped in foil or in an airtight tin. Serve it with ice cream or just a glass of vin santo or another sweet after-dinner wine. It's also lovely with coffee.

serves 6 to 8

- ³/₄ cup (1¹/₂ sticks) unsalted butter, at room temperature
- ¹/₂ cup sugar
- ¹/₄ teaspoon pure almond extract
- 1¹/₂ cups unbleached all-purpose flour
- ¹/₈ teaspoon salt
- ¹/₄ cup low-sugar apricot jam (preferably Smuckers) or grapefruit marmalade or another not-too-sweet jam
- ¹/₃ cup sliced almonds Powdered sugar, for serving (optional)

Preheat the oven to 350 degrees and set the rack in the middle of the oven. Have ready a 9-inch ungreased fluted springform pan (see note).

Beat the butter and sugar on medium speed in a standing mixer (or with a hand mixer; it will just take a little longer) for 3 to 4 minutes until very light, scraping down the sides of the bowl and the paddle from time to time. Add the almond extract and beat on medium speed for 30 more seconds to blend well.

In a small bowl, whisk the flour and salt together. Add to the butter mixture and beat on low speed to combine, just until the dough is thoroughly blended, 30 to 40 seconds. (The dough will be stiff.) Remove ½ cup of the dough and set it on a small plate in a thin layer; place it in the freezer.

Press the remaining dough into the pan evenly—it can be a little higher at the edges, but the center shouldn't be elevated. Spread the jam evenly over the dough to within an inch of the edge. Retrieve the remaining dough from the freezer and crumble it over the jam, allowing some of the jam to peek through. Sprinkle the almonds evenly over the top.

Bake the shortbread for 40 to 50 minutes, or until golden brown. Remove from the oven and let cool completely on a rack. Stand the pan on a heavy can to remove the sides—the rim will just fall away. Transfer the shortbread, still on its pan bottom, to a platter to serve, or use a spatula to remove it from the pan.

To serve, dust with powdered sugar if desired and either break it into serving pieces or let your guests break off pieces as they like.

---

cook's notes

- If you have no 9-inch springform pan, don't let that stop you. Bake the shortbread in a 9-inch pie pan.
- You can skip the jam if you'd rather, and just press all the dough into the tart pan and top it with the almonds. You might want to add the grated zest of a lemon to the dough along with the almond extract.
- You can make the shortbread, unbaked, up to a month ahead of time, wrap it twice in plastic wrap and freeze it on a flat surface. To bake it, unwrap it and set it frozen into the oven, allowing a few extra minutes.

desserts

cashew coffee biscotti

These are adult cookies —crisp, crunchy biscotti with a major hit of coffee plus the big surprise of cashew nuts. They have a lot of crunch but they're not the tooth-breaking sort of biscotti. If you're not passionate about coffee, you might want to cut the coffee powder back by half, which also strengthens the cashew flavor. Because the coffee flavor is

SOURCE

Got Milk? The Cookie Book
by Peggy Cullen

COOK

Peggy Cullen

so intense, you won't want to dip them in coffee; a cream sherry or a stronger after-dinner drink would be just right.

The biscotti make a great food gift for a coffee-loving friend, since they keep for at least a couple of days in an airtight tin. They're simple to make in the food processor, and the recipe is foolproof.

makes about 36 biscotti

- 1³/₄ cups (8 ounces) whole roasted cashews, unsalted
- 1³/₄ cups all-purpose flour
- 1 cup plus 1 teaspoon sugar
- 1 teaspoon baking powder
- ¹/₄ teaspoon salt
- 4 tablespoons (¹/₂ stick) unsalted butter, chilled and cut into ¹/₂-inch cubes

- 2 large eggs
- 2 tablespoons plus 2 teaspoons instant coffee crystals (not espresso powder, which is too bitter)
- 1 teaspoon pure vanilla extract

Preheat the oven to 350 degrees.

Toast the cashews on a rimmed cookie sheet, turning them occasionally, until golden, 10 to 12 minutes. Cool completely.

Line a heavy baking sheet with foil. In a food processor, combine the flour with 1 cup of the sugar, the baking powder and the salt.

Process for a few seconds to blend the dry ingredients. Add the cubed butter and process just until the butter pieces are the size of lentils.

In a small bowl, lightly beat the eggs with the instant coffee and vanilla. Process the wet ingredients with the flour-butter mixture. Turn the dough onto a work surface and gently knead in the cashews. Form the dough into a disk and cut it in half. Form each half into a 12-inch log. Make the logs into a rectangular shape about 2 inches wide. Sprinkle with the remaining teaspoon of sugar.

Bake for 30 minutes, or until the logs begin to turn golden. Remove from the oven and set aside to cool slightly on the tray, 5 to 10 minutes. Leave the oven on.

Using a spatula, transfer the logs to a cutting board. Using a large sharp knife and a quick downward motion, cut each log crosswise on a slight diagonal into 1/2-inch-thick pieces, discarding (or eating) the ends. Arrange the cookies cut side up on the prepared baking sheet.

Bake for 7 to 10 minutes, or until the undersides of the cookies show the barest hint of color. Don't overbake. Leave them on the baking sheet to harden and cool completely.

Store in an airtight tin for up to 5 days.

double-baked chocolate cake

A double-baked cake? Yes—and this eggy flourless cake from White-Crawford restaurant in Washington State is a true chocolate-lover's delight.

You may do a double-take when you start putting the cake together, because it's quite unlike any other cake you've ever made. First you make a very rich chocolate mousse, then bake most

SOURCE

Lettie Teague,
Food & Wine

COOKS

Sara and Jamie Guerin

of it. As it cools, the top caves in, which looks a bit alarming. Not to worry; when you spread the rest of the batter on top, refrigerate it and bake it again just before serving, the crater disappears, leaving you a slightly warm, deeply chocolate cake that's half crunchy, half moussey.

serves 8 to 10

½ pound bittersweet or semisweet chocolate, coarsely chopped

1 cup (2 sticks) unsalted butter

¾ cup unsweetened cocoa powder

7 large eggs, separated

1⅓ cups sugar

Preheat the oven to 350 degrees. Butter a 9-inch springform pan and line the bottom with wax paper. Butter the paper, then dust the pan with flour, tapping out any excess.

In a large saucepan, melt the chopped chocolate with the butter over medium-low heat. Add the cocoa powder and stir until smooth. Remove from the heat.

In a medium bowl, using an electric mixer, beat the egg yolks with ⅔ cup of the sugar until pale and light, about 3 minutes. In a large bowl, using clean beaters, beat the egg whites until soft peaks form. Gradually add the remaining ⅔ cup sugar and beat until the whites are firm and glossy.

Fold the chocolate into the egg-yolk mixture until barely combined. Fold in the egg whites just until no white streaks remain. Spoon 2 cups of the batter into a medium bowl and refrigerate. Scrape the remaining batter into the prepared pan and smooth the top with a spatula.

Bake for 45 minutes, or until the cake is puffed and a toothpick inserted in the center comes out clean. Cool the cake completely on a wire rack.

Remove the sides from the springform pan and spread the reserved cake batter over the top of the cake, leaving a 1-inch border around the edge. Refrigerate the cake for at least 1 hour.

Preheat the oven to 425 degrees. Bake the cake for 10 minutes, or until a thin crust forms on top and the batter is soft and creamy beneath the crust. Let the cake cool for 10 minutes, then cut into wedges and serve warm.

---

cook's notes

- You can make the cake ahead up to the point of adding the reserved batter for the second baking and keep both the cake base and the batter, well covered, in the refrigerator for up to 2 days.
- Parchment paper may work better than wax paper for lining the pan — the cake will release more easily.

---

desserts

plum crumb cake

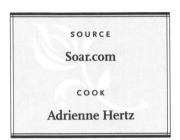

SOURCE

Soar.com

COOK

Adrienne Hertz

This humble cake began its journey to fame in Santa Fe, where chef Adrienne Hertz introduced it at the Ballyhoo Bistro. There it caught the eye of Deborah Madison, who asked for the recipe, as did a number of other diners. The Ballyhoo Bistro is no more, and Hertz has decamped to Memphis, but the cake lives on in cyberspace, where we found it.

It's moist and rich, fragrant with several spices. Cardamom is the lead singer, with good backup harmony from the nutmeg, cloves and allspice. The cake works as well for breakfast or tea as it does for dessert, served with ice cream or crème fraîche.

This amount of cake serves a mob, but you can easily cut the recipe in half to serve 8 and bake it in a 9-inch springform pan.

serves 16

CRUMB TOPPING
1 cup packed light brown sugar
2/3 cup all-purpose flour
1 teaspoon ground cardamom
8 tablespoons (1 stick) unsalted
    butter, chilled and chopped

CAKE
4 cups all-purpose flour
2 cups sugar
1 tablespoon baking powder
3/4 teaspoon baking soda

2 teaspoons ground cardamom
1 teaspoon ground nutmeg
1 teaspoon ground cloves
1 teaspoon ground allspice
1 teaspoon kosher salt
2 cups sour cream
8 tablespoons (1 stick) unsalted
    butter, melted and cooled
4 large eggs
6 red or purple plums, skin on,
    pitted and roughly chopped
    (see note)

Preheat the oven to 350 degrees. Butter a 9-x-13-inch baking dish.

TO MAKE THE CRUMB TOPPING

Combine the ingredients by hand in a small bowl until the butter pieces are the size of rice. Set aside.

TO MAKE THE CAKE

Combine all the dry ingredients and sift them into a large bowl. Make a well in the center.

In another bowl, whisk together the sour cream, melted butter and eggs. Add this mixture to the dry ingredients and whisk until the batter is silky and thick. Fold the plums into the batter. Pour the batter into the prepared pan and sprinkle the crumb coating on top.

Bake until a toothpick comes out clean, about 1 hour. Cool the cake in the pan on a rack.

When cool, cut the cake into squares for serving.

---

cook's notes

- Don't use Italian prune plums for this recipe. Other fruit options include pears and peaches.
- Try adding some chopped almonds to the topping.

---

upside-down cranberry cake

This scrumptious cake was number one on the *Los Angeles Times* food section's list of Top Ten Recipes of the Year, and it's pretty easy to see why. The fresh cranberries keep a little of their bite and all of their color on top of this completely delicious sour-cream cake. Mixing the cranberries with a butter and sugar syrup soaked

SOURCE

Los Angeles Times

COOK

Abby Mandel

with cinnamon makes them wonderfully sticky and delicious.

What a great holiday cake this is, dramatically pretty with its deep red berries shiny with syrup. It stays moist for a day or two—a bonus at holiday time—and it's as good for brunch as it is for dessert.

serves 14

TOPPING

- 8 tablespoons (1 stick) unsalted butter
- 1 1/2 cups sugar
- 2 tablespoons water
- 1 teaspoon ground cinnamon
- 4 cups cranberries, rinsed, picked over and at room temperature

CAKE

- 1 1/2 cups cake flour
- 1/2 teaspoon baking soda
- 1/2 teaspoon salt
- 6 tablespoons (3/4 stick) unsalted butter, at room temperature
- 1/2 cup sugar
- 1/2 cup packed light brown sugar
- 2 large eggs
- 3/4 cup sour cream
- 1 teaspoon pure vanilla extract

Generously grease a 9-inch springform pan and wrap the outside with foil to avoid leakage. Set aside on a baking sheet.

TO MAKE THE TOPPING

Melt the butter in a medium saucepan. Add the sugar, water and cinnamon. Cook over medium-low heat, stirring until the sugar dissolves, about 3 minutes. Stir in the cranberries, pour into the pan and spread evenly. Set aside.

Preheat the oven to 350 degrees.

TO MAKE THE CAKE

Sift together the flour, baking soda and salt and set aside. Beat the butter and both sugars on medium speed until smooth and fluffy, about 1 minute. Add the eggs, 1 at a time, mixing well after each addition. On low speed, add half of the flour mixture. Mix until combined. Add the sour cream and vanilla; mix until combined. Add the remaining flour mixture and mix until smooth. Transfer the batter to the springform pan, spreading it evenly over the cranberries.

Bake for 45 to 50 minutes, or until the top is golden brown and the edges just begin to pull away from the sides. A toothpick inserted in the center should come out clean.

Set the cake on a rack for 10 minutes to cool. Run a knife around the edge to loosen the cake. Invert it onto a plate. Remove the foil, the ring and the pan bottom. Replace any cranberries that have escaped. Cut into wedges and serve.

---

cook's note

You can make the cake up to 2 days ahead. Keep it covered airtight at room temperature.

---

coconut-lime cake

This is a cake quite unlike any other. It's crowned with strips of fresh lime zest on top of an intensely limey frosting studded with little bits of juicy lime. The overall effect has something of the thrill of biting into a margarita. And how could you not love a cake recipe that directs you to simply throw all the ingredients together? It's so

SOURCE

*Delia Smith's Summer
Collection*
by Delia Smith

COOK

Delia Smith

unorthodox that we had to try making it the "right" way, but Smith's way is much better.

The cake won't rise up to be a tall one, so do as Smith does and serve it on a raised cake stand to give it its due.

Note that you need an hour for the lime and coconut to mingle before you actually put the cake together and bake it.

serves 8

CAKE
Zest and juice of 2 limes
1 cup sweetened shredded
    coconut
1¼ cups self-rising flour
¾ cup superfine sugar
¾ cup (1½ sticks) butter, at room
    temperature

3 large eggs, lightly beaten
1½ teaspoons baking powder

ICING
2 limes
2½ cups powdered sugar

TO MAKE THE CAKE

Grate the zest of the 2 limes onto a small saucer, cover with plastic wrap and set aside. Juice the limes. Pour the coconut into a small bowl and add the lime juice. Let the coconut absorb the lime juice for an hour or so.

Preheat the oven to 325 degrees and set the rack on the middle level.

Get out a large, roomy bowl and sift the flour into it, lifting the sieve up high to give the flour a good airing. Throw in all the other cake ingredients, including the lime zest and the coconut. With an electric hand beater on high speed, beat until thoroughly combined, 2 to 3 minutes. Divide the batter evenly between two 8-inch round nonstick cake pans (no need to grease the pans), smoothing to level off the tops.

Bake for 30 to 35 minutes, or until the tops feel springy to the touch. Allow the cake layers to cool in their pans for 5 minutes, then turn them out onto a wire rack to cool. They must be completely cool before being iced.

TO MAKE THE ICING

Use a citrus zester to remove the lime zest in long, thin, curly strips that look pretty. With your sharpest knife, remove all the white pith, then carefully remove each lime segment over a small bowl to catch any juices. To release the segments, slide the knife along each side of the membrane that separates them—this is much easier to do with limes than any other citrus fruit. Drop the segments into the bowl, and squeeze any remaining juice from the skeleton of the lime and from the pith.

Sift the powdered sugar over the limes a little at a time, stirring it in carefully so as not to break up the segments too much. When all the sugar is incorporated, let the icing stand for 5 minutes. Put the first cake layer on a cake stand or a platter and frost the top with the icing. Add the second cake layer and frost just the top. Arrange the lime zest curls over the top and refrigerate for 30 minutes before serving to firm up the icing.

clementine cake

SOURCE

How to Eat
by Nigella Lawson

COOK

Nigella Lawson,
after Claudia Roden

We've been making a version of this much-stolen recipe for decades now. We were delighted to see it again, but this time credited to the original source, Claudia Roden, and with British food writer Nigella Lawson's idea of using clementines instead of oranges. It may seem like one of the more curious recipes in the world: You boil a pound of oranges—or clementines or lemons—and then grind them all up in the food processor. In the end, though, the flavor of this cake is pure orange perfume and essence. It's a very moist, incredibly tender cake, not terribly sweet, and has no butter or flour, only eggs and plenty of almonds.

Lawson claims this is the easiest cake she knows. It's great for the holidays, divine with crème fraîche for dessert or lovely on its own with coffee or tea. It keeps for a couple of days in the refrigerator. Just bring it to room temperature before serving.

serves 8

4–5 clementines (about 1 pound)
6 large eggs
1 cup plus 2 tablespoons sugar

2 1/2 cups finely ground almonds (about 3/4 pound almonds with skins)
1 heaping teaspoon baking powder

Put the clementines in a pot with cold water to cover, bring to a boil and cook for 2 hours, replacing the water as necessary. Drain and, when cool, cut each clementine in half and remove any seeds. Chop everything fine—skin and all—in a food processor.

Preheat the oven to 375 degrees. Butter an 8-inch springform pan and line it with wax paper.

Beat the eggs in a large bowl. Add the sugar, almonds and baking powder. Mix well, adding the chopped clementines.

Pour the cake mixture into the prepared pan and bake for 1 hour, or until a skewer comes out clean. You'll probably have to cover the cake with foil after about 40 minutes to prevent the top from burning.

Remove from the oven and let cool in the pan on a rack. When the cake is cool, you can take it out of the pan and serve.

---

cook's notes

- If you make the cake with lemons, increase the sugar to 1¼ cups. You can also make a glaze of powdered sugar mixed to a paste with fresh lemon juice and a little water.

- A 9-inch springform pan will work just as well as an 8-inch pan, but you'll need to reduce the baking time slightly. If you don't have a springform pan, just use a regular cake pan and butter the sides very well — or cut the cake in the pan if all else fails.

- To keep the almonds from turning into paste in the food processor, add a little of the sugar to them before grinding.

blum's coffee crunch cake

SOURCE

Los Angeles Times

COOK

Joan Kraus, after Blum's

When we saw this recipe, more than 40 years after we first tasted the cake at Blum's, the legendary sweet shop just off Union Square in San Francisco, our hearts skipped with joy. What a great cake this is! Could the woman from Palos Verdes who submitted the recipe possibly have gotten it right? Indeed she has—it's nearly five inches tall and very festive-looking, a perfect birthday cake for coffee fans. The cake is just the right foil for the real treat here—the coffee crunch. This is a coffee version of honeycomb (see page 88), foamy and crunchy, as though you'd gathered all the crema from dozens of cups of espresso and somehow managed to keep the light, airy quality while turning it into sweetly serious crunch. Every bite features the delicious cake, the whipped cream and the celestial coffee crunch.

The cake doesn't keep long once it's put together, just a few hours in the refrigerator. You can push that a bit by putting the whipped cream in a colander set over a bowl in the refrigerator so some of the liquid drains out; this thicker whipped cream will keep a bit longer. But you can also make everything but the whipped cream a day ahead and just put the cake together at the last minute.

serves 12

CAKE

- 1¼ cups cake flour
- 1½ cups sugar
- 7 large eggs, separated
- ¼ cup cold water
- 1 tablespoon fresh lemon juice
- 1½ teaspoons pure vanilla extract
- 1 teaspoon cream of tartar
- 1 teaspoon salt

COFFEE CRUNCH ICING

- 1½ cups plus 2 tablespoons sugar
- ¼ cup strong brewed coffee
- ¼ cup corn syrup
- 1 tablespoon baking soda
- 2 cups whipping cream
- 2 teaspoons pure vanilla extract

Preheat the oven to 350 degrees.

In a medium bowl, sift together the flour and ³/₄ cup of the sugar. Add the egg yolks, water, lemon juice and 1 teaspoon of the vanilla. Beat with an electric mixer on medium speed until the mixture is smooth and thick, 2 minutes.

In a large bowl, with clean beaters, beat the egg whites, the remaining ¹/₂ teaspoon vanilla, the cream of tartar and the salt until the mixture has formed peaks that roll over at the tops when the beaters are lifted. Gradually add the remaining ³/₄ cup sugar, 2 tablespoons at a time, until the meringue is firm and forms stiff peaks. Gently pour the flour-egg mixture over the meringue, and fold in with a slotted spoon or rubber spatula. Gently scoop the batter into an ungreased 10-inch tube pan. Cut through the batter with a knife 5 or 6 times to remove air bubbles.

Bake until the cake springs back when touched, 40 to 45 minutes. Invert the pan on a wire rack and let the cake cool completely. Run a knife around the edges and remove the cake onto a platter with the bottom now the top.

Cut the cake into 4 equal layers. Spread the icing generously between the layers and over the top and sides of the cake. Store the cake in the refrigerator for up to several hours before serving.

MEANWHILE, MAKE THE COFFEE CRUNCH ICING

Line a jelly-roll pan with heavy-duty foil. Combine the 1¹/₂ cups of sugar, the coffee and the corn syrup in a saucepan and bring to a boil over low heat. Cook until the syrup registers 300 degrees on a candy thermometer or reaches the hard-crack stage. Remove from the heat and immediately add the baking soda. The mixture will foam rapidly. Stir until the mixture thickens and pulls away from the sides of the pan.

Pour the mixture into the foil-lined pan. Do not spread or stir it. Let it stand without moving until cool, about 1 hour. When ready to assemble the cake, knock the candy out of the foil and crush it—you can do this most easily by placing it in a heavy-duty plastic bag (including the foil if it won't come loose) and whacking it with a rolling pin. Be sure to leave some larger pieces for more crunch.

TO ASSEMBLE THE CAKE

When you're ready to ice the cake, whip the cream until it's foamy, gradually adding the remaining 2 tablespoons sugar and the vanilla. Beat on high speed until stiff, 3 to 4 minutes. Fold the crushed candy into the whipped topping.

Spread the icing generously between the layers and over the top and sides of the cake. Store the cake in the refrigerator for up to several hours until ready to serve.

---

cook's notes

❧ Once you've mastered coffee crunch, you can make a Coffiesta Sundae, another favorite from the original Blum's. To scoops of espresso ice cream, add chocolate syrup, a very generous amount of coffee crunch, lots of whipped cream and more coffee crunch on top. Blum's always added a maraschino cherry.

❧ To make the coffee crunch release from the foil more readily, smear the foil with a thin layer of softened butter.

Allow the cake to cool in the pan for 20 minutes, then turn it out onto a wire rack to finish cooling.

While the cake is cooling, place the powdered sugar in a small bowl and slowly blend in the amaretto with a fork until the mixture is smooth.

Drizzle the cake with the glaze while the cake is still warm. Cut into slices and serve.

---

cook's note

If the glaze is too thick to drizzle, add a little water until it's the right consistency.

---

desserts

rummy pumpkin cheesecake

True cheesecake aficionados think all holidays can best be celebrated with an interesting cheesecake, and here's an excellent reason to agree. This great alternative to pumpkin pie will be welcome anytime in the fall. It's a double-decker cheesecake, with subtle flavorings of pumpkin and sweet spices, a snappy gin-

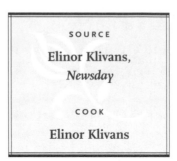

SOURCE

Elinor Klivans,
Newsday

COOK

Elinor Klivans

gersnap crust and a top layer of dark rum cheesecake. It's impressively tall, rich, smooth, creamy—everything a cheesecake should be, plus much more.

The cheesecake is best made a day ahead, and leftovers will keep for up to a week. You can even freeze it in a pinch.

serves 16

CRUST

2 cups gingersnap cookie
   crumbs (about 9 ounces)
1 teaspoon ground cinnamon
4 tablespoons ($^1/_2$ stick)
   unsalted butter, melted

FILLING

4 8-ounce packages cream
   cheese, softened for 3–4
   hours at room temperature

1$^1/_2$ cups sugar
2 tablespoons all-purpose flour
4 large eggs, at room
   temperature
2 teaspoons ground cinnamon
$^1/_2$ teaspoon ground ginger
$^1/_4$ teaspoon ground cloves
1 teaspoon pure vanilla extract
3 tablespoons dark rum
$^3/_4$ cup canned solid-pack
   pumpkin

TO MAKE THE CRUST

Preheat the oven to 325 degrees. Butter a 9-inch springform pan with sides at least 2 inches high. Wrap the outside of the pan with a large piece of heavy foil.

Mix the cookie crumbs, cinnamon and melted butter in a small bowl, combining well. Press the mixture evenly over the bottom and 1 inch up the side of the pan. Bake for 6 minutes. Cool on a wire rack.

TO MAKE THE FILLING

In a large bowl, mix the cream cheese with an electric mixer on low speed until smooth. Add the sugar and mix until smooth. Mix in the flour. Add the eggs, two at a time, mixing until smooth. Mix in 1 teaspoon of the cinnamon, the ginger, cloves and the vanilla. Spoon 2½ cups of the batter into a medium bowl, stir in the rum and set aside.

Mix the pumpkin into the batter remaining in the large bowl, stirring just until the pumpkin is incorporated and no white batter shows. Pour the pumpkin batter into the prepared pan. Place the cheesecake in a large baking pan with at least 2-inch-high sides and place in the oven. Pour hot water into the large pan to reach 1 inch up the sides of the springform pan. Bake for 35 minutes.

Carefully slide the oven rack out several inches. Pour the reserved rum batter all around the inside edge of the pan. The batter will flow evenly to cover the top of the cake. Sprinkle the remaining 1 teaspoon cinnamon over the top.

Bake the cheesecake for 25 minutes more, or until it is firm around the edges and jiggles only slightly when you jostle the pan. Cool the cheesecake in its water bath for 1 hour, covered loosely with a paper towel. Carefully remove the cheesecake from the water bath. Remove the paper towel and cool 1 hour more. The cheesecake should feel cool to the touch. Cover with plastic wrap and refrigerate for at least 6 hours or overnight before serving.

ginger peachy cobbler

SOURCE

Diner Desserts
by Tish Boyle

COOK

Tish Boyle

The very idea of diner desserts is instantly appealing, but in Tish Boyle's hands, the old classics appear in slightly tweaked versions so good they eclipse any desserts served at real diners. This lovely cobbler, for example, subtly uses three kinds of ginger—fresh, powdered and crystallized—in both the fruit and the light, flaky biscuits on top.

It's a gorgeous, homey dessert that works very well with frozen, thawed peaches (three one-pound bags is what you'll need), so it's as good in winter as it is in peach season. You can easily divide the recipe in half and bake it in an 8-x-8-inch baking dish to serve 6.

serves 12

FRUIT FILLING

- 3 pounds ripe peaches (about 6 large peaches)
- ²/₃ cup sugar
- 2 tablespoons all-purpose flour
- 1 teaspoon peeled, grated fresh ginger
- ¹/₂ teaspoon ground cinnamon
- 1 tablespoon fresh lemon juice
- 1 tablespoon heavy cream

BISCUIT TOPPING

- 1¹/₄ cups all-purpose flour
- ¹/₄ cup sugar
- 1 teaspoon baking powder
- ¹/₄ teaspoon ground ginger
- ¹/₄ teaspoon salt
- 6 tablespoons (³/₄ stick) unsalted butter, cut into ¹/₂-inch cubes
- 1 teaspoon pure vanilla extract
- ¹/₂ cup plus 1 tablespoon heavy cream
- 1 tablespoon finely chopped crystallized ginger

Preheat the oven to 375 degrees. Butter the bottom and sides of a 9-x-13-inch glass baking dish.

TO MAKE THE FRUIT FILLING

Blanch the peaches by plunging them into boiling water for 30 seconds. Remove them to a bowl of ice water and, using your hands, slip off the skins. Cut into $1/4$-inch-thick slices off the pit, and place the slices in a large bowl.

In a small bowl, stir together the sugar, flour, fresh ginger, cinnamon, lemon juice and cream. Pour the mixture over the peach slices and toss to coat. Transfer the fruit to the prepared baking dish.

TO MAKE THE BISCUIT TOPPING

Place the flour, sugar, baking powder, ground ginger and salt in a food processor and pulse until combined. Add the butter pieces and process until the mixture resembles coarse meal. Stir the vanilla into the $1/2$ cup of cream and add to the flour mixture. Pulse just until the dough starts to hold together.

Scrape the dough onto a lightly floured piece of wax paper and shape it into a disk. Roll the dough out $1/4$ inch thick. Using a 2-inch round fluted biscuit cutter, cut out as many biscuits as possible. Gather up the scraps, reroll them and cut out more biscuits, until you have a total of 12. Arrange the biscuits on top of the fruit filling, spacing them evenly. Brush the biscuits with the remaining 1 tablespoon heavy cream and sprinkle them with the crystallized ginger.

Bake the cobbler for 40 minutes, or until the fruit is bubbling and the biscuits are golden brown. Serve warm.

caramelized pineapple clafoutis

SOURCE

Rosa Jackson,
Fine Cooking

COOK

Rosa Jackson

The homey French clafoutis (CLAH-foo-TEE), just batter poured over sweetened fruit, is traditionally made with cherries. But all sorts of fruit can turn up in clafoutis — even pineapple. This clafoutis is all creamy interior and crunchy top, with the big surprise of caramelized pineapple. Most clafoutis are summer desserts, but this one is a major winter treat.

Although Rosa Jackson serves her clafoutis plain, you might want to add a pitcher of thick cream to pass at the table or a bowl of crème fraîche.

serves 6

½ large pineapple (14–16 ounces), peeled

4 tablespoons (½ stick) unsalted butter

¼ cup packed light brown sugar

3 large eggs

⅓ cup sugar

⅓ cup all-purpose flour

⅔ cup heavy or whipping cream

1 teaspoon vanilla extract or the seeds scraped from ½ vanilla bean

1 tablespoon dark rum

Preheat the oven to 350 degrees. Butter a 9-inch cake pan or pie pan.

Cut the pineapple half lengthwise into 4 wedges. Cut the core from each wedge, cut each wedge lengthwise again to make wedges about 1 inch wide, and then cut each of these crosswise into ½-inch-thick slices.

Heat the butter in a large frying pan over medium-high heat. When it sizzles, add the pineapple in a single layer if possible. Give the pan a shake and then let the pineapple release its juices without stirring. Let the liquid bubble and evaporate, giving the pan only the occasional shake and stir. In about 5 minutes, when most of the liquid has evaporated, add the brown sugar and stir again. Let the sugar bubble for about 30 seconds and then remove the pan from the heat. With a slotted spoon, transfer the pineapple to the prepared cake pan, reserving the juices in the pan.

In a large bowl, whisk the eggs and sugar until the mixture is lightly frothy and the sugar is dissolved. Sprinkle or stir in the flour and whisk until smooth. Add the cream, vanilla extract or seeds and rum and whisk again. Finally add the juices from the frying pan and give the mixture one last stir.

Pour the batter over the pineapple. Bake until the clafoutis is evenly puffed and golden and a skewer comes out clean, about 50 minutes. Serve warm.

---

cook's notes

❧ Del Monte sells a "Gold" pineapple that tends to be a bit sweeter than other pineapples.

❧ You can add a dusting of powdered sugar to dress up the clafoutis before serving.

---

pumpkin caramel pudding

This rich, creamy pumpkin-pie-like custard makes a great change from the usual pie at the Thanksgiving table. The intriguing element of the dark caramel also offsets the simple sweetness of the pudding. For pastry-phobes, making the caramel is a lot easier than making pastry (those of the easy-as-pie school may not agree).

SOURCE

The Nantucket Holiday Table by Susan Simon

COOK

Susan Simon

You're virtually required to make the pudding a day ahead, which is a great convenience. And it looks very festive with its poufs of whipped cream and jaunty little matchsticks of candied ginger. The caramel pools into a sauce around the pudding, as it does with a flan.

serves 8 to 10

- ³/₄ cup plus ²/₃ cup sugar
- ¹/₃ cup water
- 6 large eggs
- 2 cups canned solid-pack pumpkin
- ¹/₂ teaspoon salt
- ¹/₂ rounded teaspoon ground ginger
- ¹/₂ rounded teaspoon ground cinnamon
- ¹/₄ rounded teaspoon ground cloves
- 3 cups heavy cream
  Crystallized ginger, thinly julienned, for garnish

In a small saucepan, combine the ³/₄ cup sugar with the water. Bring to a boil, stirring with a wooden spoon and washing down the sides of the pan once or twice with a wet pastry brush. Cook the syrup until it's amber-colored. Immediately remove from the heat and pour into an 8-cup charlotte mold or loaf pan. Repeatedly tilt the mold in a circular motion until the sides and bottom are evenly coated. Set aside and let harden.

Preheat the oven to 350 degrees.

In a large bowl, using a whisk, beat the eggs with the ²/₃ cup sugar. Add the pumpkin, salt, spices and 2 cups of the heavy cream and whisk until smooth. Pour the mixture into the caramel-lined mold.

Place the mold in a baking pan and fill the baking pan with hot water. If you are using a charlotte mold, the water will reach only one-fourth to one-third of the way up the sides of the mold. If using a loaf pan, let the water reach halfway up the sides.

Bake for 1 hour 15 minutes to 2 hours (the loaf will cook faster than the mold), or until a tester inserted in the center comes out clean. Let the pudding cool, then refrigerate it for at least 4 hours or preferably overnight.

Just before serving, whip the remaining 1 cup cream until stiff. Transfer it to a pastry bag with a wide fluted tip.

To serve, run a knife around the edge of the mold or loaf pan and invert onto a serving platter. Decorate the pudding and the platter with rosettes of whipped cream and decorate the rosettes with the ginger strips.

---

cook's notes

❧ Before you refrigerate the pudding, it's a good idea to run a knife around the edge of the pan—this will prevent the pudding from clinging to the sides and cracking as it cools.

❧ If you have no pastry bag, just spoon dollops of whipped cream onto the pudding, or use a heavy-duty small zipper-locked plastic bag and cut off one corner to make an improvised pastry bag.

---

santa rosa plum galette

California pastry chef Mary Jo Thoresen, a veteran of Chez Panisse, is now co-owner of Jojo in Oakland, where she specializes in fruit desserts. Her favorite is this seductive plum galette (which is just a free-form tart baked directly on a baking sheet), the best we've ever tasted.

The pastry is part of the reason this galette is so good. It's the creation of Jacques Pépin, who spent a week cooking at

SOURCE

Janet Fletcher,
San Francisco Chronicle

COOK

Mary Jo Thoresen,
after Jacques Pépin

Chez Panisse and forever changed the way the restaurant's chefs make their pastry. The Pépin pastry makes a rustic free-form tart that doesn't even need to be perfectly round when you roll it out, so it's perfect for a beginner. If you're nervous about artfully arranging plum slices on top, no problem. The galette looks just as gorgeous with the plums dropped in helter-skelter.

serves 6 to 8

DOUGH

1 cup all-purpose flour
1/2 teaspoon salt
4–6 ounces unsalted butter, well chilled
Ice water

FILLING

8–10 firm-ripe Santa Rosa (or other) plums (about 1 1/4 pounds)
2–3 tablespoons all-purpose flour, depending on the juiciness of the fruit
5 tablespoons sugar, plus more for sprinkling
Melted butter, for brushing
French vanilla ice cream

TO MAKE THE DOUGH

Combine the flour and salt in a mixing bowl. Cut the butter into small pieces and add to the flour. Work in the butter with a mixer or by hand until the pieces are the size of tiny peas. Add ice water, 1 tablespoon at a time, tossing and mixing gently by hand until the dough is moist but not sticky.

Wrap the dough in plastic wrap and flatten into a disk. Refrigerate for at least 1 hour but preferably overnight.

On a floured surface, roll out the dough to a 12-inch-diameter circle. Don't worry if it's not perfectly round; the tart is beautiful no matter what shape it is.

Transfer the dough to a parchment-lined pizza pan or baking sheet. Cover with plastic wrap and refrigerate briefly.

Preheat the oven to 400 degrees.

TO MAKE THE FILLING

Halve and pit the plums. Cut each into 5 or 6 slices.

Remove the dough from the refrigerator. Leaving a 2-inch border, sprinkle the surface of the dough with the flour and 1 tablespoon of the sugar.

---

cook's notes

- If you don't have a rimless cookie sheet, use this tip from Bay Area baker David Lebovitz: Just turn over your rimmed cookie sheet and bake the galette on the bottom. This way you can easily slide the cooked tart off the sheet onto a cutting board to slice it while still warm.
- If you make the galette several hours ahead, slide it back into a low oven to warm just a bit before serving.

---

desserts

Place the plum slices on the dough, maintaining the 2-inch border. You can arrange them artfully or scatter them; either way, it will look lovely. Sprinkle the plums with the remaining 4 tablespoons sugar, or more, depending on the sweetness of the plums.

Carefully draw up the dough from the sides and fold it over to form the rim. Make sure there are no cracks where juices can run out during baking. Brush the rim of the dough with melted butter and sprinkle generously with sugar.

Bake until well browned and bubbly, about 40 minutes, rotating as needed so the tart browns evenly. Transfer to a cooling rack so the bottom crust doesn't get soggy. Use a pastry brush to dab the plums with some of the cooked plum juices to glaze them while still hot.

Serve the galette warm with a scoop of French vanilla ice cream.

---

tip

Robert Wolke writes in his *Washington Post* food column that it's silly to pay lots of money for pastry brushes, which often need replacing in any case. He buys small bristle brushes at the hardware store for a fraction of the cost and tosses them when they start looking frowzy. To clean them, just swish in warm soapy water, rinse very well and let them air-dry.

tart lemon tart

This is, to our taste, a great lemon tart. It's sunny and sharp, with a good balance of tart and sweet, a velvety custard and a rich short crust. It's also gorgeous, with little circles of

SOURCE

The Perfect Pie
by Susan G. Purdy

COOK

Harvey Edwards

glazed lemon slices on top.

This tart dough doesn't require rolling out, unless you'd prefer to do that. We think it's much easier to simply press the crust into the tart pan with fingertips.

serves 8 to 10

PASTRY

- 3/4 cup (1 1/2 sticks) frozen unsalted butter
- 2 cups unsifted all-purpose flour
- 1/4 cup sifted powdered sugar
- 1/2 teaspoon salt
- 1/2 teaspoon pure vanilla extract (optional)
- 3 large egg yolks or 2 yolks plus 1 tablespoon cream
- Grated zest of 1 lemon or orange (2 teaspoons)
- 2–3 tablespoons orange juice, as needed

GLAZED LEMON SLICES

- 2 1/4 cups water
- 1 1/4 cups sugar
- 11–13 thinly sliced (3/16-inch) rounds cut from 1 or 2 lemons, seeds removed

FILLING

- 4 large eggs, at room temperature
- 1 cup sugar
- 3/4 cup fresh lemon juice
- Grated zest of 1/2 large orange
- 1/4 cup fresh orange juice
- 1/4 cup heavy cream

- 2 teaspoons powdered sugar, for the topping

TO MAKE THE PASTRY

Cut the frozen butter into small bits. Combine the flour, powdered sugar and salt in a food processor and pulse quickly two or three times. Add the cut-up butter and pulse for 5 to 10 seconds, or until the mixture has the texture of rough cornmeal.

Add the vanilla (if using), egg yolks or the yolks and cream, and the citrus zest. Add the orange juice, a tablespoon at a time, as needed, pulsing 2 or 3 times, only until the dough begins to clump together. Stop the machine and check the dough: If you pinch it between your fingers and it holds together, it's ready. It will look rough and ragged, with little bits of butter and yolk showing. Don't let it form a ball or it will be overworked.

Turn the dough out onto a very lightly floured surface and use your hands to press the crumbs together into a ball. Form the dough into a disk about 6 inches in diameter, wrap, and refrigerate for at least 30 minutes. Butter an 11-inch tart pan with a removable bottom. Use your fingertips to press the dough into the pan. (The pastry can be made ahead to this point and placed in a buttered 11-inch tart pan, chilled until firm, partially baked for 12 minutes with pie weights, then for 3 to 5 minutes empty. Freeze and bring to room temperature before proceeding. Fill and bake the pie no more than 4 hours before serving.) If you're proceeding directly and not freezing the pastry shell, chill it until it's firm.

Preheat the oven to 425 degrees. Bake and let cool on a wire rack.

TO MAKE THE GLAZED LEMON SLICES

Combine the water and sugar in a nonreactive saucepan and heat, stirring, until the sugar is melted. Bring to a boil and add the lemon slices. Reduce the heat slightly and simmer, uncovered, for 40 to 45 minutes; remove the slices before the pulp disintegrates. Lift them from the syrup with a slotted spoon and place them around the edges of a dinner plate to drain and cool. (The slices can be made up to 1 day ahead.)

TO MAKE THE FILLING

Combine the eggs, sugar, lemon juice, orange zest, orange juice and cream. Whisk or beat until well blended and pale in color, about 1 minute if whisking by hand.

TO BAKE THE TART

Preheat the oven to 375 degrees.

Set the partially baked pastry shell in its pan on a flat baking sheet. Pour in the lemon filling, then select 8 to 10 of the best-looking glazed lemon slices and arrange them in an evenly spaced ring (to approximately fall in the center of the tart slices) about 1 inch inside the edge of the tart. Put one more slice in the center of the pie. (Don't use slices with no pulp or they'll sink beneath the filling.)

Set the tart in the center of the oven and bake for 25 to 35 minutes, or until the filling is no longer jiggly when the side of the pan is tapped. A toothpick inserted in the center should come out clean. When the tart is done, let it cool on a rack.

A few minutes before serving, sift a light dusting of powdered sugar over the tart. Remove the pan sides, keeping the tart on the pan bottom, and slide it onto a flat serving platter. Serve at room temperature. Just before slicing the tart, remove the center glazed lemon slice so your knife can make clean slices. Divide the tart so that each piece contains a lemon slice.

fig and nut torte

SOURCE
Bon Appétit

COOK
Nanda Calamandrei

The chef-owner of Tran-vai, a restaurant in Tuscany, offers this lovely, not-too-sweet, sophisticated torte that also works very well for breakfast alongside a cup of espresso. Served after dinner, the torte won't compete with a sweet wine or headier spirits. It's a particularly dense, moist torte with the full flavor of figs, a touch of fennel and toasted walnuts.

Although yeast is used, there's no real rising time, but the yeast seems to contribute to the alchemy of this very special dessert.

serves 8

²/₃ cup all-purpose flour

1 envelope active dry yeast

1 teaspoon fennel seeds
(see note)

¹/₄ teaspoon salt

4 large eggs, separated

¹/₂ cup plus 2 tablespoons sugar

4 tablespoons (¹/₂ stick) unsalted butter, melted and cooled

1 teaspoon pure vanilla extract

1 packed cup chopped dried figs (about 5 ounces)

¹/₂ cup chopped walnuts, toasted (see note)
Additional chopped walnuts (optional)

Preheat the oven to 350 degrees. Butter and flour a 9-inch spring-form pan.

Mix the flour, yeast, fennel seeds and salt in a small bowl. Using an electric mixer, beat the egg yolks and the ¹/₂ cup of sugar in a large bowl until thick and pale yellow, about 3 minutes. Gradually beat in the melted butter, then the vanilla. Stir in the flour mixture, then the figs and the ½ cup walnuts (the batter will be very thick).

Using clean, dry beaters, beat the egg whites in a medium bowl until soft peaks form. Gradually add the remaining 2 tablespoons sugar and beat until stiff but not dry. Stir half the whites into the batter to loosen it; it will still be quite stiff, but don't worry, it will all come together. Fold in the remaining whites. Transfer the batter to the prepared pan; it will be a thin layer.

Bake the cake until a toothpick inserted into the center comes out clean, about 30 minutes. Cool the cake in its pan on a rack. Release the pan sides. Place the cake on a serving platter and garnish with additional chopped walnuts, if desired.

---

cook's notes

❧ Try lightly crushing the fennel seeds before adding them to the batter to release their flavor.

❧ Moist, soft figs will be tastiest in this cake.

❧ To toast nuts, see the note on page 227.

❧ The cake will keep for at least a day in an airtight container.

---

desserts

roasted apricots
with sugared pecans and dulce de leche

SOURCE

Real Simple

COOK

Rori Spinelli-Trovato

This fruit dessert is both "real simple" as per its source and really delicious —provided the fruit is ripe, which can be a problem if your apricots aren't local. The brown sugar, butter and pecans get gooey and caramelized on top of the roasted apricots. As if that weren't enough, the dessert is served with ice cream or dulce de leche, the Latin American caramel sauce—frankly, we'll have both. Or you can take a shortcut and just serve some Häagen-Dazs dulce de leche ice cream alongside.

serves 4

DULCE DE LECHE

1 can sweetened condensed milk

APRICOTS

12 ripe apricots, halved

4 tablespoons ($^{1}/_{2}$ stick) unsalted butter, melted

5 tablespoons light brown sugar

1 cup pecan halves

$^{1}/_{2}$ cup dulce de leche

TO MAKE THE DULCE DE LECHE

Remove the top of the condensed milk can and set the can in a small saucepan. Add enough water to reach three-quarters of the way up the can. Bring to a boil and continue boiling on medium-high heat for 1 to $1^{1}/_{2}$ hours, adding water as needed to keep it at the halfway mark on the can. Give the condensed milk a stir from time to time. When the color has turned a light brown or caramel, it's done. Allow to cool before handling.

TO MAKE THE APRICOTS

Preheat the broiler.

Place the apricot halves, cut side up, on one half of a baking sheet. Brush the tops with 2 tablespoons of the butter. Sprinkle with 3 tablespoons of the sugar. In a small bowl, toss the pecans with the remaining 2 tablespoons butter and 2 tablespoons sugar and spread them out on the other half of the baking sheet.

Broil for 2 to 3 minutes, watching carefully and stirring the pecans once, until the apricots begin to brown and the pecans are lightly toasted.

Place 3 apricot halves on each plate, drizzle with warm dulce de leche, and sprinkle with the pecans. Add a scoop of vanilla or dulce de leche ice cream, if you like.

---

cook's notes

- You can make the dulce de leche several days ahead (keep it tightly sealed in the refrigerator) and just warm it before serving. Or you can buy prepared dulce de leche or cajeta, the Mexican version, which is slightly more acid.
- Peaches can be used instead of apricots. If the peaches are large, use half a peach per person. With smaller peaches, use 2 halves. Peaches take a little longer to roast than apricots, 6 to 8 minutes, so the pecans should be broiled separately.

---

oven-roasted caramel bananas
en papillote

So often, trying to cook from a book hot off the British presses from an even hotter young British chef is simply frustrating, but Gordon Ramsay is a major exception. He's aware that British ingredients are not the same as American ones and that home cooks don't have the arsenal of equipment or help that restaurant chefs do.

SOURCE

A Chef for All Seasons
by Gordon Ramsay

COOK

Gordon Ramsay

Caramel, cloves, bananas, lemongrass: This dessert is very heady, and it's all tucked into little parcels of parchment paper. When you open the parcels at the table, a great waft of lemongrass fragrance is released. If you're looking for a completely stunning dessert, you've found it.

serves 4

¹/₄ cup firmly packed light brown sugar

4 tablespoons (¹/₂ stick) unsalted butter

¹/₂ cup heavy cream

2 whole cloves

8 medium bananas, just ripe but not soft

A little sifted powdered sugar, for dusting

4 stems of fresh lemongrass

Crème fraîche, for serving

Make the caramel sauce by melting the sugar in a saucepan with just a splash of water to get it underway, stirring to dissolve the sugar. When it is dissolved and clear, raise the heat and cook, without stirring, for 3 to 5 minutes, or until a light-colored caramel is formed. Remove from the heat and immediately stir in the butter. Mix in the cream and cloves and set aside to infuse and cool (see note).

When ready to cook, preheat the oven to 400 degrees. Get four sheets of parchment paper ready, each about 8 by 12 inches.

Heat a heavy nonstick pan until nice and hot. Cut the bananas in half lengthwise and dust with powdered sugar. Add to the dry hot pan and allow the sugar to caramelize on the first side before turning carefully. This should take just seconds if the pan is hot enough. (You may have to caramelize the bananas in batches, wiping out the pan each time.) As soon as the bananas are caramelized, remove immediately to the center of the sheets of parchment, allowing 4 halves for each serving.

Slash each lemongrass stem almost to the thick end and place one on top of each serving. Remove the cloves from the caramel and spoon it over the bananas.

Holding the two long ends of a sheet of paper up together, fold over and down several times, leaving a bit of space above the bananas. Scrunch the ends in twists. Repeat with remaining sheets. Place the parcels on a baking sheet. Bake for 7 to 10 minutes, or until the parcels are puffed up. Serve each one on a plate and just slash open the top to spoon in some crème fraîche. Serve as soon as possible. Be careful opening the parcels—they release hot steam.

---

cook's notes

✺ When you're making the caramel, you may need to heat it a bit once you add the butter and cream in order to dissolve it.

✺ When the sauce is set aside to infuse and cool, stir it a couple of times during the cooling so it won't form a skin on the surface.

tip

To clean a pan that's coated in caramel, says Mediterranean cooking expert Paula Wolfert, boil an inch of water in the pan and let the caramel liquefy in the hot water.

---

toasted coconut ice cream

SOURCE
Fine Cooking

COOK
Jim Peyton

Mexican ice creams are among the best in the world, though south-of-the-border is hardly dairy country. But the superlative Mexican cooks seem to know instinctively how to make a virtue out of a deficit by creating something extraordinary with what's available. In the case of ice cream, it's evaporated milk and cornstarch that produce the richness and the velvety texture. Taking his inspiration from the heady Mexican concoctions, Jim Peyton du-plicates the wonderful texture and comes up with his own terrific flavor for this ice cream. Although he says the coconut is optional, we don't think so; you'd be depriving yourself to miss this great taste.

The ice cream is a bit softer than American ice cream, but that's a plus in our opinion. And it's easier to make, since you don't have to use a double boiler or worry about the eggs scrambling.

makes about 1 ¼ quarts

- 1 cup sugar
- 2½ teaspoons cornstarch
- Pinch of salt
- 1 cup milk
- ¾ cup whipping or heavy cream
- 2 large egg yolks

- ½ cup chilled evaporated milk
- 1 cup chilled unsweetened canned coconut milk
- ¼ cup sweetened coconut flakes, toasted, plus more for garnish

In a medium saucepan, combine the sugar, cornstarch and salt. Gradually stir or whisk in the milk and cream, bring to a boil and then reduce the heat to a simmer for 1 minute. Remove the pan from the heat.

In a large bowl, beat the egg yolks until blended, about 30 seconds. Whisk about ½ cup of the hot milk-cream mixture into the yolks and then beat in another ½ cup. Slowly whisk in the remaining hot liquid and then pour the mixture back into the pan. Heat the mixture over medium to medium-high heat until it reaches 180 degrees and begins to thicken, stirring constantly; it will look like it's about to boil.

Remove the pan from the heat and whisk in the evaporated milk and coconut milk, whisking until the mixture begins to cool. Strain to remove any bits of cooked egg and refrigerate for at least 2 hours or up to 24 hours, stirring occasionally.

Add ¼ cup of the coconut flakes and freeze in an ice cream maker according to the manufacturer's directions. Freeze until it's very thick and cold. Transfer the ice cream to a resealable plastic or stainless steel container and freeze until it's firm enough to scoop, at least 3 hours. Serve with toasted coconut flakes on top, if you like.

---

cook's notes

₡ When you open the can of coconut milk, there will be a layer of cream on top. Just stir it in.

₡ Before you put the finished ice cream in the freezer, put a piece of plastic wrap directly on the surface, pressing down to eliminate any air pockets. This will help prevent freezer burn and ice crystals.

burnt caramel ice cream

We had our own favorite source for burnt-sugar ice cream in Cambridge, Massachusetts, but once we read Corby Kummer's operatic description of his favorite one, from a shop called Toscanini's, we had to try it. Now we're hooked. The kids probably won't like this one, because it's a sophisticated, almost bitter taste, very Italian, that takes sugar beyond caramel into another realm altogether. Kummer points out that it's a great recipe for beginners,

SOURCE

Corby Kummer,
The Atlantic Monthly

COOK

Corby Kummer,
after Gus Rancatore

since it's so simple and the whole point *is* to burn the usually tricky caramel, so you don't have to worry about being exact.

In fact, this ice cream made its debut as an accident, when a regular caramel ice cream base went over the edge as the cook chatted with a friend.

If the very idea of burnt sugar sounds strange, think of the joys of crème brûlée or toasted marshmallows.

serves 4 to 6

- 1 cup heavy cream
- 2 cups milk

- ²/₃ cup sugar
- ¼ teaspoon salt, preferably sea salt

Mix the cream and milk and set aside.

In a 2-quart saucepan (and not your best one, especially if it's nonstick), mix the sugar and salt and set over moderate heat. Tip the pan back and forth to get the white sugar to the bottom of the pan. The color of the sugar will be uneven, varying from light honey to dark maple syrup.

When the first black spots appear, the steam will turn to smoke. Immediately pour in half the milk-cream mixture, all at once. Stir over moderate heat with a wooden spoon for 5 minutes, or until the caramel is calm and a light mahogany color. The caramel will initially clump or seize, and the gobs and twisted tentacles will make it look like some creature from the deep. Keep the mixture at a low simmer for 20 minutes, stirring frequently. For the last few minutes, your spoon will leave a line on the bottom of the pan. (Don't worry if the mixture gets grainy.)

Pass the mixture through a fine sieve into the remaining milk-cream mixture — push the sugar through with the wooden spoon.

Whisk the mixture, which will have cooled enough to go straight into the ice cream maker. You can also refrigerate it for at least 1 hour or up to several hours to develop flavor. Freeze according to the directions for the ice cream maker you're using.

---

cook's notes

🜋 Be careful; working with hot sugar is potentially dangerous. If it spatters on your skin, ice water will help.

🜋 You can add various flavorings before freezing the ice cream: half a teaspoon or more of pure vanilla extract, a teaspoon of instant coffee dissolved in a tablespoon of milk, or a teaspoon of ground espresso, which will give a pleasing grit to the texture (or not, depending on your taste).

caramelized orange chips

This is a magical recipe that produces an amazing shattering sliver of almost-burnt orange that may remind you of the burnt-sugar crust on a crème brûlée—with a little of the

SOURCE
Basic Baking
by Lora Brody

COOK
Lora Brody

exciting bitterness of Seville orange marmalade. Better yet, this is simple alchemy; anyone can produce these orange chips in just minutes with almost no effort.

makes about 1 cup chips

1 navel orange
About 1/2 cup sugar

Preheat the oven to 350 degrees. Line a heavy-duty baking sheet with heavy-duty foil.

Using a mandoline, a Japanese vegetable slicer or a sturdy serrated knife such as a steak knife, slice the orange into the thinnest possible slices.

Sprinkle the baking sheet evenly with about 1/4 cup of the sugar. Lay the orange slices on top and sprinkle with another 1/4 cup sugar, or enough to cover the oranges generously.

Bake the oranges for 15 minutes; check to be sure that the sugar has caramelized. If they're starting to brown on the bottom but not on the tops, turn the slices over using tongs. Cook for another 3 to 4 minutes, or until the chips are deep brown but not actually burned. Don't touch them—they're dangerously hot. They won't cook evenly, but don't worry about that.

Cool the orange slices on the foil until they reach room temperature, then peel them off. Store in an airtight tin at room temperature. No one's ever managed to keep these around long enough to know how long you can store them, but it's probably at least several days.

---

cook's notes

℘ Lora Brody suggests these are delicious crumbled over oatmeal. We also like them over yogurt. But they're best of all with after-dinner coffee.

℘ Your oven may produce better chips at 400 degrees, as ours does. Try raising the temperature if they don't brown properly at 350 degrees.

---

drinks

two drinks from the zen monastery

In New York's Catskill Mountains there's a traditional Zen monastery, Dai Bosatsu Zendo. Not only

SOURCE

Three Bowls
by Seppo Ed Farrey with
Myochi Nancy O'Hara

COOK

Seppo Ed Farrey

is the food delicious, but special attention is paid to the drinks.

Rosemary Cider

The rosemary cider is a perfect fall drink, an excellent companion to doughnuts (which they probably don't serve at the monastery). The rosemary scents the cider but doesn't overpower it, and your kitchen smells wonderful as it fills with these lovely fragrances. The recipe can easily be cut in half if it seems you'll never finish this quantity.

makes 2 quarts

½ gallon apple cider
1 sprig of fresh rosemary, about
6 inches long

Bring the cider and rosemary to a boil in a large covered saucepan. Remove from the heat and let it steep, covered, for 15 to 20 minutes. Remove and discard the rosemary and serve the cider warm.

Honey-Lemon-Ginger Tea

This deeply soothing drink sits in a pot at the back of the stove, keeping warm all winter and ready to ease sore throats and congested chests. But even if you aren't in need of its medicinal properties, it's a delicious drink on its own.

makes about 4 cups

1 2½-inch piece of fresh ginger, halved lengthwise and cut crosswise into ¼-inch-thick slices

4 cups cold water

Juice of 1 large lemon (about ¼ cup)

2–4 tablespoons honey, to taste

Place the ginger and water in a teapot or saucepan, cover, and bring to a boil. Reduce the heat to low and simmer for 20 to 30 minutes. Strain the tea and add the lemon juice and honey. Reheat, stir well, and serve hot.

ginger-berry lemonade

New York fell madly in love with lemonade this summer, and restaurants outdid themselves to come up with fascinating new versions. We especially liked the Ginger-Berry Lemonade served at Gotham Bar and Grill. It has great zing from the ginger syrup, pucker from the lemons and a sweet touch from the berries and the sugar. It's great on a

SOURCE

Alfred Portale's 12 Seasons Cookbook by Alfred Portale

COOK

Joseph Murphy

hot day, diluted a bit with sparkling water.

Be sure to serve it with plenty of ice in tall glasses to show off its stunning color. The recipe is easily divided in half if you think you won't finish off 12 glasses. This is the perfect drink for a picnic or a pool party, refreshing and delicious without alcohol, but delightful spiked with vodka.

serves 12

3 cups sugar
1¼ cups coarsely chopped fresh ginger
8 cups water

1 cup sliced strawberries or raspberries, or a combination
4 cups fresh lemon juice (from about 32 lemons)
Lemon slices, for garnish

In a large saucepan over high heat, combine the sugar, ginger and water. Bring to a boil, stirring occasionally until the sugar dissolves. Boil for 15 minutes.

---

cook's note

Don't confine yourself to strawberries or raspberries if blueberries or blackberries are in season—they'll be delicious in this drink too.

---

drinks

Let the mixture cool off the heat for 15 minutes. Strain through a fine sieve, discarding the solids, and refrigerate until well chilled.

Set aside about a third of the berries for garnish. In a blender or food processor, process the remaining berries until smooth. Strain the puree through a mesh sieve, pressing the berries with the back of a wooden spoon to extract as much of the juice as possible. Discard the solids.

In a pitcher, combine the ginger syrup, the strained berries and the lemon juice. Serve over ice, garnished with the reserved berries and the lemon slices.

white house eggnog

SOURCE

An Invitation to the White House by Hillary Rodham Clinton

COOK

Walter Scheib

Now that eggs are back and cream is back and punch is back, eggnog is also back. This isn't, however, just any old eggnog; it's a refined version, with beaten egg whites and beaten cream and three different spirits. It's become a special tradition at the White House, where it's served with a classic cherry yule log.

As Mrs. Clinton notes, it's as much a dessert as it is a drink, and we think that's a great way to serve it, with some little sweetmeats and Christmas cookies on the side. And rich as it seems, there's not even 2 tablespoons of cream in each serving.

makes 3 quarts; serves 24

- 4 large eggs, separated
- 1 cup sugar
- 1/2 cup plus 2 tablespoons bourbon
- 1/2 cup plus 2 tablespoons cognac
- 1/2 cup plus 2 tablespoons dark rum
- 1/2 teaspoon salt
- 2 cups heavy cream
- 1 teaspoon pure vanilla extract
- 1/2 teaspoon freshly grated nutmeg
- 1 quart milk

In a bowl beat the egg yolks and the sugar with an electric mixer on medium speed for 3 to 4 minutes, or until the mixture forms a rib-

---

cook's note

If you're unsure of the safety record of your egg source or you're serving people with compromised immune systems, skip this recipe, which depends on using raw eggs.

---

bon when the whisk is lifted out of the bowl. At low speed, gradually add the bourbon, cognac and rum. The mixture will become thinner.

In a very large bowl, with the mixer on medium speed, beat the egg whites and salt until foamy. Increase the mixer speed to high and beat until soft peaks form.

In a medium bowl, with clean beaters, whip the cream until it forms soft peaks. Fold the yolk mixture into the whites, then fold in the whipped cream, vanilla and nutmeg. Add the milk and mix well.

Chill the eggnog for 2 to 3 hours. When ready to serve, whisk it to form foam on the surface. If the eggnog sits for more than 4 hours at room temperature, discard it.

burns family mulled cider

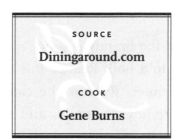

No other punch concoction is quite as warming as mulled cider, but it is so often disappointingly sweet and overly spiced, with that candle-shop aroma. Not this mulled cider, which is fresh and zesty with lots of citrus balanced perfectly with subtle spice. The recipe makes enough for a small army, but you can easily cut it in half to make 2 quarts for a smaller group. Any leftovers will keep in the refrigerator for a couple of days as long as you strain out the spices and the citrus zest promptly.

SOURCE
Diningaround.com

COOK
Gene Burns

What we like best about this brew is that it's equally good with or without the brandy, so it's a great drink for a party. Just leave the bottle of brandy next to the cider and let your guests add it at will to their glasses as they serve themselves. You may want to put a cinnamon stick into each cup for a festive touch.

As Gene Burns notes, the cider is great for sipping around the fire, après ski, and is a fine companion for holiday cookies.

makes 4 quarts

1 gallon (4 quarts) freshly pressed cider without preservatives

3–4 strips of orange zest (just the colored part of the rind)

3–4 strips of lemon zest (just the colored part of the rind)

Juice of 3–5 oranges

Juice of 3–5 lemons

1/2–1 cup sugar, to taste

5 whole cinnamon sticks, broken into about 3 pieces each

3 whole nutmegs, broken into pieces (using a nutcracker)

2 tablespoons whole cloves

Apple brandy, to taste (about 1 cup for the batch or a half shot per cup; see note)

> **cook's note**
> Apple brandy is delicious with the cider, but regular brandy also works perfectly.

drinks

Mix everything except the brandy in a pot, stirring well to dissolve the sugar, and bring to a boil. Reduce the heat to a simmer and cook for 30 to 45 minutes. Remove the cider from the heat and strain the mixture to remove the spices and zests (the cider will be bitter if you leave them in after it's cooked).

Stir in the brandy or add it cup by cup, as you wish.

lotus watermelon martini

SOURCE

Sarah Perpich,
Fashions of the Times,
New York Times

COOK

Lotus Restaurant

This very pretty martini, named for the Manhattan restaurant where it was born, is cherry red and surprisingly delicious. It's still a martini, so it packs a big punch. It's a great icebreaker drink since it's one of those "What *is* this?" concoctions. This is a good way to celebrate the Fourth of July or Labor Day.

You can speed things along by using seedless watermelon and having everything well chilled, even the fruit and the glasses. And you can use any top-shelf vodka.

This martini is frankly sweet, so you may want to try it without the sugar syrup before you make up a batch.

makes 1 cocktail

- 4 ounces freshly muddled watermelon (about 1/2 cup; see note)
- 1/2 ounce simple syrup (about 1 tablespoon)
- 2 ounces vodka (about 1/4 cup; Lotus uses Belvedere)
- 1 fresh watermelon slice (a little triangle including the rind)

Pour all the ingredients except the watermelon slice into a shaker with ice. Shake and strain into a martini glass. Serve with the slice of watermelon.

---

cook's notes

- If you don't have a cocktail muddler, just toss the watermelon into the blender and pulse a few times—just enough to crush it a bit, not to puree it.
- Simple syrup is equal amounts of sugar and water brought to a boil, then cooked until the sugar completely dissolves. Cool before using. The syrup will keep in the refrigerator for a long time and can be used to sweeten iced tea, lemonade and other drinks.

---

spumante-vodka cocktail
with lemon sorbet

SOURCE

Bon Appétit

COOK

Lucia Luhan

This great classic Italian cocktail is refreshing and tastes so good it virtually disappears in moments, so you may need to warn your guests that it's potent. It makes a terrific summer dessert but it's also very good for brunch. The Italians use a sparkling wine, such as Spumante or Prosecco, instead of Champagne in this drink, which is a bit lighter.

This classy blender drink won't hold, so serve it immediately to waiting guests.

serves 6

1 pint (2 cups) frozen lemon sorbet

1½ cups Spumante or Champagne

6 tablespoons vodka

6 tablespoons whipping cream

Spoon the sorbet into a blender. Add the remaining ingredients and blend until smooth, about 1 minute. Divide among 6 champagne flutes or wineglasses and serve immediately.

credits

Southern-Style Spicy Pecans by Ben and Karen Barker, copyright © 2000 by University of North Carolina Press. First published in *Not Afraid of Flavor: Recipes from Magnolia Grill*. Reprinted by permission of University of North Carolina Press.

Baked Greek Olives by Ainsley Harriott, copyright © 1997 by Ainsley Harriott. First published in *Ainsley Harriott's Barbecue Bible*. Reprinted by permission of DK Publishing, Inc.

Asian Tea Eggs by Marie Simmons, copyright © 2000 by Marie Simmons. First published in *The Good Egg*. Reprinted by permission of Houghton Mifflin Company. All rights reserved.

Porcini Dust Twists excerpted from *The Mushroom Lover's Mushroom Cookbook and Primer*, copyright © 2000 by Amy Farges. Used by permission of Workman Publishing Co., Inc., New York. All rights reserved.

Charred Tomatillo Guacamole with Seeded Tortilla Triangles by Mary Sue Milliken, copyright © 2000 by Mary Sue Milliken. First published in *Gourmet*, August 2000. Reprinted by permission of Mary Sue Milliken.

Bacon-Wrapped Scallops with Tamari Glaze from *Skewer It!* by Mary Corpening Barber and Sara Corpening Whiteford, copyright © 2000. Reprinted by permission of Chronicle Books, San Francisco.

Moroccan Tapenade from *Simple to Spectacular: How to Take One Basic Recipe to Four Levels of Sophistication* by Jean-Georges Vongerichten and Mark Bittman, copyright © 2000 by Jean-Georges Vongerichten and Mark Bittman. Used by permission of Broadway Books, a division of Random House, Inc.

Spinach Dip with Jicama and Sweet White Onions copyright © 2000 by The Tasting Room Restaurant. First published in *Time Out New York*, April 20–27, 2000. Reprinted by permission of The Tasting Room.

Gorgonzola Mascarpone Torta first published in *The Cheese Course* by Janet Fletcher © 2000. Reprinted by permission of Chronicle Books, San Francisco.

Crimped Shrimp by Michael Roberts, copyright © 2000 by The Los Angeles Times Syndicate. First published in *The Los Angeles Times*. Reprinted by permission of The Los Angeles Times Syndicate.

Albóndigas (South-of-the-Border Meatballs) reprinted with permission from *Cowboy Cocktails: Boot Scootin' Beverages and Tasty Vittles from the Wild West* by Grady Spears. Copyright © 2000 by Reata Restaurants Management Co., Ltd., Ten Speed Press, Berkeley, CA, www.tenspeed.com.

Martabak (Savory Indonesian Meat Pies) by Sri Owen, copyright © 2000 by Sri Owen. Used by permission.

Broccoli Soup with Stilton copyright © 2000 by Rules Restaurant. First published in *The New York Times Magazine*, April 30, 2000. Reprinted by permission of Rules Restaurant, London.

Zucchini Soup with Mint from *Simply Tuscan* by Pino Luongo. Photography by Jeff McNamara, copyright © 2000 by Pino Luongo. Used by permission of Doubleday, a division of Random House, Inc.

Scallion and Mushroom Soup reprinted with permission of Scribner, a Division of Simon & Schuster, Inc., from *Joy of Cooking: All About Soups and Stews* by Irma S. Rombauer, Marion Rombauer Becker, Ethan Becker. Copyright © 2000 by Simon & Schuster, Inc., The Joy of Cooking Trust and The MRB Revocable Trust.

Beet Soup in Roasted Acorn Squash by Kathy Massam, copyright © 2000 by Condé Nast. First published in *Gourmet*, November 2000. Reprinted by permission of Condé Nast Publications.

Brasserie Gazpacho copyright © 2000 by Luc Dimnet, Executive Chef, Brasserie Restaurant. First published in *The New York Times*, June 28, 2000, article by Florence Fabricant. Reprinted by permission of Brasserie Restaurant.

Chilled Curried Cucumber Soup from *The Greenmarket Cookbook* by Joel Patraker and Joan Schwartz, used by permission of Viking Penguin, a division of Penguin Putnam Inc.

Avocado Vichyssoise copyright © 2000 by The New York Times Co. First published in *Paris in a Basket* (Konemann). Reprinted by permission of The New York Times Co.

Asian Chicken Soup by Bonnie Tandy Leblang, copyright © 2000 by Universal Press Syndicate. First published in *Express Lane Cooking*. Reprinted by permission of Universal Press Syndicate.

Fresh Corn Soup from *The Essential Cuisines of Mexico* by Diana Kennedy, copyright © 2000 by Diana Kennedy. Used by permission of Clarkson Potter/Publishers, a division of Random House, Inc.

Garlicky White Bean Soup with Chicken and Chard by Judith Barrett, copyright © 2000 by Judith Barrett. First published in *Food & Wine*, November 2000. Reprinted by permission of Judith Barrett.

Crab Soup with Sweet Spices and Ginger Juice from *Raji Cuisine* by Raji Jallepalli, copyright © 2000 by Raji Jallepalli. Reprinted by permission of HarperCollins Publishers, Inc.

Scallop and Corn Chowder by Richard Blais, copyright © 2000 by Richard Blais. First published in *The Atlanta Journal-Constitution*. Reprinted by permission of Richard Blais.

Green Salad with Grapefruit and Warm Shrimp from *The Secrets of Success Cookbook* by Michael Bauer, copyright © 2000. Reprinted by permission of Chronicle Books, San Francisco.

Jicama-Mango Tortilla Salad with Citrus Vinaigrette from *Southwestern Vegetarian* by Stephan Pyles and John Harrison, copyright © 2000 by Stephan Pyles. Used by permission of Clarkson Potter/Publishers, a division of Random House, Inc.

Herbed Farfalle and Grilled Chicken Salad by Joanne Weir, copyright © 2000 by Joanne Weir. First published in *Fine Cooking*, July 2000. Reprinted by permission of Joanne Weir.

Warm Mushroom Salad by Marcia Kiesel, copyright

© 2000 by *Food & Wine*. First published in *Food & Wine*, December 2000. Reprinted by permission of *Food & Wine* .

Fennel, Red Pepper and Mushroom Salad by Martha Rose Shulman, copyright © 2000 by Martha Rose Shulman. First published on www.martha-rose-shulman.com. Reprinted by permission.

Haitian Coleslaw by Pusser's Limited, copyright © 2000 by Pusser's Limited. First published in *Bon Appétit*, August 2000. Reprinted by permission of Pusser's Limited.

Fennel Slaw copyright © 2000 by River's End Restaurant. First published in *Gourmet*, September 2000. Reprinted by permission of River's End Restaurant.

Singapore Salad by Chris Schlesinger and John Willoughby, copyright © 2000 by The New York Times Co. First published in *The New York Times*. Reprinted by permission.

Beet and Spinach Salad with Lemon, Cilantro and Mint by Deborah Madison, copyright © 2000 by Deborah Madison. First published in *The Los Angeles Times*. Reprinted by permission of Deborah Madison.

Roasted Bell Pepper Salad with Pine Nuts by Rozanne Gold, copyright © 2000 by Rozanne Gold. First published in *Bon Appétit*, December 2000. Reprinted by permission of Rozanne Gold.

Tomato, Avocado and Roasted Corn Salad by Elizabeth Falkner, copyright © 2000 by Elizabeth Falkner. First published in *Food & Wine*, August 2000. Reprinted by permission of Elizabeth Falkner.

Turkish Bulgur Salad with Tomatoes and Nuts from *The New Book of Middle Eastern Food* by Claudia Roden, copyright © 1968, 1972, 1985, 2000 by Claudia Roden. Used by permission of Alfred A. Knopf, a division of Random House, Inc.

Quick Pickled French Green Beans by Harry Schwartz, copyright © 2000 by Harry Schwartz. First published in Oxford Health Plan's newsletter *Healthy Mind, Healthy Body*, Summer 2000. Reprinted by permission of Harry Schwartz.

Christmas Morning Melon Wedges reprinted with permission from *Caprial Cooks for Friends* by Caprial Pence. Copyright © 2000 by Caprial Pence, Ten Speed Press, Berkeley, CA, www.tenspeed.com.

New Orleans Broiled Grapefruit from *Commander's Kitchen* by Ti Adelaide Martin and Jamie Shannon, copyright © 2000 by Commander's Palace, Inc. Used by permission of Broadway Books, a division of Random House, Inc.

Inc. By permission of Little, Brown and Company, Inc.

Crispy Snapper Tacos with Avocado and Tropical Fruit Salsa by Lisa Ahier, copyright © 2000 by Lisa Ahier. First published in *Gourmet*, March 2000. Reprinted by permission of Lisa Ahier.

Herbed Salmon Baked on Rock Salt reprinted with permission from *Wildwood: Cooking from the Source in the Pacific Northwest* by Cory Schreiber. Copyright © 2000 by Cory Schreiber, Ten Speed Press, Berkeley, CA, www.tenspeed.com.

Salt-Seared Swordfish with Garlic and Mint by Arthur Schwartz, copyright © 2000 by Arthur Schwartz. First published on www.food-maven.com. Reprinted by permission of Arthur Schwartz.

Cured Salmon and Potato Gratin by Marcus Samuelsson, copyright © 2000 by Marcus Samuelsson. First published in *Food Arts*, April 2000. Reprinted by permission of Marcus Samuelsson.

Olive Oil–Poached Cod with Roasted Tomatoes and Broccoli Rabe reprinted with permission from *Charlie Trotter Cooks at Home* by Charlie Trotter. Copyright © 2000 by Charlie Trotter, Ten Speed Press, Berkeley, CA, www.tenspeed.com.

David's Famous Fried Chicken excerpted from *Staff Meals from Chanterelle*. Copyright © 2000 by David Waltuck and Melicia Phillips. Used by permission of Workman Publishing Co., Inc., New York. All rights reserved.

Quick and Easy Chicken Breasts with Fresh Mozzarella reprinted with permission of Simon & Schuster from *The Cheese Lover's Cookbook and Guide* by Paula Lambert. Copyright © 2000 by Paula Lambert.

Port-and-Black-Currant-Glazed Chicken Thighs by Susan Westmoreland, copyright © 2000 by The Good Housekeeping Institute. First published in *Good Housekeeping*, July 2000. Reprinted by permission of The Good Housekeeping Institute.

Butterflied Chicken with Crisp Potatoes by Dawn Yanigahara, copyright © 2000 by *Cook's Illustrated*. First published in *Cook's Illustrated*, March/April 2000. Reprinted by permission of *Cook's Illustrated*.

Chicken Cooked Under a Brick by Joseph Verde, copyright © 2000 by Joseph Verde. First published in *Fine Cooking*, January 2000. Reprinted by permission of Joseph Verde.

Hot-Roasted Turkey with Sausage, Black Olive and Walnut Dressing copyright © 2000 by Karen Hess. First published in *The New York Times Magazine*, March 19, 2000. Reprinted by permission of Karen Hess.

Turkey in a Bag copyright © 2000 by Reynolds Consumer Products. Published in *The Washington Post*, November 15, 2000. Reprinted by permission of Reynolds Consumer Products.

Skirt Steak with Shallot-Thyme Butter by Steve Johnson, copyright © 2000 by Steve Johnson. First published in *The New York Times*, May 31, 2000. Reprinted by permission of Steve Johnson.

Beef Fillets with Stilton-Portobello Sauce by Diane Sparrow, *Southern Living* holiday contest winner for "Entrees with Eight Ingredients or Less," copyright © 2000 by Southern Progress Corporation. First published on www.recipecontest.com. Reprinted by permission of Southern Progress Corporation.

Beef Tenderloin with Garlic by Stew Leonard, copyright © 2000 by Stew Leonard. First published in an advertisement for Stew Leonard's Farm Fresh Foods. Reprinted by permission.

Beef and Onion Stew by Andy Harris, copyright © 2000 by Weldon Owen Magazines, Inc. First published in Williams-Sonoma's *Taste* magazine, Holiday 2000. Reprinted by permission of Weldon Owen Magazines, Inc. and Williams-Sonoma.

Kuala Lumpur Lamb by Josh Parsons, copyright © 2000 by Josh Parsons. First published in *Connecticut Chefs 2000*, edited by Lee White. Reprinted by permission.

Algerian Lamb Shanks from *The Wine Sense Diet* by Shafer and Mondavi, copyright © 2000. All rights reserved. Reprinted by special permission of Regnery Publishing, Inc., Washington, D.C.

Seven-Hour Leg of Lamb by Paula Wolfert, copyright © 2000 by Paula Wolfert. First published in *Food & Wine*, October 2000. Reprinted by permission of Paula Wolfert.

Pork Chile Verde with Posole by Mary Sue Milliken and Susan Feniger, copyright © 2000 by Mary Sue Milliken and Susan Feniger. First published in *The Boston Globe*. Reprinted by permission of Mary Sue Milliken and Susan Feniger.

Aromatic Lemongrass and Pork Patties excerpted from *Hot Sour Salty Sweet*. Copyright © 2000 by Jeffery Alford and Naomi Duguid. Used by permission of Artisan, a division of Workman Publishing Co., Inc., New York. All rights reserved.

Tuscan Pork Roast with Herbed Salt by Sally Schneider after Piero Ferrini, copyright © 2000 by Sally Schneider. First published in *Food & Wine*, October 2000. Reprinted by permission of Sally Schneider.

Miami Black Beans reprinted with permission from *Bruce Aidells' Complete Sausage Book* by Bruce Aidells. Copyright © 2000 by Bruce Aidells and Denis Kelly, Ten Speed Press, Berkeley, CA, www.tenspeed.com.

Slow-Roasted Chipotle Pork by Michele Anna Jordan, copyright © 2000 by Sasquatch Books. First published in *The New Cook's Tour of Sonoma*. Reprinted by permission of Sasquatch Books.

Pulled Pork from *How to Cook Meat* by Chris Schlesinger and John Willoughby, copyright © 2000 by Chris Schlesinger and John Willoughby. Reprinted by permission of HarperCollins Publishers, Inc.

Pan-Roasted Asparagus from *Think Like a Chef* by Tom Colicchio, copyright © 2000 by Tom Colicchio. Used by permission of Clarkson Potter/Publishers, a division of Random House, Inc.

Blasted Broccoli by Tina Ujlaki, copyright © 2000 by *Food & Wine*. First published in *Food & Wine*, March 2000. Reprinted by permission of *Food & Wine*.

Buttered Sugar Snap Peas with Fresh Mint from *The Greenmarket Cookbook* by Joel Patraker and Joan Schwartz. Used by permission of Viking Penguin, a division of Penguin Putnam Inc.

Stir-Fried Spinach with Pine Nuts from *Big Bowl Noodles and Rice* by Bruce Cost with Matt McMillin, copyright © 2000 by Bruce Cost. Reprinted by permission of HarperCollins Publishers, Inc.

Roasted Green and Yellow Wax Beans with Hazelnut Oil from *The Tribeca Grill Cookbook* by Don Pintabona, copyright © 2000 by Don Pintabona. Used by permission of Villard Books, a division of Random House, Inc.

Spicy Mustard Greens with Cumin from *The Modern Vegetarian Kitchen* by Peter Berley with Melissa Clark, copyright © 2000 by Peter Berley. Reprinted by permission of HarperCollins Publishers, Inc.

Asparagus Baked with Roncal Cheese by Florence Fabricant, copyright © 2000 by The New York Times Co. First published in *The New York Times*, May 10, 2000. Reprinted by permission of The New York Times Co.

Cauliflower with Garlic and Paprika by Joyce Goldstein, copyright © 2000 by Weldon Owen Publishing. First published in *Savoring Spain and Portugal*, The Williams-Sonoma Series.

Reprinted by permission of Weldon Owen Publishing.

Roasted Red Onions with Thyme and Butter by Jamie Oliver, copyright © 2000 by Jamie Oliver. First published in *The Naked Chef*. Reprinted by permission of Hyperion.

Walla Walla Onion Rings by Jean Galton, copyright © 2000 by Weldon Owen Publishing. First published in *The Pacific Northwest Cookbook*, The Williams-Sonoma Series. Reprinted by permission of Weldon Owen Publishing.

Indian Ratatouille by Floyd Cardoz, copyright © 2000 by Floyd Cardoz. First published in *Bon Appétit*, January 2000. Reprinted by permission of Floyd Cardoz.

Roasted Potatoes with Garlic, Lemon and Oregano by Aglaia Kremezi, copyright © 2000 by Aglaia Kremezi. First published in *The Foods of the Greek Islands*. Reprinted by permission of Houghton Mifflin Company. All rights reserved.

Mashed Potatoes with Toasted Coriander reprinted with permission of Scribner, a Division of Simon & Schuster, Inc., from *The Herbfarm Cookbook* by Jerry Traunfeld. Copyright © 2000 by Jerry Traunfeld.

The Best Grated Potato Pancakes from *Julia's Kitchen Wisdom* by Julia Child with David Nussbaum, copyright © 2000 by Julia Child. Used by permission of Alfred A. Knopf, a division of Random House, Inc.

Sweet Potatoes with Southern Comfort by Barbara Rochatka Riley, copyright © 2000 by Barbara Rochatka Riley. First published on www.diningaround.com. Reprinted by permission of Barbara Rochatka Riley.

Orange-Ginger Cranberries by Sheila Lukins, copyright © 2000 by Sheila Lukins. First published in *Parade* magazine, November 12, 2000. Reprinted by permission of Sheila Lukins.

Mesa Grits by Bobby Flay, copyright © 2000 by Mesa Grill. First published in *Time Out New York*, April 3–10, 2000. Reprinted by permission of Mesa Grill.

Almond Currant Couscous from *The Secrets of Success Cookbook* by Michael Bauer, copyright © 2000. Reprinted by permission of Chronicle Books, San Francisco.

Couscous cooking tip by Claudia Roden. *The New Book of Middle Eastern Food* (Knopf), copyright © 2000 by Claudia Roden. Reprinted by permission of Claudia Roden.

Rice with Lemon from the Piedmont from *Pot on the Fire* by John Thorne with Matt Lewis Thorne,

credits

index

THE B·E·S·T AMERICAN SERIES ™

THE BEST AMERICAN SHORT STORIES 2001

Barbara Kingsolver, guest editor · Katrina Kenison, series editor

0-395-92689-0 CL $27.50 / 0-395-92688-2 PA $13.00
0-618-07404-X CASS $25.00 / 0-618-15564-3 CD $35.00

THE BEST AMERICAN TRAVEL WRITING 2001

Paul Theroux, guest editor · Jason Wilson, series editor

0-618-11877-2 CL $27.50 / 0-618-11878-0 PA $13.00
0-618-15567-8 CASS $25.00 / 0-618-15568-6 CD $35.00

THE BEST AMERICAN MYSTERY STORIES 2001

Lawrence Block, guest editor · Otto Penzler, series editor

0-618-12492-6 CL $27.50 / 0-618-12491-8 PA $13.00
0-618-15565-1 CASS $25.00 / 0-618-15566-X CD $35.00

THE BEST AMERICAN ESSAYS 2001

Kathleen Norris, guest editor · Robert Atwan, series editor

0-618-15358-6 CL $27.50 / 0-618-04931-2 PA $13.00

THE BEST AMERICAN SPORTS WRITING 2001

Bud Collins, guest editor · Glenn Stout, series editor

0-618-08625-0 CL $27.50 / 0-618-08626-9 PA $13.00

THE BEST AMERICAN SCIENCE AND NATURE WRITING 2001

Edward O. Wilson, guest editor · Burkhard Bilger, series editor

0-618-08296-4 CL $27.50 / 0-618-15359-4 PA $13.00

THE BEST AMERICAN RECIPES 2001–2002

Fran McCullough, series editor · Foreword by Marcus Samuelsson

0-618-12810-7 CL $26.00

HOUGHTON MIFFLIN COMPANY / www.houghtonmifflinbooks.com